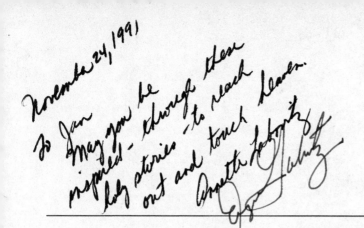

November 24/1991

To Jan

May you be inspired — through these holy stories — to reach out and touch Heaven.

Annette Labovitz

A Touch of Heaven

A Touch of Heaven

*Eternal Stories
for Jewish Living*

Annette Labovitz
Eugene Labovitz

Jason Aronson Inc.
Northvale, New Jersey
London

Library of Congress Cataloging-in-Publication Data

Labovitz, Annette.
   A touch of heaven : eternal stories for Jewish living / Annette
Labovitz, Eugene Labovitz.
     p.   cm.
     Includes bibliographical references.
     ISBN 0-87668-886-5
     1. Ethics, Jewish. 2. Jewish way of life. 3. Parables, Jewish.
I. Labovitz, Eugene.   II. Title.
BJ1287.L328 1990
296.3'85—dc20   90-166
                                                CIP

Manufactured in the United States of America. Jason Aronson Inc. offers books and cassettes. For information and catalog write to Jason Aronson Inc., 230 Livingston Street, Northvale, New Jersey 07647.

Throughout our history, there were many holy souls who by their writings and exemplary living guided our people toward a more ethical and moral life.

In their memory:

"I shall not die, I shall live,
I shall recount the deeds of God."

Psalms 118:17

Contents

Acknowledgments

The Torah thoughts in *A Touch of Heaven* were translated from the works of the holy masters that appear in the footnotes of those sections. These spiritual thoughts would not have been possible without the legacy that they left for posterity.

The authors suggest that, for further bibliographic resources, the reader consult the references listed in the footnotes.

Our special thanks to Arthur Kurzweil for his guidance, to Muriel Jorgensen for her editorial direction, to Gloria Jordan for her work as production editor, to Brenda J. Haight for her artistically designed jacket, and to the entire staff at Jason Aronson Inc., who create magnificent books.

Prologue

At the turn of the twentieth century, when millions of Jews arrived in the United States from the old country, their goal was to "make it" in the *goldena medinah,* the golden land. For many, Judaism stood in the way of their becoming "Yankees." The more they became Americanized, the more comfortable they felt in this blessed democracy, and the more they surrendered their Jewish practices.

Today, we are seeing the pendulum swing in the opposite direction. We are living at a time when many Jews are reawakening spiritually to their Jewish commitment. America has permitted Jews the freedom to choose a Jewish lifestyle in which it is not uncommon to hear the words, "the more Jewish observances, the better."

We have discovered through this spiritual reawakening that the only way to attract our people back to their roots is with the language of love, the language in which we envision the Heavenly Angels praise the Almighty.

The spiritual reawakening has also motivated our people to search for a sense of higher purpose, in addition to their observance of the *mitzvos.* So many want to be uplifted; they want to envision a world that is holy and spiritual, a world where people act in a manner that bespeaks their true creation in the image of God.

To attain this holy spiritual world, we need to practice *midos tovos,* good character traits that imitate God, such as *gemilus chasadim, ahavas harayah,* and *hachnasas orchim.* These are only some of the topics that you will find discussed in selected Torah thoughts in this book, illustrated with stories whose heroes can be role models for today.

Let us consider: if *midos tovos* are so important, why does the Torah not specifically delineate them in the form of *mitzvos,* commandments? The reasons why they are not so delineated is because the goal of the *mitzvos* is to bring us to the practice of *midos tovos,* which is the highest service of God.

The more a Jew observes the *mitzvos,* the more he will practice the *midos.* Just as *mitzvos* are the road maps of life, so the *midos* are the highways toward a more ethical, more complete, more perfect existence.[1] Therefore the *midos* are the wings to the service of God. Just as birds cannot fly without wings, so man, even though he is immersed in Torah, cannot rise to the highest spiritual levels without *midos.* The more man purifies his *midos,* the holier he becomes.[2]

Our patriarch Jacob dreamed of a ladder stretching between heaven and earth. He envisioned angels climbing up and down the ladder and exclaimed: "How holy is this place; it must be the House of God, the Gate of Heaven!"[3]

It is our hope that the Torah thoughts and stories within the pages of this book, *A Touch of Heaven: Eternal Stories for Jewish Living,* portray a holy, spiritual world, and inspire you to touch a little of heaven as our patriarch Jacob did.

[1] Rebbi Chaim Vital. *Sayfer Sha-ar Ha-kedusha.*
[2] Rebbe Shalom Berzovsky. *Netivos Shalom.* Jerusalem: Slonim, 1982.
[3] Genesis 28:10–17.

Listen to Me, My People

Listen to me, my people, I speak to you from the soul
From the bond of life which binds me to you all,
From that same deep feeling
That you, only you, are the substance of my life.
With you, my life has the same substance
Which is called: LIFE.
Without you, I have nothing.
All the hopes, all the aspirations,
All I find within me, exists only when I am with you.
I must love you with an unending love,
I am incapable of feeling any other emotion.
You give substance to my life;
To work, to Torah, to prayer,
To song, to hope.
On the airy wings of your passion
I am carried aloft to the love of God.
With you I soar to the corners of the earth
With your eternity I live forever,
With your glory, I, too am noble and glorious.
With your suffering I am filled with pain,
With the anguish in your souls I am embittered.
With the knowledge and understanding in your midst
I am filled with knowledge and understanding.

Rabbi Abraham Isaac HaKohen Kook.

Simchah— JOY

imcha is the religious expression of joy as described in the following passages:

And rejoice in your holy days, and you will be happy.
—Deuteronomy 16:14–15

Rejoice in the Lord, you righteous,
And give thanks to His Holy Name.
—Psalms 97:12

Serve the Lord with joy, come before Him with
gladness.
—Psalms 100:2

Torah Thoughts

Joy

"*Ashraynu, mah tov chelkaynu*; we are happy and our portion is good."

Every Jew should rejoice for the privilege of having been born a Jew, for the privilege of saying *Sh'ma* twice each day, for the privilege of declaring the Oneness of God in the morning and in the evening. It is the simple joy of expressing this faith that promises meaningful life in this world and its reward in the world to come.[1]

The greatest of all *mitzvos* is to be joyful at all times.[2]

Some people think that the commandment to rejoice is merely another *mitzvah*, while others think that it is unimportant. In reality, the essence of Judaism and the existence of

---

[1]Excerpted from the daily morning blessings as explained by Rebbe Nachman of Bratslav, from the commentary on his siddur, *Sha-aray Ratzon*. Kollel Bratslav, B'nay B'rak, Israel.

[2]Rebbe Nachman of Bratslav. *Likutay Maharan*. Reprinted Brooklyn, NY, Mesivta Chasiday Bratslav, 1978.

mankind depend upon serving God with joy. It is impossible to reach any level of holiness without joy; the more one rejoices, the closer one comes to God.

One should not be embarrassed at being happy.

Thinking of the past or worrying about the future forces a person to digress from the path of joy to the point where he cannot enjoy the present. It is best to seize the momentary joy and dance with it.

Real joy is recognizing that God cares for the world.

Joy is the essence of holiness. Sadness is the epitome of defilement.

It is impossible to be joyful unless one is humble. The arrogant are insatiable and can therefore never experience true joy.

People who are slaves to their occupations are sad; on the other hand, those who serve one Master experience the joy of freedom.

A person who wears a happy face spreads joy wherever he goes. When sad people encounter happy people, they are prepared to be joyful. When they meet a happy person and are inspired to follow his example, their sadness disappears.

A person should accustom himself to dance as he walks, thereby spreading joy from his feet upward through his entire body.

A person must learn to stand before God.
A person must learn how to walk before God.
A person must learn how to pick himself up after he
   falls.
What do you do if you feel that you can't pick yourself
   up?
Then you keep on walking and keep on dancing until
   you dance your way into heaven.[3]

[3]Rebbe Nachman of Bratslav. *M'kor Hasimcha.* Jerusalem: Mesivta Chasiday Bratzlav, 1982.

What has passed is no longer,
And what the future will bring is unknown,
So we have only this moment, use it to rejoice.
Like a sailor who is measuring the knots of his rope,
The knots that have passed through his hand are gone,
He hasn't yet reached the other end of the rope,
He holds only the one knot that he grasps with his
    hand.[4]

When a person performs a commandment with great joy, the memory lingers, as if he would continue to perform it.[5]

---

[4]Rebbe Shmuel Tzvi Me Aleksander. *Tiferes Shmuel.* Vol. II. Lodz, Poland. Reprinted Brooklyn, NY, 1969.

[5]Rabbi Yisrael Klapholtz. *Sayfer Hachasidus.* Jerusalem: Mosad Belz, 1965.

Stories

Don't Delay

Cracow, Poland, a city of magnificent synagogues, built in the ninety-year period between 1553–1644, was one of the flourishing centers of Jewish life. Other cities with a vibrant Jewish life were Lublin, Lemberg, Brisk, and Polona.

Autonomy, granted by Polish kings, generated a strict moral, ethical, and religious way of life in these cities under the leadership of its rabbis, particularly Rabbi Yoel Sirkes.[1]

Rabbi Yoel Sirkes personally provided room and board for the many yeshiva students who flocked to Cracow—home of the

Yisrael Klapholtz. *Sepuray Bays Din Shel Ma-aleh.* Tel Aviv: Pa'er Hasayfer, 1978,

[1] Rabbi Yoel Sirkes (1561–1640) was known as "the Bach" (for *Bayis Chadash* his major work, a masterful comprehensive commentary on the Code of Jewish Law).One of the eminent rabbinical leaders of Cracow Jewry during this period, he was a descendant of a long line of Kabbalists whose influence inspired his commentary on our prayer book. When he was appointed to lead the Cracow Jewish community, people described him by quoting from the Talmud *Bavli, Gittin* 59a: "Torah merged with the understanding of worldly affairs in one place."

largest yeshiva in Poland—from the "four corners of the world" to learn Torah under his guidance.

Once, one of his intimate friends asked, "Rabbi, do you think that I have been blessed with such wealth because I meticulously tithe my income?" Rabbi Sirkes answered, "We do not understand the ways of the Almighty. We are only required to help Him do His work."

The two friends spent a great deal of time together, most of it usually devoted to the study of Torah. However, before they parted company, they chatted about current market conditions.

One day, just as his friend was leaving, a village innkeeper who lived in the outlying district around Cracow knocked on Rabbi Sirkes's door. Always ready to help those who sought his advice, he welcomed the innkeeper cordially. After making him comfortable, Rabbi Sirkes asked him how he might be of help.

"This is my problem," began the innkeeper hesitantly. "I have lived on the *Poretz* Vladovistov's estate for the last ten years. My lease will be up for renewal very soon. I earn my livelihood by managing the inn on his property. The peasants stop for food and drink during the day. Sometimes, wayfarers sleep over for a night or two. Life has not been easy for me and my family, but I manage to eke out a living. I manage to pay the *poretz* his rent on time. We have a fairly amicable relationship. Now, I have recently discovered that Shlomo Chayim, the fisherman, offered the *poretz* more money than I can afford to pay him. I fear the *poretz* will give my lease to the fisherman, for why shouldn't he accept more money for the same property? If he does not renew my lease, I will have no way to earn a livelihood. Shlomo Chayim is clearly overstepping his bounds by encroaching on my territory. After all, his livelihood is not in danger of being lost. He desires something that is not rightfully his."

The innkeeper finished and waited for Rabbi Sirkes's reply.

"I wonder if you saw the man who left this house just as you approached?" he asked gently.

The innkeeper shook his head, wondering what connection the rabbi's previous guest had with his problem.

"Well," continued the rabbi, "that man is a very close friend of mine. He is also a prominent merchant who happens to be friendly with the *Poretz* Vladovistov. I want you to go to see him. When he asks you how he can help, tell him the story you just told me. Be sure you conclude your story by asking him, in my name, to speak to the *poretz* on your behalf. I'm sure he will do it. I also know that you will have no more problems with Shlomo Chayim."

The innkeeper thanked Rabbi Sirkes and set out to find the merchant, confident that his problem would be solved.

The merchant was as cordial to the innkeeper as the rabbi had been. He listened patiently to the details of the innkeeper's story and when he had finished, the merchant responded: "I shall be very happy to speak to the *poretz* when I return from the semiannual summer fair in Jaroslav, for he is a good friend of mine, and he will certainly consider my request. I have a great deal of merchandise involved in this fair. I am just about ready to leave town and had only gone to bid Rabbi Sirkes farewell."

The innkeeper was visibly shaken.

"What I am asking you to do will only take a few minutes. My livelihood depends on the *poretz* renewing my lease. Can't you speak to him before you leave town?"

The merchant answered, "Surely you know the talmudic saying in the name of Rabbi Judah ben Rabbi Shalom: 'A man's earnings for the year are determined for him from Rosh Hashanah, as are his losses for the year determined for him from Rosh Hashanah.'[2]

"You must have faith in the goodness of the Almighty. It is still a few months until Rosh Hashanah, when your earnings for next year will be determined. I shall surely return from the fair before our holy days. Believe me, nothing will happen before then."

The innkeeper seemed satisfied with the merchant's sincerity, so he returned home. His wife, however, was not placated.

"Faith in the Almighty?" she screamed. "How is He going to stop Shlomo Chayim from interfering in your livelihood? If the *poretz* listens to the fisherman, we will starve!"

She gave the innkeeper no peace. She cried and cursed day

[2] Talmud Bavli, *Bava Basra* 10a.

and night. Nothing the innkeeper did could calm her fears, and they spent the next two months in utter misery.

True to his word, as soon as the merchant returned from the fair, he hurried to speak to the *Poretz* Vladovistov.

"That's not a problem," the *poretz* agreed cheerfully with the merchant. "The innkeeper has done a fine job of managing my inn until now; he has always paid his rent on time. The customers seem happy enough. Why should I change horses in midstream? I will renew his lease for another ten years."

The innkeeper and his wife were naturally overjoyed with the news.

That year, right after Sukkos, the merchant passed away. Every Jew in Cracow honored him by attending his funeral and escorting his remains to the cemetery.

About two months after the week of *Shiva* had ended, the soul of the merchant appeared to Rabbi Yoel Sirkes in a dream. The soul spoke. "I have returned to tell my friend what the eternal world is like. When I first arrived, I found many souls wandering about the heavenly abode, waiting for judgment. I feared the outcome of my final judgment. Finally, I was ordered to appear before the Heavenly Court. I shook with trepidation, for although I had tried to live my life righteously, a man's priorities are not always the priorities of the Almighty. I was relieved when a chorus of angels greeted me as I stepped before the Heavenly Court. The Court ordered that I be immediately admitted to my eternal resting place in Paradise. The chorus of angels gathered around me, rejoicing, ready to escort me. But suddenly, an angel dressed in black stepped into our path. He held up both hands."

"Stop!" he ordered.

"Who are you?" I gulped. "Who are you that dares block my way to Paradise?"

"I am the angel that you created by your act of kindness when you spoke to the *poretz* on behalf of the innkeeper."

"Then why are you blocking my entrance to Paradise?" I demanded. "You should be escorting me with all these other angels. Why are you standing in my path? Didn't I hurry home from the fair in Jaroslav just to speak to the *poretz*?"

"Yes, you truly saved a family's livelihood, but you don't

know how much pain and anguish they suffered for two months while you multiplied your business assets a hundredfold at the fair. The innkeeper's wife cursed and cried. They never stopped arguing the entire time you were gone."

"Wasn't I justified in hurrying to the fair? After all, the delays would have cost me thousands of *zlotys* in profit," I argued.

"All my arguments were of no avail. The angel dressed in black insisted that I remain outside the gates of Paradise for a period equivalent to the time I had spent at the fair. I sat and waited for two months. I have just been escorted to my final resting place in Paradise. Although I am relieved now, even happy with my reward, I came to tell you to emphasize to all your friends and followers that if they have the opportunity to do a *mitzvah*, they should never delay doing it, not even for one minute. One never knows the suffering caused by delaying a *mitzvah*, nor the joy of its fulfillment.[3]

[3]"Do not delay the opportunity to do a *mitzvah*" (Mechilta Bo Pesikta Zutrati).

Expectation

Rebbe Zusia[1] walked through the marketplace along cobblestoned streets. He was trying to reach that particular wall
where important announcements were posted.

His progress was slow, for people stopped his every step to
greet him, to ask his advice, while he, in turn, wanted to know
about their families and their livelihood. Because he had become so involved with their personal lives, they clung to him.

[1] Rebbe Zusia of Anipoli (died 1800) was a disciple of Rebbe Dov Baer, the
Maggid of Mezeritch during the second generation of chasidim. Because his sole
purpose was to exemplify one who clings to the ways of the Almighty, he was a
model for thousands. His stated goal was to influence every Jew to develop the
spark of holiness within his soul to its utmost potential. To accomplish this goal,
he wandered among the people, in order to teach them, to inspire them, to instill
in them the respect and fear of God. His friends said that even the Heavenly Court
stood in awe of his deeds. Burdened with misery and afflicted with poverty, he
would respond in the third person to people who asked him how he could thank
God for the good by saying, "Zusia suffering? He is not suffering. Zusia is happy
to live in the world that He created. Zusia lacks nothing, Zusia needs nothing."
His major concern was his personal Day of Judgment, of which he said, "I will
not have to explain why I was not as great as Abraham, Isaac, Jacob, or Moses.
I will have to explain only why I was not as great as Zusia could have been."

Finally, he reached the wall. He scanned the announcements on the bulletin board and found a very important notice. He read an invitation calligraphed on ivory-colored, linen-weave paper, "Chaim Layb and Hinde announce the marriage of their only daughter Rachel to Moshe ben Aleksander. The *chuppah* will take place on Tuesday, *rosh chodesh,* the first day of Kislev. The following people are invited . . ."

"This will be a big wedding," thought Rebbe Zusia. "After all, Chaim Layb and Hinde are the richest Jews in this shtetl." He read the names carefully. Near the bottom of the list, he noticed his own name.

"Oh!" he called out joyfully, "Chaim Layb and Hinde are inviting me to their daughter's wedding!" He danced a rhythmic step to a melody he started to hum. "I'm so happy that they invited me. I never expected to find my name on that list. I will be the first of the guests to arrive, I'm so happy!" And he continued singing and dancing.

Ten minutes later, Mottel, a very wealthy man, stood in front of the board, scanning the list for his name. He had walked through the marketplace, ignoring the crowd as usual. He did not mix with the multitude, nor did he go out of his way to do anyone any favors.

"Let me see where my name is on this list," he thought. "I am one of the wealthiest people in this town. Because of my importance, my name should be first or second on that invitation list." He scanned the list and saw that his name was also near the bottom.

"What *chutzpah!*" he cried angrily. "I am such an important person. Since my name is near the bottom of the list, and they don't recognize that I am one of the pillars of this *shtetl,* I will not go to the wedding!" By the time he had walked away from the wall, he was seething.

Rosh chodesh Kislev arrived. As soon as the afternoon prayer service ended, Rebbe Zusia started to walk briskly toward the wedding hall. He wanted to be the first guest. He sat down on the front bench, very close to the *chuppah,* and waited patiently for the other guests. When other people entered the wedding hall, they sat down diffidently behind him.

After the *chuppah,* the people who had been seated in the front row were asked to sit at the front table for the wedding dinner; the people who had been seated in the second row were asked to sit at the second table. Therefore, Rebbe Zusia was seated at the same table as the bride and groom and their respective parents, and he was accorded the same honor as they.

After the first course was served, there was a big commotion at the back of the wedding hall. Mottel, who had reconsidered the invitation, decided to make an appearance at the wedding. He stormed into the hall, demanding to know where his seat was. Because he had arrived late, there were only a few empty places left at the back table. Grumpily, he sat down and waited to be served. It was clear that Mottel was seething with anger. The longer he sat, the more livid he became. He looked around the room and noticed that Rebbe Zusia, considered to be one of the poorest people in the *shtetl*, was sitting at the most important table, seemingly enjoying himself.

He walked over to Rebbe Zusia's table.

"I don't understand what happened," he muttered. "You are one of the poorest people in this *shtetl*, yet you have the honor to sit at the head table. I am one of the wealthiest people in this *shtetl*, yet I was seated in the back. My presence alone should guarantee that I have the most honored place at this wedding!"

"You see," whispered Rebbe Zusia, "I was so happy to see my name on the invitation list. . . I really didn't think I would be invited, because I don't expect anything. You, on the other hand, think that everyone in this world owes you honor, that everything is coming to you. If a person doesn't expect anything, he gets everything, but if he expects everything, you see, he gets nothing."

The Fixer

Each night, the King of Sadness walked the length and breadth of his kingdom to determine if his subjects were obeying his law, for he had decreed that no one was to be happy. The king was happy only when all his subjects were sad.

Rebbe Nachman of Bratslav. *Sippuray Maaseyos*. Jerusalem and New York: Bratslav Yeshiva and Research Institute, 1959.

This story was first printed in Hebrew and in Yiddish in Jerusalem around 1905 by Rabbi Tzvi Dov ben Avraham of Berdichev. It was originally told by Rebbe Nachman on the fourth day of *Elul*, 5566 (August 19, 1806). To prepare his disciples to understand this story, he first taught them to accept suffering with love and faith.

Rebbe Nachman of Bratslav (1772–1810), the great grandson of the Baal Shem Tov, founder of the chasidic movement, spent his childhood in assiduous study, fasting, praying at his grandfather's tomb, and meditating in the fields. He regarded every minute of his life as a precious gift, never to be wasted. Because he believed that the highest attainment of holiness could be reached only in Eretz Yisrael, he set out, at the age of 26, to visit the holy land. He stayed for a year, visiting graves of his spiritual ancestors, the Kabbalists. His writings include books on morals and joy, commentaries on the *siddur* and *halachah*, as well as the famous *Thirteen Stories*. Soon after he returned to Bratslav, he moved to Uman, one of the infamous sites of the Chmielnicki pogroms. He lived there for three years. Today, the Soviet government wants to create a national shrine at the grave of Rebbe Nachman.

Disguised as a commoner, he visited a different neighborhood each night. He usually stood behind a hovel, peered through the cracks in the wall, and strained to hear the conversation of his subjects.

"My business is not going well," complained one merchant. "I will have to make an appointment to see the king."

The eavesdropping king smiled when he heard the merchant's complaint. Behind the baker's shanty, he learned that the flour was lumpy. The tailor bemoaned the fact that he had to work day and night to eke out a livelihood. The king smiled at his subjects' problems. Then he walked toward the farthest shack.

"The person who lives in this dilapidated place can certainly not be happy," he mused. "The roof is leaking, the door swings noisily on its hinges, one of the windows is broken, the fence has a big gap, and the weeds are knee high."

The king peered through the broken window. He was shocked to see the owner sitting on a three-legged stool at a chipped, tilted table, enjoying the feast that was spread before him. A half-bottle of wine stood in the center of the table next to a plate of potatoes, a few slices of meat, and a piece of *challah*. The king watched while the man ate and drank. When he finished, he lifted his fiddle from the floor and pulled the bow across the strings. To his dismay, the king heard a happy melody flowing from the fiddle.

"This man is disobeying my orders," muttered the king. "I'll have to find out why he is so happy."

He knocked on the door and entered. The man stopped playing and stood to greet the stranger. Then he poured some wine and gave it to the king. The king sat down on the mattress nearest the wall and fell asleep.

When he arose in the morning, he said:

"Before I return home, I would like to ask you a few questions. Tell me, who are you? What do you do for a living? What were you celebrating last night?"

"I'll answer the first question first," replied the man. "I am a fixer. I can fix anything that is broken. Each morning, I wait in the marketplace for people to hire me to fix their broken articles. I refinish and paint wooden furniture, repair broken fences, install window panes, fasten book shelves to walls.

When I finish my work, I collect my wages. Before I return home, I purchase all the ingredients for my nightly feast. I prepare my food slowly, carefully. When I finish eating, I play my fiddle and I rejoice in the fruit of my labors. You see, being able to have a feast each night gives me great joy!''

"I understand," responded the king, bidding the fixer farewell. He returned to his palace.

"Call my scribe," he shouted as soon as he was seated comfortably on his throne. "I want to decree a law to stop the fixer from any further joy. From now on, no one in this kingdom is permitted to fix anything for anyone else!"

The next morning, the fixer went to the marketplace in search of work. Usually, a long line of people waited for him. That morning, however, no one seemed to need his services.

"Don't you have anything around to repair?" he asked one of his usual customers.

The customer replied, "Didn't you hear the king's new law? The king decreed yesterday that no one could fix anything for anyone. If something we own needs repair, we must either fix it ourselves or throw it away!"

Realizing that he would earn no money to buy his feast if he stayed around the marketplace, he wandered off in search of work. He was not too worried, for he trusted in God.

The fixer happened upon the wealthiest man in town chopping trees near his luxurious mansion, trying to stockpile wood for the coming winter months.

"Excuse me," he said, addressing the rich man. "Why are you chopping that wood by yourself? Isn't it beneath the dignity of the wealthiest man in town to chop his own wood?"

"I couldn't find anyone to chop the wood for me, so I decided to do it myself."

"Please, give me the ax," answered the fixer. "I will be only too glad to chop all the wood you need to prepare a stockpile for the cold weather ahead."

When he finished chopping the wood, the rich man paid him his wages and he walked farther, trying to find more people for whom he could work. He worked hard as a wood chopper that day, and toward evening, he had accumulated enough money to buy his feast. Returning to his shack, he prepared his food, sat down on his three-legged stool at his chipped, uneven table, ate, and drank. When he finished eating and drinking, he played joyful tunes on his fiddle. The fixer was very happy.

The king had no peace that day. He couldn't wait for nightfall to return to the fixer's dilapidated shack to see how sad he was.

The king peered through the broken window. To his surprise, he saw that the fixer fiddled and sang. Leftover food was spread on the plate on the table. He entered the shack. Once again the fixer rose to greet him and again offered the remainder of his wine.

They both slept. In the morning, the king inquired, "Where did you earn money to purchase food for your feast last night?"

"Well," hesitated the fixer, "the king passed a law prohibiting anyone from fixing anything for anyone else. So I had no way of earning any money. But that didn't bother me. I wandered around trying to find work. I found a rich man chopping his own wood. I offered to chop it for him and he paid me, so I enjoyed the work and earned enough money to buy my feast."

The king rushed back to his palace and called his scribe. "I want to enact another law. From now on, no one in this kingdom is permitted to chop wood for anyone else. Any person who needs wood must chop it himself." The king smiled. He was satisfied with his new law.

News of the king's decree spread rapidly throughout his realm.

The fixer was a bit disturbed with the new decree, but he had faith in God. He decided to search out other possibilities for earning enough money for his nightly feast.

He walked in the direction of the open fields, where the farmers lived. As he passed a stable, he noticed the farmer cleaning it by himself.

"Let me help you," he offered. "I'm sure you have other chores that need your attention. I can certainly do this job for you." The farmer agreed on the wages he would pay the fixer at the end of the day, and the fixer set to work.

With the money the farmer paid him, he bought what he needed for his evening meal. He returned home, cooked his supper, relaxed on his three-legged stool at his chipped table, ate, drank, and rejoiced. He was very happy.

That night, the king once again made his visit. And again after drinking the remainder of the wine, he fell asleep. In the morning, he demanded to know how the fixer had earned enough money for his feast. "I earned my money as a farmhand. Yesterday, I cleaned stables," replied the fixer sheepishly.

The king then rushed posthaste to his palace and decreed that no farmer could hire a helper.

The next morning, the fixer searched for another farmer who might employ him, but the first one he approached informed him that the king had decreed that hiring farmhands was prohibited.

The fixer was upset, but he trusted in God. He sat down in the field to think. "What can I do to earn a little money every day," he wondered, "without the king decreeing that job prohibited?"

He thought for a long while. "I know what I can do," he finally realized. "In this kingdom the national guard is drafted, but foot soldiers can enlist any time. I will enlist on the condition that the recruiting officer pay me my wages on a daily basis."

Happy with his decision, he went to talk to the recruiting officer. Since the officer was always searching for new soldiers, he agreed to the fixer's condition and gave him a uniform and a sword.

The fixer soldiered all day. Toward evening, he collected his money, changed into his regular clothes, and bought the food for his feast in the marketplace. He ate and drank and fiddled and was very happy.

The king was curious to see how the fixer fared, so he paid him his nightly visit. They drank wine and talked. The king again spent the night in the fixer's shack.

In the morning, he again inquired as to how he had earned money to pay for his feast.

"That's not a problem," replied the fixer. "His Majesty, the king, decreed yesterday that farmers may not hire farmhands to clean their stables. It becomes difficult to find a different job every day, so I decided to enlist in the army on condition that they pay me my wages daily."

"Now I understand," replied the king. He bid farewell to

the fixer and returned jubilantly to his palace. "Call my scribe to the throne room," he shouted to a servant. "I need to decree a new law. From now on, soldiers serving in the king's army are not to be paid every day."

The fixer soldiered all day. That evening, when he went to collect his wages, the officer said, "The king has decreed a new law. Soldiers are not to be paid daily!"

"But," moaned the fixer, "we made an agreement when I enlisted that you would pay me daily wages."

"Yes, I agreed," muttered the officer. "That was before the king's new decree. I dare not do anything to break the law."

The fixer pleaded with him for his wages, but he would not change his mind.

"I'll tell you what I can do," he said, "I'll pay you tomorrow for two days."

The fixer walked toward the marketplace. He knew he would have to devise a plan to earn some money for his nightly feast. He walked aimlessly, still believing that his faith in God would lead him to a solution. Suddenly, he thought to himself: "I know what I can do. I can remove the metal blade from my soldier's sword and replace it with a wooden blade. I can pawn the metal blade and use that money to buy my feast tonight. After I collect my money tomorrow, I will replace the wood with the metal blade. No one will know the difference."

That night the fixer feasted and sang. He was very happy.

The king was beside himself that night when he peered through the broken window. Sullenly, he watched the fixer rejoice for a few minutes. Then he knocked on the door, entered, drank, talked a bit with the fixer, and fell asleep.

The next morning, the king again asked how he had earned the money for his feast.

"That's easy," replied the fixer. "I removed the metal blade from my sword and I pawned it. I replaced it with a wooden blade. Tonight, when I collect my money, I will replace the metal blade and and no one will know the difference, since I can fix anything!"

The king ran back to his palace, fuming, for the fixer had broken the law of happiness in addition to changing the blade on his sword, which was also forbidden. He called the recruiting officer and said:

"I command you to order that soldier whom you hired on a daily basis to decapitate a criminal who is awaiting execution."

The recruiting officer summoned the fixer and told him of the king's command.

"I want you to know that the king has chosen *you* to be the executioner. The commanding officers were ordered to watch the execution. The king wants them all to witness the proceedings."

The fixer ran to the palace and threw himself at the mercy of the king. "Your Majesty!" he pleaded. "You have summoned me to decapitate a criminal. Please, don't make me fulfill your command. What if the man is innocent and doesn't deserve the death penalty? I have never killed a man in my life."

"I have no doubt in my mind that the criminal is guilty. I am certain that he deserves the death penalty. You must carry out my order!"

The fixer knew that he had no recourse but to obey the command. He turned his eyes heavenward. With perfect faith, he prayed, "Master of the Universe! I have never killed a man in my life. If the criminal is innocent, let the blade of my sword turn into wood!"

The fixer drew his sword from its sheath. The moment he lifted it, all the officers saw that the blade was made of wood. They all laughed. Even the king laughed. The laughter was contagious. The king roared: his body shook to an inaudible joyous melody.

Finally, he raised his hand and announced, "I now know why this man is called the fixer." Turning to the fixer, the king said, "You may return to your home in peace!"

That night, as usual, the fixer enjoyed his feast!

Joy

People flocked to Lublin from all over the Pale of Settlement,[1] for Lublin was the center of Polish *chasidus*. They came to see the Chozeh, the Seer of Lublin, Rebbe Yaakov Yitzchak Halayve Horowitz,[2] for they believed that when his soul was created, it was given the power to perceive the wonders of the world.

A group of *chasidim* were traveling in the back of a wagon, on the road to Lublin. When the wagon reached the outskirts of Lublin, the wagoner turned around from his seat at the front of the wagon and raised his voice to get the attention of the jovial people who were his passengers.

"Where are you going?" he shouted.

Seforim Kedoshim: Me-talmiday Baal Ha Rebbe Shem Tov, Niflaos Ha-rebbe. Brooklyn, New York: Bayt Hillel, 1985.

[1]See Glossary, p. 284.

[2]The Chozeh of Lublin (1745–1815) was revered by his disciples for his holy actions and righteous deeds. For this reason, they honored him with the title chozeh or prophet. One of his contemporaries, the Maggid of Mezeritch, said of him: "A soul has come to us that has not appeared in this world since the time of the prophets." His *Bays Midrash* at Sroka Street 28 was the university, the training center for many other chasidic *rebbes* who established illustrious dynasties, some of which endured more than 150 years until the Holocaust. Other dynasties that were threatened with annihilation were rebuilt afterwards in New York and Eretz Yisrael.

"We are on our way to vist the Seer," they answered joyfully.

"Well, in that case," he continued, "do me a favor. Will one of you please give the Seer this *kvitel*? I wrote it a few days ago, and I have carried it in my pocket ever since. I have asked many of my passengers their destination, but you are the first to visit the Seer."

He took the *kvitel* from his pocket and handed it to the *chasid* who sat closest to him. The *chasid* promised to put it directly into the hands of the Seer.

The wagoner thanked him, turned around, tapped the horses with the tip of his whip, and they lurched forward. He stopped the wagon in front of the *bays midrash* of the Seer of Lublin.

As he had promised, the *chasid* immediately handed the *kvitel* to the Seer. The Seer unfolded the *kvitel* and held it to the light. He turned it over and over, then stared at the message for a moment.

Finally, he said, "The writer of this *kvitel* is a special human being. He brings blessings wherever he goes!"

The *chasidim* looked at one another and at the Seer. They were dumbfounded. They did not understand how the Seer could know anything about the wagoner without having spoken to him. To them, he was a simple wagoner. While they were wondering, the Seer whispered, "Even at this moment, he is bringing blessings!"

The *chasidim* knew that the Seer did not chatter idly. Immediately, they ran out of the *bays midrash* through the alleys and streets of the city, scurrying around the marketplace, searching for the wagoner. They searched the vegetable stall, the fish stall, the cheese and butter stall, and came to an abrupt halt in front of the flour stall. Throngs of people were crowded around the flour stall. They were shouting, shoving, clapping their hands to an inaudible rhythm. The *chasidim* pushed their way through the crowd to the center. The wagoner was dancing energetically, his feet flying through the air. The crowd encouraged him:

"More, more, higher, higher!" they shouted.

"What is going on here?" the *chasidim* demanded of one of the spectators.

"Wait," he said, "wait and watch. When he finishes dancing, he will tell you himself why he is so joyous."

While they waited, the *chasidim* joined the singing and clapping.

Finally, he stopped dancing. The crowd dispersed slowly, and the *chasidim* formed their own circle around the exhausted wagoner.

"Please tell us," they pleaded, "what was your occasion to rejoice!"

"After I left you in front of the Seer's *bays midrash,* I went to the marketplace in search of something to do. As I approached, I realized that there was a celebration of some kind about to take place, for I heard a flute and a violin in the distance. As I drew closer, I recognized the sounds of an approaching wedding, but I also heard a great tumult over the sounds of the music. I was told that the wedding celebration was for two orphans.

"But I found out that the tumult was an exchange of angry words, not joyous excitement. It seemed that the groom's side threatened to back out because the bride's side had not supplied a new *tallis* for the groom, as is the custom. They simply did not have the money to buy one. The people argued vociferously. The young groom stood under the *chuppah* in tears, surrounded by his people. The bride's people screamed that she was waiting in a house on the edge of the marketplace for the ceremony to begin.

"I was absolutely heartbroken. I couldn't stand the pain of the bride and groom, so I took all the money you had paid me for the trip, ran to the stall where religious items were sold, bought the *tallis,* and gave it to the groom. I have never seen such joy when he took the *tallis* from my hand. I was so happy when both the groom's side and the bride's side agreed to proceed with the wedding ceremony.

"When the ceremony was over, I started to dance, for there is no greater *mitzvah* than rejoicing with the bride and the groom."

The *chasidim* understood what the Seer meant when he said that the wagoner was a special human being who brings blessings wherever he goes.

A Touch of Heaven

What kind of person was Rebbe Yaakov Yosef Halayve Horowitz, the Chozeh of Lublin?[1]

Why did people flock to his *bays midrash* from all over southwest Poland and Russia? Was it to hear his words, to seek his advice, to observe his deeds? Were they trying to imitate the man they revered as their spiritual leader? Perhaps this story will tell us what kind of a human being he really was.[2]

Rumors flew all over town about how the *chasidim* carried on in the *bays midrash* of the Chozeh of Lublin. People whispered that they sang and danced even on the solemn night of Rosh Hashanah. The *misnagdim* scoffed.

[1]For biographical information, see the story titled "Joy" on p. 28

[2]*Chasidim* believed that the uneducated could also approach the Heavenly Throne of the Creator through prayer and good deeds. Serving God with joy, song, and dance in addition to the study of Torah created an emotional environment of love and caring. The *misnagdim* insisted on intensive Torah study and the strict interpretation of *halachah* (Jewish law). They believed that the performance of the *mitzvos* was the ladder to reach the Heavenly Throne of the Creator. Although their styles were different, both *chasidim* and *misnagdim* had the same goal—namely, to raise the Jewish people to the highest possible level of holiness.

"I think I will go to see for myself," said Tzvi, a *misnaged*. "I don't like to listen to rumors."

That year, on Rosh Hashanah night, after the conclusion of the evening service, Tzvi headed for the *bays midrash* of the Chozeh. He thought that people should be sad on Rosh Hashanah, as a new year was beginning and the old year ending with most people not having lived up to their fullest potential. Imagine his surprise when he saw the *chasidim* dancing with all their strength. "Alas," he thought, "the rumors are indeed true." He stared at the sight. The floor shook in the *bays midrash* from the pounding of their heels, the walls reverberated with their *niggun*, their smiles radiated joy as each *chasid* wished his neighbor, "May you be inscribed and sealed in the book of life!"

Tzvi stood at the edge of the dancers' circle, watching for a long time.

"I can't believe my eyes!" he muttered. "Tomorrow is the Day of Judgment. Who knows what is in store for us for the coming year? Who knows how we will be inscribed? Why are these people dancing?"

Hostility glared from his eyes. He walked over to where the Chozeh sat, calmly watching his *chasidim* rejoice.

"I can't believe my eyes!" he shouted. "This is blasphemy. I wanted to see for myself. I hoped the rumors were not true, but this is worse than anything I have heard. People are supposed to be serious tonight. It is the eve of the Day of Judgment. How can you permit your *chasidim* to dance? This is a terrible desecration of the Holy Name!"

The Chozeh of Lublin, a very gentle man, answered Tzvi quietly, "Please, come closer." He put his hand over Tzvi's eyes, held it there for a few moments, then whispered, "Tell me, what do you see?"

It seemed to Tzvi that he saw a vision of the Heavenly Court. He stammered, "I see that all the people who are dancing in the *bays midrash* have been inscribed in the book of life; not only those who are dancing, but their wives and children have already been inscribed. Now I understand why they are dancing and singing, why they are filled with so much joy."

The Chozeh removed his hand from Tzvi's eyes and continued. "Now, look over in that corner. What do you see?"

"Why," said Tzvi, "I see a *chasid* who is by himself. He is the only one who is not singing or dancing."

The Chozeh covered Tzvi's eyes once more. "Tell me what you see this time."

Tzvi hesitated to speak, for what he saw disturbed him greatly. Finally, with a choked voice, he uttered, "I see that man has not yet been inscribed. No wonder he is not dancing. No wonder he is so sad."

Suddenly Tzvi realized that he, too, was not dancing or singing. He shuddered at the thought that maybe he had not yet been inscribed in the book of life. He cried out, "Rebbe, holy master, please show me the way to be inscribed in the book of life. Please help me to inscribe my wife and my children!"

"There is only one way, there is only one way," whispered the Chozeh. "Don't stand here. Join everyone else. Dance your way into the book of life. Sing your way into the book of life. By dancing and singing, you will be able to touch heaven!"

Ahavas Harayah—

LOVE Your Fellow Man as You Love Yourself

ove your fellow man as you love yourself.

—Leviticus 19:18

When Hillel was approached by a heathen who asked him to explain the essence of the Torah, he replied "What is hateful to yourself, do not do to your neighbor. That is the whole Torah, while the rest is the commentary thereof; go and learn it."

—Talmud *Bavli, Shabbos* 31a

Rabbi Akiva said that to love your fellow man as you love yourself is the fundamental principle of Torah.

—*Sifra, Kedoshim*

Ben Zoma said, "Who is respected? He who respects others."

—*Avos* 4:1

My beloved children, do I lack anything that I have to demand it from you? All I ask is that you love and honor each other, nothing more.

—*Sayfer Hachinuch Mitzvah* 243

Treat all men with respect and amiability. Bring happiness to one another by kindly social relations. Let there be no dissension of any kind, only love and friendship. Forgive one another and live peacefully for the sake of God.

—Rabbi Elyahu ben Shlomo, the Vilna Gaon,
in a letter to his family

Love, nurtured on the knowledge that every human being is created in the image of God, is the basis for peace and happiness.

—Meir Meiseles. *Judaism.* Jerusalem: Feldheim Publishers

Torah Thoughts

Love

You shall love the Lord your God with all your heart, with all your soul, and with all your might.[1]

"With all your heart" means not to hate anyone in your heart.

"With all your soul" means not to hate anyone even if you perceive that you are more ethical than he is.

"With all your might" means not to hate anyone even if he is more talented than you and you harbor feelings of jealousy.[2]

Before praying each morning, Rabbi Yitzchak Luria, the father of Lurianic kabbala, deemed it proper to pronounce:

"Herewith I take it upon myself to perform the commandment to love your neighbor as you love yourself."

He felt that he could not turn to God in prayer with any hate in his heart.[3]

[1]Deuteronomy 6:5

[2]Rabbi Yeshaya Halayve Horowitz. *Sh'nay Luchos Habris.* Kitzur Shila.

[3]B. S. Jacobson. *Meditations on the Torah.* Tel Aviv: Sinai Publishing Co.,1956.

One day, Rebbe David Lelever (1746–1814), told a student that he overheard two peasant friends discussing how much they loved each other.

The first peasant asked, "Do you love me?"

His friend answered, "Of course, I love you. I love you very much."

The first peasant persisted, "But do you really love me?"

"I've already told you that I love you," his friend responded.

"In that case," continued the first peasant, "Do you know what hurts me?"

His friend countered, "Do I know what hurts you? How can I know what hurts you?"

The first peasant cried, "If you really loved me, you would even know what hurts me."[3]

Why were certain special commandments, particularly the one to love your fellow man, given in the presence of the entire Jewish people? This commandment was given because a person who desecrates *any* commandment brings pain to his fellow human being, who is also part of the community, thereby disregarding the commandment to love your neighbor.[4]

Communal leaders who love and respect one another have the power to guide the entire community, for they include the Almighty in their deliberations.[5]

I love everything.
I cannot keep from loving all beings, all peoples.
In the depths of my heart
I wish for the splendor of all: the mending of all.

[3] Meir Meisels. *Judaism*. Jerusalem: Feldheim Publishers.
[4] *Tiferes Shmuel*, vol. 2.
[5] Rebbe Nachman of Bratslav (*Sayfer Hamidos*).

My love for Israel is more fervent, more profound,
But the inner longing expands in its power of love
Over all, literally all.[6]

[6]Rabbi Abraham Isaac HaKohen Kook. *Arfaly Tohar.* Born in Grevia,
Latvia, Rabbi Abraham Isaac HaKohen Kook (1865–1935) was a rabbinic authority, the first Chief Rabbi of Ashkenazic Jews in Eretz Yisrael, prior to the
establishment of the state. He was in England in November 1917, when the
Balfour Declaration was issued. He declared it a step in the process of the redemption of the Holy Land. Referring to the land as *Medinat Yisrael* (State of
Israel) years before the state was proclaimed, he encouraged cooperation between secular and religious Jews in the process of rebuilding.

Stories

Soulmates

Imagine Jewish life in Vienna during the thirteenth century![1] One of the great centers of Jewish learning, Vienna was a haven for Jews who fled the devastation as the Crusaders marched eastward through the cities along the Rhine River basin.

The influence of the sages of Vienna spread far beyond its boundaries and continued for many generations. The responsa

This story was told by Rabbi Shlomo Carlebach in January 1985, at a housewarming in Petaluma, California. It was subsequently printed in *Agada*, Spring-Summer, 1986. The historical background was added by the authors.

[1] Records of the first synagogue in Vienna date from 1204. The Jewish community prospered under a charter of privileges, "the Fredericianum," granted by Duke Frederick II of Babenberg in 1244 and confirmed by Emperor Rudolf of Hapsburg in 1278. The Jews were autonomous, held important administrative positions, served as tax collectors and minters for the royal treasury, and engaged freely in trade. They developed into a middle class, which served as a link between the royalty, the nobility, and the serfs. Measures were taken to generally ensure the safety of the Jews, so they would not want to leave.

J.D. Eisenstein, ed. *Otzar Yisrael*. Jerusalem: Shilo Publishing.

Annette Labovitz. *Secrets of the Past, Bridges to the Future*. Miami, FL: Central Agency for Jewish Education, 1983.

of these sages, besides being a record of their halachic decisions, shed light on the way the Jewish people lived at that time
and in that part of the world.

Among the topics dealt with in one of the foremost halachic works of the time, *Or Zarua,* is the imposition of taxes on
the Jews by Emperor Rudolf, the holding for ransom of Rabbi
Mayer ben Baruch of Rothenberg, the relationship between
Jews and their Christian neighbors, and the manner in which
matchmakers arranged marriages.[2]

Chaim Eliezer, the son of Rabbi Yitzchak Or Zarua, at the
age of 15 was the most outstanding student in his yeshiva. It
was only natural that the wealthiest merchant in Vienna would
want him for a son-in-law.

The merchant approached the *rosh yeshiva* and said, "I
want to arrange a match between Chaim Eliezer and my
daughter. I will guarantee to support them for the
next ten years, so that he may devote himself entirely to
study without worrying about earning a livelihood. That way
he will truly become a light to all Israel." And so it was
arranged.

The parents and the matchmaker took care of all the
arrangements. In those days, the bride and groom didn't see
each other before the wedding.

As the day of the wedding approached, the bride's father
invited all the Jews of the city, rich and poor alike, to his
daughter's wedding. His servants began preparing a sump-
tuous wedding dinner.

Moments before the young couple were escorted to the
chuppah, the groom approached the bride to place the veil over
her face. It was then, seeing her for the first time, that he
realized how beautiful she was.[3]

The first part of the wedding ceremony proceeded without

---

[2]Rabbi Yitzchak ben Rabbi Moshe (approximately 1200–1270), the author of *Or Zarua,* studied in yeshivos in Vienna, Regensburg, Wittenberg, Paris,
and Speyer with the most outstanding scholars of that time. Recognized as a
rabbinic leader, he was appointed to head the Jewish court in Vienna. Besides
his halachic works, he wrote an anthology explaining the ethical values of each
of the letters of the Hebrew alphabet.

[3]The ceremony is called *badeken.*

incident, but just after Chaim Eliezer placed the ring on his bride's finger, a mob broke into the synagogue, set fire to the richly embroidered curtains, smashed the windows, and desecrated the Torah scrolls. Fire spread to the edges of the *chuppah*, flames engulfed it. The panic-stricken guests ran for safety. Outside the synagogue, peasants, waving flaming torches, clamored, "Death to the Jews!"

Not satisfied with the destruction of the synagogue, the mob ran uncontrolled throughout the Jewish section of Vienna. They smashed windows, set fire to buildings, threw stones, beat and killed indiscriminately. Bodies were strewn all over the street.

The survivors of the pogrom walked around dazed, unable to understand how their neighbors could harbor such hatred, how they could perpetrate such evil.

Lucky to be alive, Chaim Eliezer crept back into the city the next day, after he had spent the night hiding on the other side of the Danube River. He questioned the survivors, "Have any of you seen my bride? Do you know if any other member of her family survived the attack?"

"Most everyone who was invited to the wedding was killed," they told him. However, Chaim Eliezer strongly believed that his bride had survived, so he decided to search for her. He wandered from city to city in the Germanic lands, to Wurzburg, Regensburg, Neustadt, Cologne. He inquired in each of the Jewish communities if by chance a family had been ransomed from captivity soon after the date of his wedding. Unsuccessful in finding them, he decided to return to his yeshiva in Vienna.

A few years later, the *rosh yeshiva* approached Chaim Eliezer saying, "The Jews have rebuilt their lives. It's time you did the same. A wealthy merchant asked me for my most promising student. I would like to arrange a match for you with his daughter."

"I will consent only if I may meet my future father-in-law first. I have to discuss something with him," responded Chaim Eliezer.

At their meeting, he said, "I will marry your daughter on two conditions. I want you to invite all the poor people in the

Germanic lands to the wedding and to the seven days[4] of the marriage festivities afterwards. I also want you to know that I will not be able to live with your daughter until after the seven days of marriage festivities have passed. You must trust me. I cannot explain the reasons for my request."

Deep in his heart, Chaim Eliezer still hoped that his first wife was alive.

"If she is alive, and if she is poor, then when all the poor people receive the invitation to come to my wedding, maybe she will come also. It will be my last chance to find her," he thought.

The wedding took place on Tuesday.

He insisted that all the guests who came to the wedding sign their names to a specially prepared scroll that he labeled "Guests Who Came to Honor the Bride and Groom."

Each of the first three nights after the marriage festivities, he checked the scroll. Her name was not listed. Then, on Friday afternoon, when he checked the scroll for the guests who would spend *Shabbos* with them, he found her name scrawled at the bottom.

Overwhelmed, he cried, "She is alive! She is alive!"

At the *Shabbos* meal, bride and groom sat among the poor people, for they were the most honored guests at wedding festivities. The groom's eyes wandered from face to face, desperately searching for his first wife. Their eyes met.

"She was so beautiful five years ago, " he mused. "She is disheveled and bedraggled now. She must have suffered so much. I still love her. I wonder if she still thinks about me."

Chaim Eliezer knew he had time to reveal himself to her, for no one would leave the city on *Shabbos*. There were two tents erected for the comfort of the *Shabbos* guests, one for the men, one for the women. After the *Shabbos* afternoon meal, he excused himself from his bride and walked in the direction of the women's tent. He found his first wife resting near the

---

[4]The number seven in Jewish life denotes completion; for example, the seven days of the week parallel the seven days of creation. Therefore, it is customary for the bride and groom to rejoice for seven days following their wedding. The seven blessings of marriage are repeated after each festive meal during that week.

tentpole. He beckoned her to come outside. "I want to talk to you," he whispered.

She didn't recognize him and was very suspicious. "What do you want?" she hesitated.

"I want to thank you for coming to my wedding."

"Are you thanking all the guests individually?" she asked.

"No, I just wanted to thank you," he murmured. "I want to know how it is that such a beautiful young woman does not have a husband to provide for her?"

"Beautiful? I'm not beautiful anymore," she said softly. "Do you want me to tell you when I was beautiful?"

He nodded.

"Five years ago," she continued, "I was beautiful. I was beautiful for one moment in my life, the moment I stood under the *chuppah*. I was the daughter of the richest merchant in Vienna. Just as my groom placed the ring upon my finger, a vicious mob broke into the synagogue. A terrible pogrom followed. People were tortured or killed indiscriminately. A few people escaped. I have no idea what happened to my groom or to my family. Most people told me that he was killed, but I would not believe them. Somewhere, in my heart, I believed that he was alive. I have been wandering for the past five years trying to find him.

Chaim Eliezer was speechless. Tears streamed down his cheeks. He hurried away, so that she would not see his pain.

On Sunday morning, Chaim Eliezer called together his father-in-law and his rabbis. "You might think it strange that I asked you to meet with me during the seven days of the marriage festivities, but I have to reveal something to you."

He turned to his father-in-law.

"I hope you will understand what I am about to tell you. I beg you to forgive me. I could not marry your daughter without one final attempt to find my first wife. I have found her, and I have to go back to her."

The father-in-law reacted angrily.

"How can you do this? I made you the most lavish wedding! I invited all those poor people! I am the richest man in Vienna. How can you go back to someone who has been wandering in filth for the past five years?"

Chaim Eliezer was patient. "Please," he pleaded, "listen to what happened."

He retold the entire story of his five-year search for her slowly and in great detail. He explained why he insisted that all the poor people be invited to the wedding. He emphasized that the conditions that were agreed upon regarding inviting the poor and not living with the bride until after the seven days of marriage festivities were with the hope that he would still find his first wife.

His father-in-law jumped up from his seat, ran over to Chaim Eliezer, hugged and kissed him.

"My anger was a test of your sincerity. Yes, I wanted you to marry my daughter because I knew instinctively that you were a very special person, a very holy man. If you would have told me that you were not going back to your first wife, I would not have wanted you for my son-in-law anyway. I only want you to do me one favor. Let me give all the money that I would have given to my daughter as a dowry . . . let me give it to your first wife. I want her to be my daughter, also."

Yossele, The Holy Miser

Can you imagine living in a Jewish community where a *kahal* controlled the religious and communal life of the entire city? The *kahal* was mandated to govern for the benefit of the entire Jewish population. It levied taxes on the rich and comfortable, and the money collected supported the poor, the widows, and the orphans; it cared for the ill and paid for the work of the *chevrah kadisha;* it ensured that the children were educated.

About four hundred years ago, Jews who lived in various Polish cities were governed by such a *kahal.* Some were successful merchants; some were great scholars. Others earned their livelihood as bakers, bookbinders, weavers, craftsmen, or artisans. They lived in Jewish neighborhoods and were part of a cohesive community.

Most Jews in the community paid the taxes the *kahal* assessed them, for no one wished to defy them; no one except Yossele, the wealthiest Jew in Cracow. Yossele was an exception. He refused to pay the taxes the *kahal* levied against him, or give one *zloty* on his own for charity, and therefore

Rabbi Shlomo Carlebach originally told us this story.

he became a social outcast. The Jews of Cracow called him "Yossele, the Miser," but he paid no attention to their taunting.

In fact, Yossele had the strange habit of inviting poor people to his elegant mansion from time to time. He made them comfortable in the luxurious surroundings by serving them schnapps and honey cake. Then he asked: "Where do you live?"

The poor person might answer, "I live on that street near the marketplace. You can recognize my house by the broken fence."

"Please write down your name and the description of your house," Yossele would reply.

By that time the poor man felt so comfortable that he would ask for a few *zlotys*.

"What?" Yossele would shriek,"I invited you here to find out your address, not to give you any money. Get out of my house, immediately!"

He would rise from his chair and chase the poor man into the street without helping him.

Yossele grew old and the *kahal* appointed a committee from the *chevrah kadisha* to visit him and demand that he pay his fair share for the upkeep of the community before he died. As was his custom, Yossele invited the members of the committee into his house, served them some schnapps and honey cake and asked them the reason for their visit.

"We have come to inform you that you owe the community charity fund a lot of money. You have never deemed it necessary to pay one *zloty* until now. If you pay up, all will be forgiven. However, if you do not pay what you owe before you die, we warn you that the *kahal* has decreed that you will not be buried in the Jewish cemetery."

Yossele listened and laughed. "Not bury me in the Jewish cemetery?" he scoffed. "Who cares! Now leave my house, fast, leave immediately and don't come back!" Yossele paid no heed to the warnings of the *chevrah kadisha*.

He died on Monday. His body lay unattended all that day, all of Tuesday, and most of Wednesday. The *chevrah kadisha* refused to prepare the body for burial or make any arrangements for a funeral. Finally, late Wednesday evening, a compassionate neighbor dug a hole outside the fence of the Jewish cemetery and buried the corpse.

Immediately following the morning prayer service on Thursday, a long line of agitated, indigent Jews pushed for a place outside Rabbi Yom Tov Lipman Heller's[1] study hall.

The *shamish* invited the first person inside. Rabbi Heller tried to calm him. "Why are you so perturbed?" he inquired gently.

"Rabbi, I came to tell you that I have no money to buy food for *Shabbos*," answered the poor man, moaning.

"How is it that you never had to come for help before? The *kahal* provides money for people who need help. Your name is not on their list! I don't understand why your situation today is different from last week," insisted Rabbi Heller.

"Rabbi, listen to me, please. I never had to come to the *kahal* because every Thursday morning I would open the door of my little house, pick up the loose board by the fence and find enough money for *Shabbos* and the whole week. I don't know who helped me, but I found money there every Thursday for the past twenty years. Today, there was no money and I don't know what to do. I have no money to buy food for *Shabbos*," he repeated sadly.

Rabbi Heller wrote a note for the poor man and said compassionately, "Take this note to my *shamish*, and he will give you enough money to buy food for *Shabbos*."

The first person left and the second poor person told a similar story to Rabbi Heller. All the people who stood in that line repeated a similar story. It did not take long for Rabbi Heller to realize that Yossele the Miser had been supporting most of the city's indigent Jews for many years. Because he had not been aware of Yossele's kindness, he was clearly distressed that he had not allowed the *chevrah kadisha* to bury Yossele.

Around ten o'clock that morning, Rabbi Heller entered the

---

[1] Rabbi Yom Tov Lipman Heller, the Tosefos Yom Tov (1579–1654), was the leader of the Cracow Jewish community at this time. He is famous for his commentary on the Mishnah, which is always printed alongside the standard text. In addition to his commentary, he wrote religious poetry whose themes describe historical events: the upheaval of the Moravian government in 1618–1620 and the Chmielnicki pogroms in 1648–1649. His prayer poems are recited by some congregations on Yom Kippur to this day.

shul, called his *shamish* and instructed him to assemble all the Jews of Cracow. The people came running, for it was not often that the rabbi summoned them to leave their work.

When the *shul* was filled to capacity, Rabbi Heller ascended the *bimah* and spoke. "I have discovered," he said, "that we are guilty of mistreating a fellow Jew who has supported most of our city's poor people for many years. We did not provide a proper burial for this holy man who lived in our midst. In order to atone for this terrible wrong, which we have all committed, I hereby decree this as a day of public prayer and fasting."

They prayed the remainder of the morning, then returned to their jobs, still fasting. Rabbi Heller stayed in the synagogue, distraught, despondent, sitting in his chair at the front, his head buried in the crook of his elbow, deep in thought. After a while, he fell into a deep sleep and dreamed that Yossele was standing before him and that he pleaded with Yossele to forgive him, the *kahal,* and the entire Jewish community. "Please, Yossele, tell us how we can atone for all the wrongs we have committed against you. We mocked you and threatened you. We shamed you and embarrassed you and we did not bury you in the Jewish cemetery!"

Yossele answered, "I want you to know that you committed no wrong against me. I never wanted the members of the *kahal* or the Jewish community to know how I distributed charity. I never wanted the poor people of Cracow to know who was supplying them with money. You did me a favor by not burying my body properly. . .there was such a tumult in the Heavenly Court over who should have the privilege of burying the man who gave charity in such a secret way. . .the patriarchs Abraham, Isaac, and Jacob demanded the honor. . .Moses and Aaron contested that decision. . .finally, Elyahu, the prophet of peace, prepared my body and buried it." The dream faded.

Rabbi Heller awoke, startled. He immediately summoned a stonemason and commissioned him to carve a monument[2] for

---

[2] Visitors to Cracow have reported finding this monument outside the fence of the Jewish cemetery. However, on a trip to Poland in July, 1989, the authors were shown the grave of Yossele next to that of Rabbi Nassan Shapiro, the Megalleh Amukos (1585–1633). Engraved on that tombstone are the words "He spoke to the prophet Elyahu." The caretaker told us that according to tradition Elyahu revealed himself to Rabbi Shapiro and commanded him to move Yossele's body inside the cemetery.

Yossele's grave. "I want you to inscribed the words 'Here lies Yossele the Holy Miser.' I, Yom Tov Lipman Heller,[3] am a witness," he said. "It will be a fitting memorial for a man who practiced the highest form of charity."

[3] Although we have known this story for many years, we never knew the name of the rabbi, for Cracow was blessed with illustrious rabbinical leadership during that historical period. His name was revealed to us by Rabbi Yaacov Katz, a Gerer *chasid*, the *shochet* (ritual slaughterer) in Munich, West Germany, as we sat in his living room one evening in July 1982, sharing stories with him and his wife. He told us that he had heard this story from his father, who had heard it from his father, who had heard it from his father.

One Never Knows

Poretz Sigizmund Polski was a Polish landholder with vast holdings; he boasted ownership of *shtetlach* and villages, forests and lumber mills, towns and trade routes, lakes and fisheries. The peasants living in the vicinity were forced to work his land. The *shtetlach* were inhabited predominantly by Jewish merchants who ensured the success of the *poretz's* investments with their business acumen, operating under an unrestricted free enterprise system. Because he was dependent upon them, he treated them in a kindly manner.[1]

Polish kings and princes had limited the power of the church for centuries. They chose economic success (ensured by supporting Jewish autonomy) rather than religion (the church) to gain control of the country. However, when the aristocracy

Beth Chanah School Graduates. *Der Lichteker Kuk Fun Baal Shem Tov.* Brooklyn, NY: Empire Press, 1985.
[1]He followed the precedent of King Casimir the Great, who had reconfirmed the Charter of Privileges in 1344–1346 when he invited the Jews fleeing persecution in Western Europe to settle in his country.

lost its power, the church stepped in to fill the void. It was at this time that a new priest, an immigrant from Germany, arrived in *Poretz* Polski's mansion to replace the deceased priest who had been Polski's religious advisor. The new priest was filled with hatred against the Jews and incited people to protest the success of the Jewish merchants. When he felt powerful enough, he went to the *poretz* with a proposal:

"Your territory has more Jews than any other. Years ago, you may have needed them to develop the economy. You thought they were indispensable, so you protected them. Now, we have a new generation of businessmen. Many of them are immigrants from Germany who have all become Polish citizens. They are skilled and can do a better job than the Jews you protect. I think it is time that you expel the Jews from your realm."

Poretz Polski was taken aback by the priest's audacity. "I can't do what you demand. The Jews have served me faithfully for years and years. You are asking me to betray their faithful service."

"I don't mean that you should expel them immediately," explained the priest, hesitatingly. "After all, we Christians are compassionate, we believe in loving our neighbors. We just don't want to be victimized any more by Jewish merchants. On the contrary, give them six months to sell their businesses, to settle their affairs, and to relocate anywhere else in this vast country. And if you listen to me, you will benefit in two ways. First, I can promise you salvation. In addition, any property that the Jews are unable to sell in the stated time can be confiscated. You can divide the property with me as a reward for my sagacious advice. We will both have an opportunity for financial gain. Think about what I have told you and tell me your decision."

Tormented by the decision he had to make, the *poretz* lay awake for many nights. Finally, repressing conscience and compassion, he signed a decree in the presence of the priest expelling the Jews from his realm in six months.

No sooner had the decree been signed than "the couriers went forth hurriedly by order of the *poretz*, and the edict was distributed . . . they sat down to drink (to celebrate the decree of annihilation) and the city was in an uproar. (the Jews cried and wailed loudly while the priest shouted with joy)."[2]

The Jews could not believe this turn of events. Having been protected by this *poretz* and his predecessors, who had been kindly, decent human beings for many years, they hurried to the *shul* in a quandary, to pray and to determine what to do. The rabbi decreed a fast day with the recitation of psalms, but to no avail. When the sun set, the decree had not been rescinded.

The *kahal*, the communal governing council, appointed a representative to plead with the *poretz* and to present him with a sizable sum of money in order that he might rescind the decree. The *poretz* invited the priest to participate at the meeting, so even had the *poretz* wavered in his decision, the haughty mien of the priest paralyzed his ability to reconsider.

Entirely distraught with the knowledge of impending doom, the rabbi decided to seek the advice of Rebbe Yisrael ben Eliezer, the Baal Shem Tov,[3] Master of the Good Name, whose reputation as a mystic, a pietist, and an advisor, had begun to spread throughout the region.

Accompanied by two leaders of the *kahal*, the rabbi set out for Medziboz, the *shtetl* of the Baal Shem Tov, who received them warmly and listened attentively as they told him about the terrible decree of expulsion.

"This is what you have to do," he said slowly, softly, directly to the three men who stood before him, shuddering with grief. "You must select someone from your *shtetl* to travel to St. Petersburg to appeal to Gregory Mikhail Gogol to rescind the decree. He is Minister of the Interior, and the most impor-

---

[2] *Megillas* Esther 3:14–16, paraphrased metaphor.

[3] Rebbe Yisrael ben Eliezer, the Baal Shem Tov (the master of the good name) (1700–1760), succeeded in infusing life and vitality into the Jewish people living in the misery of the Diaspora. He taught them to serve God with great joy, despite their personal feelings of hopelessness and helplessness; he imbued them with a love for Eretz Yisrael and a yearning for the days of the Messiah; he nurtured a deeper understanding of learning and observance; he emphasized prayer as a focal point of Jewish life; he stressed an abiding love for every Jew. These were his legacies, the tenets of the emerging chasidic movement, a movement that still pulsates with life around the world, more than two hundred years after his death.

tant member of the *Zemski Sobor*, the Land Council. He is the only one who can override the *poretz*'s decree, and he is the final authority regarding these matters. Moreover, I suggest you send Pinchas, the old *melamed*, who is in my opinion the only person qualified to speak to Gregory Mikhail Gogol on behalf of the Jewish community."

"Pinchas, the old *melamed?* He is so soft-spoken! How will he be able to plead for us before the Minister of the Interior? St. Petersburg is so far! Even if he succeeds in reaching that distant city, Jews are not permitted into it, unless their business is important to the economy. There are only a few Jews who are permitted into St. Petersburg."

"Don't worry! I know that Pinchas's mission will be blessed with success. There are enough *shtetlach* along the way for him to stop and rest among his people. He can travel through Tzernobel, Liadi, Vitebsk, and straight to St. Petersburg. I have a feeling that he will not have a difficult time arranging an appointment with the Minister of the Interior."

The Baal Shem Tov blessed them and they returned to their *shtetl*. They called a meeting of the *kahal* and were immediately besieged with questions.

"How do we know that Pinchas will be able to arrange an appointment with the Minister of the Interior? What if he is not successful in presenting our case? Should he go alone? Maybe we should send a committee to accompany him? What if, what if. . .?"

Finally, the rabbi raised his hands to silence the tumult.

"Listen, my friends, we sought the advice of the Baal Shem Tov. He blessed us and told us exactly what to do. I believe that he is a man of great wisdom, that his soul sparkles with holy inspiration. If Pinchas agrees to undertake this mission, he should leave tomorrow!"

Pinchas did not know why the Baal Shem Tov had singled him out for this important mission. Nevertheless, since he was chosen, he reluctantly accepted the responsibility. "I have only one request of the community leaders. Please appoint a younger person to accompany me, to help me along the way," Pinchas said.

The two men set out for St. Petersburg, following the route the Baal Shem Tov had suggested. They stopped only to rest, for Pinchas knew that his mission was urgent, a matter of life or death.

Arriving in St. Petersburg, Pinchas found that the few Jews who had permission to live in the city discreetly maintained a cloak of silence. Although they were hospitable, they hesitated to extend themselves to a government official.

"You are asking us to do the impossible," one of the St. Petersburg Jews volunteered. "Even if you were to send a letter requesting an appointment with the Minister of the Interior, he would probably not answer. We have had our experiences with him."

"I have come a long way on an urgent mission. One of you," he pleaded, "must take a chance and write a letter immediately to the Minister of the Interior, requesting an appointment for an emissary from a distant Jewish community. Time is running out. The Baal Shem Tov said that Minister of the Interior Gregory Mikhail Gogol makes the final decisions in these matters. I must see him! You must help arrange an appointment!"

Finally, one of the St. Petersburg Jews agreed to write the letter and to deliver it personally to the minister's appointment secretary. He wrote, "An emissary of a faraway Jewish community, named Pinchas, the teacher of young children, has arrived in St. Petersburg to seek an audience with you. He says that you are the only one who can solve his problem, which involves many people who are faced with a life or death situation. He respectfully requests an appointment at your earliest convenience."

Shock gripped the St. Petersburg Jews when the minister replied that he would see the emissary in two days. Pinchas fasted and prayed.

They accompanied him to the gate of Gogol's mansion and departed. Pinchas took a deep breath, and on gaining admittance walked steadily toward the center staircase, stopping only to ask a servant the direction of the room indicated in the letter he held in his hand.

He recited psalms as he climbed to the top of the staircase, turned right, proceeded down a long corridor, passed three unmarked doors and stopped before the minister's office. The appointments secretary asked him to be seated. "You will have to wait a short while for the minister to see you," he said.

Pinchas experienced fear and faith at the same time. On one hand, he feared that the minister would ignore his plea, that the decree of the *poretz* would remain in effect. On the other hand, he believed that in some way the blessing of the Baal Shem Tov would prevail.

One hour later, he stood before Gregory Mikhail Gogol.

"I am a very busy man," Gogol began curtly. "Your request for an appointment stated that you had to see me on a matter of life or death. I hope that I will consider the matter as important as you do. Now, tell me what it is that you want!"

Without speaking, Pinchas removed a copy of the decree from his pocket and handed it to him.

He read the decree slowly, folded the paper and placed it on the desk next to him. For some inexplicable reason, he stared intently at Pinchas. "Tell me about yourself," he asked. "How is it that *you* were appointed to be the emissary of the Jewish community?"

"Your Honor," uttered Pinchas, the words tumbling forth from his mouth. "I am truly not worthy to stand before you. I was singled out for this most important mission. I do not know why. I am not a member of the communal governing council, nor am I a man of wealth, power, or influence. I am a *melamed*, a teacher of young children. I have been a *melamed* all my adult life. I have a wife and five children. My children are all grown. I was born in the same *shtetl* where I now live."

When Pinchas finished, Gogol signaled for his appointments secretary. "Call my bodyguards, Fyodor and Peter at once," he ordered. He looked away from Pinchas. Pinchas wondered why the minister's seemingly polite attitude had changed so suddenly.

In an instant, he was grabbed under the arms by the bodyguards, lifted, and carried roughly from the room.

He pleaded, he cried, he screamed, but they paid him no heed. "Where are you taking me?" he shrieked. "What did I do to incur the minister's wrath? Two minutes ago he was listening to my request. What happened?"

They carried him along the corridor, down the stairs, out

the door, across the courtyard into a small, high-walled, square, sloped-roof building. Icons and paintings of the mystical symbols of the Eastern Orthodox church covered the walls. A priest signaled them to release him.

"You came to the Minister of the Interior for a favor. He will not consider the plea of a Jew. He insists that you kiss the icon I am holding above your head. You must convert or die!"

Pinchas's heart palpitated. He felt his blood pulsating violently through his body. He quivered; his head throbbed.

"Master of the Universe!" he prayed. "What have I done to deserve this fate? *Sheluchay mitzvah aynan nezakin!* [4] I came to St. Petersburg to plead for Your people. I came with faith that somehow, some way, You would inspire the Minister of the Interior to rescind the decree of doom that hangs over us. I will never convert as they demand. I was born a Jew and I will die a Jew. Is this what happens to people who risk their lives in the performance of *mitzvos*? Do You want me to die a martyr? If You will not help me, will You at least help Your people?"

The priest waved the icon again over Pinchas's head. "Convert or die," he demanded once again. "If you refuse our demands, I will pour that pot of boiling wax down your throat! You have three minutes to decide."

Sobbing, Pinchas recited the deathbed confessional, "May my death be an atonement for all my errors, iniquities, and wrongs that I have committed before You. Grant me a share in the Garden of Eden and permit me the privilege of residing in the World to Come." And then he added brokenly, "*Hayn yikletayne Lo ayachel.* [5] *Sh'ma Yisrael Adonay Elohaynu Adonay Echad.*" [6]

He lay on the floor motionless, ready to meet his Creator.

The priest blindfolded Pinchas and tied his hands together. He forced his mouth open. Pinchas waited for the hot wax to sear his mouth, his palate, his tongue, but the next thing he knew, he was tasting honey!

The priest removed the blindfold and untied his hands.

---

[4] Those sent to perform a religious duty will not suffer hurt (Talmud Bavli, *Pesachim* 8b).

[5] Though He slay me, yet will I trust in Him (Job 13:15).

[6] Hear O Israel, the Lord our God. The Lord is one.

Placing his hands under Pinchas's arms, he helped him rise to his feet. Then he said, "The Minister of the Interior ordered me to try to convert you. Now he is waiting to see you. Return to his office."

Fyodor and Peter walked an unsteady Pinchas back to the minister's office where Gregory Mikhail Gogol awaited him.

Pinchas shook his head, puzzled. He did not understand the game that Gogol was playing with him. All at once, Gogol asked his bodyguards and appointments secretary to leave the room. He sat down at his desk and looked compassionately at Pinchas. "I know that you have lived through an awesome experience, " he began. "Please sit down and I will explain everything to you. First, I want you to know that the mission for which you came to St. Petersburg has been accomplished successfully. While you were being tested, I issued a decree that *Poretz* Sigizmund Polski rescind his order to expel your people from his territory. He must obey because I have jurisdiction over the entire area. My decree is already on the way, in that hands of trusted messengers. Now, I need only ask you one question before I clarify what happened to you. In all the years that you have been a tutor of young children, have you ever taught a child who wasn't Jewish?"

Pinchas leaned his head on the palm of his right hand. Suddenly, memories of hundreds of young children that he had taught flooded before him. He recalled the Chaims, who had become prosperous merchants, the Eliezers, who left the *shtetl* for yeshivos, the Shimons, whose fathers had been *vasser traygers*. So many young children had sat in his *cheder*! But did he ever teach a child who wasn't Jewish?

"I can't remember ever teaching a child who wasn't Jewish," he whispered.

"Please try to remember," the minister urged.

Pinchas sat silently, pensively, for a few moments. After a while, he mumbled, "Yes, yes, I recall now. Once, I taught a child who wasn't Jewish. He used to sit on a bench in the back of the *cheder* with some of the other children. He had a very good mind. He used to listen attentively to the lessons. He also lived in my house."

Gregory Mikhail Gogol insisted, "How was it possible for you to raise a child who wasn't Jewish?"

"As far as I can recall," Pinchas proceeded, "he was an orphan. No one else would take him in. He was the son of the *poretz* and a Polish princess. The marriage had been arranged for political and economic reasons. The princess was very unhappy with the *poretz* because she perceived that he was mismanaging his inheritance. When he lost all his money, she ran away. He was heartbroken, despondent, alone, and poor. Apparently, he saw no future for himself, so he committed suicide. Neighboring *poretzim* refused to have anything to do with the child. The peasants did not want to support another child. The villagers shunned him. So my wife and I brought him into our house. We fed him, clothed him, and educated him along with our own children." Pinchas stopped speaking. He looked up to see tears flowing down Gogol's cheeks.

"What happened to the orphan?" he gulped.

"A few years later, the princess returned to our *shtetl* in search of her son. She found him in our house, thanked us for caring for him, and disappeared with him. I don't know what happened to him after that."

"Look at me," pleaded Gregory Mikhail Gogol. "Is there any resemblance between me and that orphan boy?"

Pinchas stared at him, stunned. "Was it you?"

"Yes. I vowed never to forget what you and your wife did for me. I did not know how I would ever repay my debt to you, especially after my own people rejected me.

"My mother returned with me to her father's house. My grandfather was a very wealthy man, a very influential, very powerful man. I grew up under his tutelage and was educated in the best schools in St. Petersburg. When he died, I inherited everything from him, including his title. I never forgot my oath. I didn't know if I would ever find you, but I carefully checked every petition that crossed my desk that originated from the southern part of this country, hoping that one would concern itself with you or your *shtetl*. When I received your petition for my appointment, I knew my opportunity had come. But I wanted to fulfill my oath in a manner worthy of my deepest respect for you. With what could I reward you? Money, a larger house, splendid clothes? I knew that these things were meaningless to you, so I devised a plan.

"I remembered learning about Rabbi Akiva[7] when I sat on the back bench in your *cheder*. You told us that he died to sanctify God's name. You taught us that this is the highest service that a Jew could perform. I wanted to give you that same opportunity, to experience serving God with all your soul. For a few moments you believed that you were dying to sanctify His name. This is the way I have repaid you.

"Now you may return to your *shtetl*. Be assured that as long as I am Minister of the Interior, nothing evil will happen to you or your family, to the people who live in your *shtetl*, or to other Jewish people who live in the territories under my control."

Pinchas rose, shook hands with his former student, and walked slowly out the door, along the long corridor, down the steps, out the door of the mansion. All the while he sang, "*Hodu Lashem ke tov, ke l'olam chasdo*" ("Give thanks to the Almighty, for He is good, His kindness endures forever!"[8])

---

[7]During the oppressive Roman rule of Eretz Yisrael, Rabbi Akiva was one of the prominent religious leaders who led the struggle for Jewish independence. He believed in the primacy of Torah along with the struggle for redemption. The Romans charged him with treason on two counts: teaching Torah and organizing the rebellion. He was tried, found guilty, and condemned to death. Early in the morning, on the day of execution, Rabbi Akiva's students watched as Roman soldiers flayed the flesh from his body with iron combs. They heard him reciting the *Sh'ma*. They asked him how he could affirm the Kingship of God under such unbearable torture. He replied, "I never knew the meaning of the phrase in the Sh'ma: 'You shall love the Lord Your God with all your soul.' I now understand it to mean, even if He takes your soul" (Deuteronomy 6:5; Talmud *Bavli, Berachos* 61b).

[8]Psalms 118:1.

And You Shall Love

"I remember so clearly," reminisced Rebbe Naftali Ropshitzer,[1] "how I learned the meaning of the *mitzvah*, 'and you shall love your neighbor as you love yourself, I am the Lord. I was a young man of only 16 when my family permitted me to *daven* in Rimanov, in Rebbe Mendel Rimanover's[2] *shul*, that Rosh Hashanah.

Eliyahu Kitov. *Sayfer Haparshey, Kedoshim*. Jerusalem: Alef Publications, 1970.

[1]Rebbe Naftali Tzvi Ropshitzer (1760–1827) was descended from a long line of illustrious rabbis. As a young man, he followed three leading chasidic rebbes: Rebbe Yaakov Yitzchak Halayve Horowitz (the Chozeh of Lublin), Rebbe Yisrael Haupstein (the Maggid of Koshnitz), and Rebbe Menachem Mendel of Rimanov. With the passing of his teachers, he settled in Ropshitz. His chasidic court was famous for the intensity of beautiful *niggun*, which he introduced. His followers believed that his melodies connected the soul of the singer to his Creator.

[2]Disciples of Rebbe Menachem Mendel Rimanover (1745–1815) said that "holy sparks flowed from his head." He believed that Napoleon's early victories were an omen heralding redemption for the Jewish people, because of the liberalization of restrictive laws. See detailed biography in the story "Three Conditions," in Part III, p. 124.

The strangest thing happened before the sounding of the *shofar*. Instead of proceeding with Psalms 47:1, "Clasp hands, all you nations, call forth to God the tribute of the shofar, sound it with rejoicing," the Rebbe stopped the service and said, "Before we proceed, I have to ask you a question that has bothered me for a long time. The Torah instructs us 'to love your neighbor as you love yourself,' but concludes the verse with 'I am the Lord.' What does loving your neighbor have to do with God? It is easy to understand the relation between the *mitzvah* of sitting in the *succah* or eating *matzah*, when the passage ends with 'I am the Lord'—but loving your neighbor?

"To help you understand the connection, I will tell you a story."

* * *

Many years ago, in a *shtetl* not far from here, two children grew up and became the closest of friends. Yaacov and Moshe went to *cheder* together, they played together, sometimes they ate their meals together. They were almost inseparable. Their friendship was so intense that by the time they became working men, they swore to each other that no matter what they were doing *erev Shabbos*, they would meet to share the week's events. One Friday afternoon they met at Yaacov's house, the next Friday afternoon they met at Moshe's house. Their weekly meeting continued after they married and had children.

Yaacov had a very hard time earning a living as a merchant in his native *shtetl*. He made inquiries in the neighboring *shtetlach*, and found that in one particular place there was no merchant who bought household supplies from the twice-yearly fair. He thought it possible to earn a comfortable living where he had no competition. His dilemma was soul-wrenching. How could he leave his parents and relatives? And how could he leave his best friend, Moshe?

The following Friday afternoon he discussed his problem with him. "I have never had to make such a difficult decision," he confessed. "It seems that opportunity beckons, yet I am so used to living in this *shtetl*. We have been inseparable since we were children. How will we manage not being able to see each other? And if I move, I will have to settle my wife and children among strangers. I might have to travel a lot among the various fairs to buy merchandise. On the other hand, I have found that there is no competition in that area. I could become very successful. I am really so tired of being poor.''

"Whatever you decide to do," Moshe assured him, "we will always remain the best of friends. If you do decide to move, we will still maintain our friendship. Let's promise that no matter what happens we will write each other long letters every Friday in place of our weekly visits.''

Yaacov was grateful for Moshe's emotional support and decided to make the move. He settled his family in the new *shtetl*, traveled to the fair, stocked up on merchandise, and opened a household supplies store in the marketplace. People flocked to his shop, for his merchandise was of good quality and his shop was conveniently located.

Yaacov worked diligently all week, but closed his shop two hours before *Shabbos* in order to have time to write his weekly letter to Moshe.

After a few years, Yaacov felt that his decision to move had been a wise one, for he had established himself as one of the leading businessmen in the *shtetl*.

Meantime, Moshe had made some bad business investments. Slowly, he lost all the money that he had saved for emergencies. At first, he tried to hide his financial difficulties from his wife, but she was a clever woman and realized something was troubling him. Finally, she came right out and said "You are not the same man I married. That man shared everything with me. Obviously, something is troubling you. Please tell me what's the matter.''

At first Moshe, protective husband that he was, refused to share his troubles, but when it was difficult to put bread on the table to feed his children, he told his wife that he had misjudged certain business deals and the consequences were that they simply had no more money.

"Listen to me," she said quietly. "I have an idea. Your friend, Yaacov, has become a very wealthy businessman. You trust him more than any person in the whole world. Knowing you, I realize that he may not know of our plight, for I'm sure you never mention such things in your weekly letters. Why don't you go see him? Maybe he will help us.''

Moshe did not want to share his pain with his friend, but finally he realized that he had no choice. Having no money for coach fare, he packed a loaf of bread and some fruit in a bag, slung it across his shoulders, and took off on foot for Yaacov's *shtetl*. He arrived after many weeks of tramping through grassy fields, and trudging along muddy roads.

"Since it is already dark," he thought, as he crawled exhausted into the town, "I will spend the night under the tree in the town square and seek Yaacov in the morning." He lay down under the tree and fell into a deep sleep.

That night, someone set fire to the local church. Sleeping people, awakened by the acrid smell of smoke, rushed from their houses. "Who could have done this, who could have done this," they yelled and screamed at each other. The commotion was ear-shattering.

The police searched the *shtetl* for a suspicious character and found Moshe sleeping under the tree. "We have the culprit," they shouted gleefully. "Who, except this vagabond, this beggar, this Jew, could possibly have set fire to our church?" Ten witnesses stepped forward to corroborate the police constable's suspicion.

They arrested Moshe and placed him in the stock. Townspeople passed, and threw stones, kicked and spat at Moshe. "After all," they sneered, "isn't he the scum who set fire to our church?"

In the morning, Yaacov came to town to open his shop. He heard the commotion in the square and walked toward the throngs who still milled around hours after the blaze had been extinguished, scorning the man in the stocks.

As he approached, he heard the jeering call of "Jew! Jew!" His curiosity was aroused. What Jew would dare set fire to the church? he wondered. Stealthily, he tiptoed closer to the stocks, trying to remain as unobtrusive as possible. He wanted to see the face of the man who had disgraced and endangered the entire Jewish community. Finally, he reached a tree directly facing the stock. Standing behind it, he recognized his best friend whom he had not seen in many years.

"It's Moshe! It's Moshe!" he whispered, aghast. "It's my friend, Moshe!" He is so emaciated and bedraggled. Poverty must have affected his mind. That's why he set fire to the church. Yaacov ran to the police station. Breathlessly, without thinking of his own safety, he shouted at the constable, "You have the wrong man! You have the wrong man! I am the one who set fire to the church."

The constable arrested Yaacov and ordered a policeman to set Moshe free. Then he hustled Yaacov to the town square and set him into the stock. Moshe wanted to flee that town as soon as possible, knowing that his mission to see his friend Yaacov had failed, but first he decided to find out who the guilty man was.

He remained near the square until the accused had been set into the stock, then walked by pretending that he was about to throw stones with the rest of the crowd. As he raised his hand to throw the stone, his eyes sought the face of the man sitting in the stock.

"Yaacov, my dear friend Yaacov," he whispered to himself thinking "His wealth must have gone to his head. He must have lost his mind from the power the Jewish community bestowed upon him. He must have thought that he could get away with setting fire to the church."

Moshe ran to the constable and shouted, "You have the wrong man! You have the wrong man! I am the one who set fire to the church."

The constable was puzzled. He had two confessions but only one crime. In all his years of experience as an officer of the law, he had never had such a problem. He decided to turn the case over to a higher judicial court.

The judge who was assigned to review the case could not reach a verdict, for the circumstances of the arrest of the two confessed criminals were very peculiar. That judge decided to transfer the case to a still higher court. In the meantime, Yaacov and Moshe were transferred each time the case was transferred, but were never permitted to see each other. Finally, the case was presented to the tzar.

Moshe and Yaacov saw each other for the first time when they were both brought before the ruler of Russia. Instantaneously, they realized what each one was willing to do for the other. In that moment of recognition, they embraced lovingly, sobbing uncontrollably.

"Silence, silence," interrupted the tzar. "I have read the details of this case, and I find the circumstances very peculiar.

The way the case was presented to me, I can't find either of you guilty of setting fire to the church. However, I understand what each of you was willing to do. I want you both to know that I have never met, in my entire life, two such loyal friends who were willing to die for each other."

Pensively, he rested his head on his raised palm. After what seemed to be an eternity, the tzar turned to Yaacov and Moshe and spoke to them very softly, very gently. "There is no question in my mind that both of you are innocent. I have, however, one request. You know that I am the tzar of all Russia. I have more power and more wealth than anyone in the world. Yet I do not have a friend as loyal as either of you. Please, please, won't you include me in your friendship?"

Rebbe Mendel Rimanov paused. He wanted his story to have an impact on the worshipers who waited for him to sound the *shofar.* He waited a few moments, and then resumed.

"From this story we may learn the answer to my original question. What does 'I am the Lord' have to do with 'you shall love your neighbor as yourself'? As the tzar rules Russia, so does God rule the world. He asks us to love one another. When we fulfill the *mitzvah* of 'love your neighbor as you love yourself,' as Moshe and Yaacov loved each other, then God asks to be included in that friendship. Now you understand the relationship between the words, 'love your neighbor as you love yourself,' and 'I am the Lord.' "

A hushed silence settled over the *shul* until the piercing sound of the *shofar* resounded throughout.

* * *

"Since that Rosh Hashanah, I try to keep in my mind," concluded Rebbe Naftali Ropshitzer, "the connection between 'love your neighbor as you love yourself' and 'I am the Lord' that I learned from Rebbe Mendel Rimanov."

A Renewed Friendship

When I first moved to Ushpetzin, I used to study with Rebbe Berish once or twice a week.[1] I was delighted to be in his presence, listening to his words of wisdom. It seemed that any question I had about a talmudic passage that I couldn't grasp, a halachic decision I couldn't understand, or a midrashic concept that evaded me . . . he always knew what bothered me. He never waited for me to ask. Somehow, when he sensed I had a problem, he would quote verses from the Torah and explain them, always clarifying my problems. It never ceased to amaze me how he could focus in on my problems without my having pointed them out to him.

Gradually, I became part of the inner circle of his closest disciples, the ones who were invited for *shalosh seudos*, the third meal of *Shabbos*.

It was during the second year of my being part of the

Menachem Menli Sofayr. Shlosha Esray Tzon. Tel Aviv, Jerusalem: Hotzaas Sinai, 1958.

[1]Rebbe Berish was a contemporary of Rebbe Yaakov Yitzchak Halayve Horowitz, the Chozeh of Lublin (1745–1815).

rebbe's inner circle, on the *Shabbos* eve between Rosh Hashanah and Yom Kippur, that he whispered to me after the evening prayer service: "After all the others have left, I'd like you to stay for a few moments. I have something private to discuss with you."

I waited impatiently for them to leave, but each one wanted to wish him a *gut voch* individually, shake his hand, dip the tips of their fingers into the spilled wine from *havdalah*, and brush their eyelids and pocket linings with it. The wait seemed interminable. I could not fathom what the rebbe wanted, why he chose me, a relative newcomer from among all his disciples, for a private discussion.

Finally, we were alone, standing face to face. Rebbe Berish spoke: "I have been looking for a young man like you for a long time, one whom I could trust to do special favors for me. Now, if you will consent, I want you to undertake a secret mission. I want you to know now that you will never be able to divulge the details of this mission to anybody, nor will you understand completely why I want you to do it. Nevertheless, I beg you to trust me. Will you agree to do my bidding?"

I stood in awe before Rebbe Berish, intrigued that he had chosen me from among all his disciples for a secret mission. Slowly, I nodded my head in assent.

Rebbe Berish continued. "Remember," he warned, "you can tell nobody. If the wrong people find out what you are doing, it might endanger many Jews."

I was eager for him to explain what he wanted me to do. He began speaking again, very softly, solemnly. "You know, of course, that we Jews believe that prayer, charity, and repentance nullify an evil decree.[2] I have dreamed night after night, ever since Rosh Hashanah when man's fate is decreed, about a harsh judgment from the Heavenly Court against Isaac Ungar, a wealthy Jew who lives in Yanderchof, Galicia, not far from here.

"I want you to find him. Tell him you have a message from an anonymous Jew who understands the mysteries of creation. Explain to him that we believe that prayer, charity, and repen-

---

[2]*U'Nesaneh Tokef, Musaf* prayer for Rosh Hashanah and Yom Kippur.

tance nullify an evil decree. Naturally, he will ask you what he has to do. These are the instructions.

"First, the minute he awakens each day, he must wash his face and hands and dress. Second, even before he recites his morning prayers, he must put aside all the money left over from his business dealings the day before in a specially marked charity box. He must distribute it secretly to those students who are devoting their days to the study of Torah. He is to make a daily habit of this charity distribution, doubling the amount on Friday, so that the people he supports will have enough for *Shabbos*. Tell him that if he does this conscientiously, every day, until Rosh Hashanah next year, he will be able to stand before the throne of judgment in great joy, knowing that the decree against him was annulled."

I left immediately for Yanderchof, weighed down with the responsibility of fulfilling my special mission. It did not take me long to find Isaac Ungar, for he was one of the wealthiest Jews in town.

Although he greeted me warmly, his manner changed to skepticism when I told him the message from the anonymous Jew. He considered himself to be an upright, charitable man, and he did not understand why he had to carry the burden of supporting students of Torah on a daily basis.

I repeated Rebbe Berish's words in order to impress upon him the seriousness of the Heavenly Court's decree against him. I also told him that prayer, charity, and repentance nullify the evil decree. Finally, he acceded. "I promise to do my best to follow your instructions."

When we parted, I honestly believed that I had successfully accomplished my mission.

During that year, I kept my eyes and ears open for any news of Isaac Ungar and his family. Because I was the harbinger of his fate, I was curious to know how he would fare that year.

I heard that bandits had set fire to the trees in front of his house, but miraculously, the fire did not spread and no one was hurt. Only a very small chest, containing a few pieces of jewelry, disappeared in the melee that followed. Apparently, the bandits had used the fire as a ploy to break into the house.

I heard that a note in Polish, threatening his life, was tacked to his front door one morning. It warned, "You will be shot and no one will know your murderer!"

I heard other harrowing stories about Isaac Ungar, but it always turned out that he had escaped unharmed.

Then, I heard that Isaac Ungar was awarded a government contract to import and export raw materials. It seemed that the Austrian government was planning to build a blast furnace in which to process pig iron for its emerging industries. The plant would be located in Krompahi, near Lvov, in the district of Galicia.

He rushed to the government administrative offices to bid on the contract as the supplier of the raw material for the plant. The government official realized the advantages of dealing with one responsible supplier, so he signed the contract proposed by Isaac Ungar.

In his role as the central government supplier, he had to deal with Jews and non-Jews alike, for both shaft mine owners and open-pit mine owners were forced to channel their raw materials to him.

I was relieved at this turn of events in Isaac Ungar's life. And then there was no more news. I found out the rest of the story when he came to see Rebbe Berish a few months later.

I was in the *bays midrash* that Friday afternoon when he arrived. He agitatedly told the rebbe that his success had become apparent to his neighbor, a non-Jew named Villtshik, who had been very friendly until the awarding of the government contract. Haltingly, he blurted out the details. "Villtshik, angered by my coup, gathered a group of his friends together for the purpose of defaming me. I found out that Villtshik had goaded his friends. "Why should that Jew have exclusive right to supply the government blast furnaces? We should all have part of the same business," he thundered at them, "we should all have the right to share the government profits! We should be entitled to half the business!"

Villtshik's friends agreed with him. It didn't take much to rouse their envy. They decided they would petition the government official concerning their grievance and if he paid no attention to their plea, they would take matters into their own hands.

Ungar continued, "I was horrified when I discovered the plot against me. I was not concerned for my personal safety. I was worried more about my family and the many students that I support with my daily distribution of charity. I am also concerned with the welfare of my miners and the drivers of carts and wagons who deliver the ore and wood to the blast furnaces."

Since Rebbe Berish knew all about Isaac Ungar, he was not surprised at his story. His eyes twinkled. A smile creased his cheeks. He held out his hands and beckoned Isaac Ungar to stand close to him. Then he placed his outstretched arms on his shoulders and looked him straight in the eyes.

"I want you to know that Villtshik will not get his way. No matter what he does, he will not interfere with your government contract. Now, go and prepare for *Shabbos*."

Isaac Ungar looked skeptical. It was apparent that he wanted to believe Rebbe Berish's words, but he was known as a practical man. It was impractical to believe that things would work out in his best interest. He seemed troubled that whole *Shabbos*, because he could not stop thinking what would happen if Villtshik did take matters into his own hands.

His mind was no more at ease when he took leave of the rebbe Sunday morning. Again, I didn't hear any news about Isaac Ungar for a while, but a few months later, he burst into the *bays midrash* and happily revealed the end of the story.

"A few days had passed since my last visit here. One night, I was awakened by a heavy pounding on the front door. Nervously, I ran down the stairs from my bedroom, remembering the threatening note that had been tacked to my front door months ago. The frightened servants ran from their sleeping quarters toward the foyer, parted the draperies and peered into the darkness, trying to determine the identity of the intruder. One turned to me and said, 'It is only your neighbor Villtshik on the porch. He is crying.'

"I calmed myself and signaled the servants to let him in. As soon as Villtshik stepped into the foyer, he fell to his knees and began pleading. 'Please forgive me for trying to cause you harm. Your success made me envious. All the land I own and the rents I collect never satisfied me, when I imagined how much profit you were earning on the government contract. I swear to you that I will drop all my plans to cause you grief, if only you will forgive me.'

"I stood glued to the spot, unable to react. After a few silent minutes, I raised the kneeling man to his feet, and gave him a handkerchief to dry his tears. I signaled a servant to bring some whiskey and led the distraught man into my study.

"Please sit down. Try to calm yourself," I said to Villtshik. "I don't know what convinced you to change your plans, but you must have had good reason to do so. Would you like to tell me the reason for your change of heart?"

Hesitatingly, he began. "I really wanted that government contract, and I made plans to accomplish my goal. But during the past five nights, I have been unable to sleep. As soon as I fell asleep, I would be awakened by terrible nightmares. I awoke screaming in panic, because the nightmares haunted me so. I dreamed that the horrible plans I had for you were really being carried out against me."

He dropped his voice and continued in a whisper. "My wife is a very wise woman. Tonight she said to me sternly, 'Villtshik, you have brought these sleepless nights, these horrible night-mares upon yourself. Don't you remember all the kindness Isaac Ungar did for you? Don't you remember how he lent you money to buy your first tract of land? Don't you recognize how fine a neighbor he's been, how he has given you responsible business advice? How can you plot to hurt him? How can you repay good with evil? What kind of human being are you, anyway?'

"I was dumbfounded. My wife never spoke to me so harshly . . . but her words penetrated my soul and I realized she was right. Therefore, I came to you in the middle of the night to beg for forgiveness. I swear I will not harm you. I couldn't bear another sleepless night. My conscience is hurting too much. Please tell me that you forgive me!"

"By the time Villtshik had finished speaking, my servant had brought the whiskey. We raised our glasses. "To our renewed friendship, *L'Chayim*," I said, downing the warm amber liquid.

"*L'Chayim!*" echoed Villtshik, swallowing the whiskey. He shook my hand, turned toward the door of the study, and backed his way out of the foyer through the front door.

"I sat alone until daybreak, pondering the events of my life during the previous year. I wondered who the anonymous Jew was, the one who understood the mysteries of creation, who the messenger was. Slowly, I began to comprehend the meaning of the verse 'prayer, charity, and repentance nullify an evil decree.'

"When I saw the rays of dawn break the night sky, I quickly washed my face and hands, dressed, separated the portion of the money from yesterday's business dealings that I would give to charity, prayed, harnessed my horses to a wagon, and set off again to see Rebbe Berish Ushpetzin.

"I wanted Rebbe Berish to know that Villtshik promised that he would not interfere with my government contracts. I wanted the rebbe to know also that I now understand how prayer, charity, and repentance nullify the evil decree."

A Jew Has to Know How
to Do a Favor

"I remember my rebbe Kalonymous Kalmish Shapiro of Piasetsno so well; he left an indelible impression on me," said the
hunchbacked street cleaner, beginning his story as he hobbled
on his deformed legs along the beach in Tel Aviv with Rabbi
Shlomo Carlebach.[1] His face was contorted, as if his nose and
jawbone had been broken and never healed. Ugly disfigurations
surrounded the blue concentration camp number that had been
tattooed onto his arm. "Although many years have passed," he
said softly, "I think about the lessons of life he taught me in the
years between the world wars when I was a student in his
Yeshiva Daas Moshe. Even after the Nazi invasion of Poland,
when they shrank the boundaries of the cities and incarcerated
the Jews behind barbed wire, my rebbe moved the yeshiva
inside the Warsaw ghetto and continued to teach us. I re-

[1]This story was told to us by Rabbi Shlomo Carlebach, creator of thou-
sands of chasidic melodies, Talmud scholar, and one who was instrumental in
founding the *Baal Teshuvah* movement. The biographical data about Rebbe
Kalonymous Kalmish Shapiro was taken from the introduction to *Rebbe
Kalonymous Kalmish Shapiro*, Derech Hamelech, Tel Aviv, Chasidim of
Piasetsno, 1976.

member that early in 1943 he had to relocate the yeshiva again. He camouflaged it in an underground bunker beneath the Schultz Shoe Factory.

"Actually, he saved my life. If you have time, I will tell you the whole story."

"Of course, I have time. I have been searching for people who knew the rebbe of Piasetsno," insisted Shlomo. "No matter how many stories I hear about him, it is never enough. You know that my family escaped from Baden Bei Wien in Austria, right after the Anschluss in March 1938. Somehow, every time I meet a survivor, I am compelled to listen to his story so that as I travel, I can retell the details of the greatest of Jewish tragedies."

They walked side by side together for a few silent moments. The hunchbacked street cleaner tried to organize his thoughts, not knowing where to begin his story. After a while, he spoke softly.

"Once the blitzkrieg was over, Poland crumbled. The Nazis, in their determination to find a final solution to the Jewish problem, followed a specific pattern of annihilation. They ravaged the synagogues and study halls as soon as they overran each *shtetl*. Sometimes they turned them into stables or latrines, but their priorities were always to confiscate the precious ritual objects and burn the Torah scrolls and the holy books.

"Barbed wire was strung around the Jewish quarter of Warsaw. The Jews were herded into a confined, overcrowded area that was continuously narrowed with every additional deportation. Their plan was to isolate the victims, to starve them, to dehumanize them. Food was rationed; smugglers were severely beaten or shot immediately, no questions asked. The Jews knew that they would be susceptible to typhus and other diseases or that they would die of starvation.

"There were two prisons in Warsaw. The Pawiak prison was used to incarcerate Jews who were found on the Aryan side of the city. It was a fortress of terror before death for 8,000 Jewish men, women, and children. The other prison, Gesia, was nearby. There, the inmates' instincts were brutalized in order to turn man into beast, willing to kill for a crust of bread.

"I have not always been a hunchback. The beatings in Treblinka permanently deformed me." Sighing painfully for a few minutes, breathing deeply, he attempted to continue walking.

"It is so difficult to talk, yet I know it must be told," he whispered brokenly. "I will try to go on.

"Did you know how some of the children survived in the Warsaw ghetto a bit longer than others? There was a Jewish orphanage, Dom Sierot, that was also transferred inside the ghetto wall after the Nazi invasion. The children lived by their wits, stealing to survive, crawling through sewage pipes to reach the Aryan side, hoping to beg for a *zloty* to buy a crust of bread or a potato peel. But I'm sure you know all this from what you've read."

Shlomo turned to his companion. Tears streamed down his cheeks. His body quivered. As they walked along the Mediterranean coast, the white breaker waves foamed and swelled, rippling against the shore line.

"Let me tell you the part that you don't know. Let me tell you about my rebbe. Now that I have opened up to you, I have to tell you everything. I feel that my speaking today is in place of the eulogy that was never delivered."

* * *

He was born on 19 Iyar, 1889, to Rebbe Elimelech and Chana B'racha Shapiro. Although his father prophesied at his *bris* that his young son would grow to be a dedicated servant of God, he did not live to see his vision fulfilled, for he passed away three years later. When my rebbe was 16, he married Rachel Chaya Miriam, the daughter of Rebbe Yerachmiel Moshe of Koshnitz. His father-in-law was his mentor, and he succeeded him to the rabbinate of Piasetsno when he died four years later.

It was 1909. People came from all over the surrounding area to learn from him. He was like an overflowing well of magnificent Torah thought. His chief concerns were teaching the love of God and Torah, the sanctity of *Shabbos*, doing favors. But his most important priority was teaching children, for he was known as the "rebbe of children."

After World War I, he moved to Warsaw and established a *bays midrash* which gradually turned into Yeshiva Daas way, my rebbe kept whispering to me, "Don't forget . . . If you come out of this alive . . . remember. . . . Tell everyone you Moshe, named for his deceased father-in-law. In order to maintain contact with his followers in Piasetsno, he spent the summer months with them, but his main educational efforts were expended in Warsaw. He was committed to rearing a generation of Torah scholars. People sought his blessings, his advice. They entered his room downtrodden and forlorn, but emerged full of hope, their minds at ease.

Like his predecessors, Rebbe Layve Yitzchak of Berditchev and Rebbe Avraham Yehoshua Heschel Apter, he was known as an 'Ohayv Yisrael,' a lover of every Jew.

He arranged and supervised a course of study in Yeshiva Daas Moshe that would produce students immersed in Torah thought as well as students committed to living the ways of Torah. His students were the jewels in his crown.

"Please tell me how your rebbe celebrated *Shabbos*," Shlomo interrupted.

"I can only tell you that until the Messiah comes, there will never be another *Shabbos* like those we celebrated together," he reminisced. "I remember hundreds of children, his kingdom of children, between the ages of 5 and 17, singing together 'L'cha Dodi' and 'Shalom Aleichem.' I was one of his children. The chorus of our voices ascended on the wings of angels directly to the gates of heaven. Maybe our song was even higher than heaven.

After he made *Kiddush*, he would speak to us about the Torah reading for that particular week. Then he would ritually wash his hands, distribute pieces of *challah*, and continue his discourse. We ate and he taught. After each course of the meal, he continued teaching us. As he came to the end of each thought, he always ended with: 'Remember, my children, *a Jew has to know how to do a favor.*'

We celebrated *Shabbos* this way as long as I can recall. There were always younger children who joined his "kingdom of children," and as we grew older, we left for other *yeshivos*. During his Warsaw years, he wrote an educational manual titled *Chovos Hatalmidim, Duties of the Students*, that served as a written guide to his educational philosophy.

His only son, Rebbe Elimelech Bentziyon, and his young wife were murdered almost immediately after the outbreak of the war. His personal pain was intense, but aware that all his people suffered, he attempted to cover his own anguish by doing everything in his power to help them: by praying, by teaching, by studying, and by attending to their physical and spiritual needs. He found tattered blankets and clothing where none could be found. He begged for a little extra food for 'his children' from those people who still had a little money and were able to purchase extra rations. He refused to stop doing favors; instead, he worked untiringly to help his people survive, to maintain some semblance of dignity where none was permitted. He continued to teach in hidden cellars and in underground bunkers.

His work *Esh Kodesh* (*Holy Fire*), Torah thoughts he taught during the Holocaust, was recorded by his scribe, Rebbe Nesanel Radziner. The manuscript was smuggled into Treblinka. The scribe intended to hide it, hoping it would be found after the war and that someone would reprint it, hoping that it would remain for posterity. Most of it was lost. The fragments that remained were printed many years later by some students who survived and were able to carry them to Eretz Yisrael.

You know, we survived the Warsaw Ghetto uprising, which lasted almost four weeks beginning at Pesach 1943. The German SS General Jurgen Stroop did not expect such heroic Jewish resistance. His Nazis fought to regain every house on Zamenhof Street, on Mila Street, on Smocza Street, on Gesia Street, every building, every inch of the ghetto. They used cannons, tanks, flamethrowers, demolition engineers. We used primitive weapons to defend our position and a network of underground bunkers for first aid stations, to hide the defenseless children, the infirm, and the aged.

Toward the end, the Warsaw Ghetto was a flaming inferno. Some Jewish fighters escaped to safety through the sewers, joining the Polish partisan units. The Nazis responded by dropping gas into the sewer manholes around the ghetto wall. All forms of resistance stopped by the middle of May.

We were taken to Treblinka concentration camp.[2] On the
meet. . . . A Jew has to know how to do a favor. . . . A Jew has
to know how to do a favor."

He was martyred on the fourth day of Marcheshvan 1944,
at the age of 55.

* * *

The hunchbacked street cleaner stopped breathlessly. He
paused in his tracks for a long minute. Finally, he lowered
himself to a sitting position on the sand. He looked up at
Shlomo.

"Now you know the story of Rebbe Kalonymous Kalmish
Shapiro. You must also know how his teachings saved my life in
Treblinka. I always tried to follow his instructions to do a Jew a
favor. When I had absolutely no more strength, when I thought
I would collapse from lack of food and sleep, I only had to think
of my rebbe, and somehow I could go on. I knew my entire
family had been murdered, and when I couldn't bear it anymore, I tried to commit suicide. But I always heard my rebbe's
words . . . 'a Jew has to know how to do a favor.' Do you know
how many favors you can do in a concentration camp? Every
time I did a favor, I had enough strength to go on a little bit
longer. I went on until the Allied liberation. Then I wandered
around Europe as a displaced person for three years. I arrived in
Eretz Yisrael shortly after the establishment of the state. Since
then, I have been cleaning streets during the day, but at night,
I think of the words my rebbe whispered to me on the train to
the concentration camp. Sometimes I can hear his voice com-
pelling me to act. I hear him whispering to me, 'Remember, a
Jew has to know how to do a favor!'"

[2]During the authors' trip to Poland in July 1989, they located the marker
for Piasetsno among the 18,000 memorial markers in Treblinka commemorating the *shtetlach* that had once lived throughout the Polish countryside.

Gemilus Chasadim–

Acts of
KINDNESS

emilus chasadim (act of kindness) is defined as any assistance extended to anyone in need. There are no parameters to kindness; it is incumbent upon everyone to act in a kindly manner.

Shimon HaTzadik said: The world depends on three things for its existence, the study of Torah, the service of God, and acts of kindness.

—*Avos* 1:2

These are the precepts that have no prescribed measure: leaving the corner of a field for the poor, bringing the first fruit offering to the Holy Temple, acts of kindness, and Torah study.

—*Payah* 1:1

These are the precepts whose fruits a person enjoys in this world but whose principle remains intact for him in the world to come . . . acts of kindness. . .

— Talmud *Bavli, Shabbos* 127a

The Jewish people are characterized by modesty, mercy, and benevolence.

— Talmud *Bavli, Yevomos* 79a

Whoever is merciful to his fellow men is certainly of the children of our father Abraham.

—Talmud *Bavli, Baytzah* 32b

This is my God and I will adore Him.

—Exodus 15:2

Abba Shaul explained that this means: I will be like Him, just as He is gracious and compassionate, so be you gracious and compassionate.

—Talmud *Bavli, Shabbos* 133b

As He clothes the naked, so clothe you the naked[1];

As He visits the sick, so visit you the sick[2];

As He comforts the mourners, so comfort you the mourners. . .

—Talmud *Bavli, Sotah* 14a

Even a poor man can practice *gemilus chasadim* by showing genuine care, speaking soft words, and extending good will to his neighbor who is in need.

—Rabbi Yona Gerondi, *Yesod Hateshuvah*

[1]Despite their (Adam and Eve's) wrongdoing in eating from the Tree of Knowledge, the Almighty did not withdraw His care from them; and He made for the man and the woman garments of skin and He clothed them (Genesis 3:21).

[2]And the Lord appeared to him (Abraham) to visit him in his sickness, for it was the third day after his circumcision (Genesis 18:1, Rashi).

Torah Thoughts

Kindness

Kindness is the most significant of all character traits, for God created the world because of His lovingkindness for mankind. The verse "the world is built with kindness" (Psalms 89:3) means that lovingkindness is inherent to the proper functioning of the world.[1]

—Rabbi David Kimchi (1160–1230), Bible commentator

The following acts of kindness have no limit. In fact, they are included in the category of positive, active *mitzvos:* visiting the sick, comforting the bereaved, burying the dead, dowering the bride, hospitality to guests . . . these are all included in the category of "love your neighbor as you love yourself." This means that anything you wish others to do for you, you are obligated to do for them.

—Maimonides. *Ayvel* 14:1

The Torah begins with *gemilus chasadim*[2] and ends with *gemilus chasadim*[3] to emphasize its major theme. By inte-

---

[1]See note 1, p. 89.
[2]See note 2, p. 89.
[3]And the Holy One, Blessed be He, in His glory, buried him (Moses) (Deuteronomy 34:6).

grating *gemilus chasadim* into the Torah from beginning to end, the Almighty instructs us how to conduct our lives.[4]

"The Lord is your shadow . . ." (Psalms 121:5). God is overjoyed when man acts kindly. He then illuminates the world with His own kindness, thereby increasing gentility in the world. When kindness increases, happiness prevails. This passage means therefore that God's kindness is a reflection of man's deeds
                —Rebbe Yisrael ben Eliezer, the Baal Shem Tov

The uniqueness of being part of the Jewish people is that when one Jew suffers, the pain is felt by every Jew. The essence of an act of kindness is first to feel his pain and then to try to alleviate his suffering.
                —Rebbe Shmuel Tzvee MeAleksander, *Tiferes Shmuel*

If you see your fellowman suffering, and you are indifferent to his pain, it is as if you have contributed to its cause.
                —Rebbe Nachman of Bratslav, *Sayfer Hamidos*

"Do what is right and good in the sight of the Almighty. . ."
                —Deuteronomy 6:18

If the Torah instructs us in the observance of 613 commandments, we know what is expected. Aren't these words 'to do what is right and good' redundant? There are certain acts of lovingkindness that are not required by specific laws. Yet, when they are performed, one fulfills doing what is right and good. The more acts of kindness we do beyond the requirement of the law, the more we do what is right and good, and the more we imitate and cling to the characteristics of the Almighty.
                —Rebbe Yehuda Layb Ayger, *Toras Emes*, Volume II

[4]Rabbi Chaim Kapusi (1540–1631) was a leading Sephardic rabbi. His synagogue in Cairo was considered an especially holy place, attracting worshipers from the surrounding area, particularly students of Kabbala. As long as two hundred years after his death, Jews poured oil on the monument over his grave when they visited its site.

There are people who personify lovingkindness. They are synonomous with the verse, "and be a blessing."

—Genesis 12:2

This means that everyone who comes in contact with them is influenced by their actions. They feel the pain of their fellow man and act to alleviate this pain, thereby becoming a source of hope. Just as truly kind people lift the burden of pain, so they share expressions of joy. Since they love their fellowman, they deal peacefully, lovingly, and kindly with all.

—Rebbe Shalom Noach Barzovski MeSlonim, *Netivos Shalom*

Stories

A Sacred Trust

Two Jewish business partners, José and Alberto, emigrated from Barcelona, Spain to Italy, entirely stripped of their material possessions.[1] They settled their families and decided on a daring attempt to return and regain their wealth. To escape observation

Mordechai ben Yechezkel. *Sayfer Hamaseyos.* Tel Aviv: Hotzaas Devir. First edition 1928. Reprinted 1977.

[1]Since the destruction of the second Holy Temple, shortly after the beginning of the common era, Jews wandered from country to country, seeking a place of refuge in a generally hostile world. Spain was one of the countries that extended its hospitality for a period of approximately five hundred years.

During that period, known by historians as the Golden Age, Jews lived with Moslems in a mutually productive environment. There were no differences in language, dress, and culture and no discrimination in areas of political, intellectual, or economic achievement. Only religion separated the two peoples.

Then the Moslems lost their stronghold in Europe to Christendom. At first, the new conquerors maintained a friendly relationship with their Jewish subjects, but within a short period of time they gradually imposed restrictive measures similar to those their co-religionists had imposed upon Jews throughout western Europe during the latter part of the Middle Ages.

Some Jews who had been comfortable in an environment of religious freedom and economic success migrated to Poland where they were welcomed. Some Jews wandered around the Ottoman Turkish Empire, eventually settling

by the Inquisition's spies, they disguised themselves as prosperous Spanish merchants and spoke only Spanish.

They traveled from city to city, from Granada southwest to Malaga, northwest to Seville and Cordova, north toward the center of the country to Toledo, northeast toward the Mediterranean city of Barcelona. They traded in silk fabrics and precious stones, earning huge profits with their beautiful merchandise.

In each city to which they traveled, they rented rooms in the top floor of the inn where they would have complete privacy to practice their religion secretly.

They awoke each morning an hour before sunrise, taking time to study a page of Talmud and review the weekly Torah portion from the books they carried with them. Then they prayed, ate a breakfast of fruits and nuts, arranged their merchandise neatly in sacks that they slung over their shoulders and set off on foot for the center of town.

They returned each evening to their room, unloaded their merchandise, counted their profits, prayed, shared a simple meal consisting of food they had themselves bought in the marketplace that day, and retired for the night. They did this for five or six months. When they had sold all their merchandise and earned enough money to sustain their families for the rest of the year, they returned to their new homes in Italy.

Their secret adventure created so loyal a friendship between the two men that there were no bounds in their love or devotion to each other.

Three years passed. No one ever questioned their identity. No one suspected that the two merchants were Jews and so they thought they would be able to continue the masquerade indefinitely.

However, shortly after their arrival in the port of Malaga for the fourth time, Alberto fell ill. They decided to work their way

---

in Eretz Yisrael, their homeland. Many others converted officially, but remained hidden Jews (*conversos*) after the Spanish government decreed baptism or forced expulsion. The *conversos* were suspected of heresy, and therefore the Inquisition, whose job it was to ferret out heretics, set up a spy system. Jews who were suspected of heresy were arrested, tortured, and burned at the stake. By the 1500s the concept of "limpieza de sangre," racial purity, had taken hold in Spain. Henry Kamen, *The Spanish Inquisition*. New York: New American Library.

slowly northward toward Granada, hoping that if they slowed their pace, his health would improve. But by the time they reached the inn in Granada where they usually stayed, Alberto was feverish. At first, he sat on the balcony on the top floor of the inn, overlooking the Sierra Nevada mountains and rested, but his condition worsened. After a few days, he could not move from his bed. José attended to him, refusing to leave his side except to fetch food from the marketplace. Days passed and Alberto seemed to grow weaker and weaker. José believed that each passing day they remained secluded in their room would heighten the suspicion of the innkeeper who would inform the Inquisition. An investigation would reveal their true identity. He tried not to show his fears to his sick friend.

Finally, Alberto felt that his end was near. Tearfully, he turned to José and pleaded:

"My dear devoted friend, I know I shall not survive this illness. I have only one request and I beg you not to refuse me. Swear to me that you will bury my body in a Jewish cemetery. I know you will be facing great danger but as we have been loyal to each other in life, so, I pray you, be loyal to me in death. Please, bury me among our people. I am confident that God will protect you and guide you in your quest to find a Jewish burial ground. May He reward you for this great act of kindness."

Now, José's eyes filled with tears. He embraced his friend warmly. "I swear to you that I will do what you request," he stammered.

Alberto died that night. José was alone, not knowing what to do. His immediate reaction was anguish and despair, anguish at the loss of his friend, despair at not knowing how to carry out his friend's request. At first he wept. He sat on the floor opposite the body of his friend and wept for hours. Then he pulled himself to his feet, walked over to a table where a few newly printed holy books lay, books that he carried with him on his travels, picked up his Book of Psalms, opened it to the twentieth chapter, and prayed:

Lam-na-tze-ach a psalm of David
May God answer you on the day of distress
May the Name of Jacob's God make you impregnable,
May He send you help from His sanctuary, and support
  you from Zion. . ."

Then he recited the entire Book of Psalms, going back to the first psalm, concluding with Psalm 150 the last. He prayed that God would open his eyes to find a way to fulfill the vow he made to his friend. When he finished, he noticed the first rays of dawn breaking across the horizon. He washed his hands, changed his clothes, recited his morning prayers, and walked out of the room, shutting the door behind him. He set out for the center of town, not knowing for certain what he was going to do. He walked for about half an hour. Rounding a corner, he realized that an old man, seemingly a beggar, had joined him. The old man spoke first.

"May I join you? I like to walk."

José had no objection to the old man's company. They chatted as they walked. Along the road, they found a café. José turned to the old man and asked, "Would you like to stop for a cold drink?"

The old man nodded his head and they entered. Sitting over their drinks, the old man and José continued their conversation. Finally, the old man whispered, "I've been following you. You seem to be a stranger here with plenty of spare time. I've lived here all my life. I know some interesting Jewish and Moslem sites. Actually, before I became too old to work, I earned my living showing people around. Would you like me to show you some interesting places? I need the money. You can pay me what you think it's worth."

José didn't hesitate. "I very much want to see those old places and I can pay you handsomely."

The two set out in search of Jewish and Moslem sites. They passed mosques that had been converted into churches and empty weed-filled synagogues, with ivy crawling up their smashed windows.

The old man commented, "When I was a young boy, Jewish people lived here in comfort and security. Some were doctors, advisors to ministers of state and kings, many were merchants. Then they were expelled, their property confiscated by the government.

"Look, there in the distance is the eleventh century palace of Samuel ibn Nagrela (993–1056). The Jews called him Rabbi Shmuel ben Yosef Halayve Hanagid (the Prince). He was the Chief Rabbi of this city. He was appointed minister of state to Caliph Habus. He gave the caliph a wonderful gift, twelve fountains, each one shaped like a lion, and they still stand in the courtyard of the Alhambra palace. We will pass through the gardens and you will see them. The Jewish quarter was called Los Tiros Juderia. I remember telling so many people, 'Whoever has not seen the splendor of the Jews in Granada, their good fortune and their glory, has never seen true glory, for they were great with wisdom and piety.' "

José's heart ached. He remembered having grown up in Barcelona. He remembered how his father had uprooted himself and his family, along with 160,000 other Jews whose family trees could be traced back for five centuries since the beginning of the Moslem conquest in 711 c.e. Among his personal friends were Jews who chose to leave rather than renounce their faith.

They walked on. In the distance they saw the Alhambra palace, a classic example of magnificent Moorish architecture and design. As they approached, the old man said, "In that palace, overlooking the Sierra Nevada mountains, whose gardens are lush with the perfume of jasmine and orange trees, whose magnificent fountains recall a once majestic culture, Ferdinand and Isabella signed the edict of expulsion in the Hall of Ambassadors on March 31, 1492."

José asked, "Are there any other Jewish sites?"

"Yes," answered the old man, "there is one more, the ancient cemetery. It has a very high wall with iron gates that are always locked. It is very far, but I will take you there if you will pay me extra for the additional time it takes us to reach it. When I worked, I never worked at night, and it will be dark soon."

José trembled at the old man's words. "I will pay you whatever you wish. I don't know if I shall ever have the opportunity to return to this city again. I want to see all the ancient sites."

The two men set off for the Jewish cemetery. José paid very close attention to the route they walked, making mental notes of signs he would be able to recognize by moon light when he returned with Alberto's body.

When they reached the cemetery, the old man stretched out his hand. José placed in it the money he had promised, and thanked the old man for showing him all the sites. They bade each other farewell. The old man continued on his way and finally disappeared from sight.

José ran all the way back to the inn and raced up the stairs to his room on the top floor. Without stopping to catch his breath, he began to wash the body of his friend, in preparation for burial. He removed the blanket from the bed and laid it on the floor. He then wrapped Alberto's body in it, gathering the four corners to form a sack. He placed the sack over his shoulders, went slowly down the stairs, and set out for the Jewish cemetery.

When he reached it, he lowered the sack gently to the ground. He walked around and around, trying with no success to find an opening in one of the gates. Not despairing, for he was so close to fulfilling his vow, he lifted his eyes toward Heaven and prayed once more, "Master of the Universe! Yesterday, at this time, I made a vow that I did not know I would be able to fulfill. I prayed for mercy and compassion and You opened my eyes. I have come so close to fulfilling my vow. Please help me complete this great act of kindness. Help me find a way into the cemetery to bury my friend!"

Suddenly, the rusty iron gate directly in front of him squeaked. Cautiously, he approached and pushed it. It moved a little. He pushed again and the gate opened more. He lifted the sack, carried it inside the cemetery, searching for a plot where he could bury his friend. Near an open space, he found a shovel glistening in the moonlight and started to dig. When the hole was large enough to bury his friend, he slid the body into the grave as he removed the blanket. Shoveling the dirt to cover the body, he recited the *Kaddish*, because he knew that no one else would ever recite *Kaddish* at Alberto's grave.[2]

José had fulfilled his vow. He left the cemetery with the blanket under his arm. Now he felt faint, for he had not eaten all day, having been so preoccupied with burying his friend.

Walking toward town, he realized he could go no farther until he rested. He sat down, emotionally and physically drained, and leaned his head against the wall of a small house at the side of the road. He breathed slowly and deeply, his eyes closed. He knew his only source of strength was from God, so he prayed again, "Master of the Universe! All day I was involved in the *mitzvah* of burying the dead. Now I must deal with life. Show me the way out of this cursed land."

[2]Ordinarily, the recitation of *Kaddish* requires a *minyon*.

As he uttered these words, he opened his eyes, lifted his head, and turned ever so slightly. He noticed a small bottle on the window ledge directly above his head. He stretched his hand, grasped the bottle, opened it, and sniffed at it. It contained whiskey. He raised the bottle to his lips, took a drink and waited for the liquid to warm his body. He returned the bottle to its place, stood up and walked toward the inn. It was almost daybreak again when he stealthily unlocked the door and let himself into his room.

Once more he washed, changed his clothes, recited the morning prayers, and ate his remaining fruit and nuts. He then gathered his belongings, made his way to the port, and purchased passage to Italy. He knew he would never set foot in Spain again.

When he arrived and told the story of Alberto's death to the mourning family, he told them also the story of how he had buried him and how he had miraculously escaped from Spain undetected. When he finished, he poured himself a glass of whiskey, and shouted *"L'Chayim! L'Chayim!"*[3]

---

[3]From that time on, within certain families who adhere to the Sephardic tradition, it has been the custom to drink *"L'Chayim"* on returning from the cemetery to the house of mourning. It is based upon the passage:
Give drink unto him that is ready to perish,
And wine unto those with heavy heart.—Proverbs 31:6.

A Dowry for the Bride

"Did you hear, did you hear?" the *shamish*[1] ran through the marketplace in Koretz shouting "that the tailor finally died, and now no one wants to go to the funeral!" He panted as he ran, adding: "You know the one I mean, the one who never gave a ruble for charity or went to *shul*, the one who never bought from the kosher butcher!"

Normally, the *shamish* was an organized and reserved man, and news of death rarely disturbed him. However, in spite of the fact that the tailor was not deserving of normal respect due the dead, the *shamish* felt that some people should attend the funeral.

Sh'moneh Seforim: Tzeror Hachayim. Bulgaria. Printing House of Rabbi Natan Neta Kronenberg, 1903. Reprinted in New York, 1983.

[1]The root of the Hebrew word for beadle is *shimesh,* meaning "to serve or function within the Jewish community." The person who served in this capacity was called a *shamish.* Throughout Jewish history, his role varied: he was a messenger of the Jewish court, a scribe, a janitor in the synagogue, the caller who announced the start of the Sabbath from the marketplace, the runner who knocked on doors to awaken people for the morning prayer service.

As he ran past the *bays midrash*, Rebbe Pinchas[2] heard his agitated voice and sent a student to call him inside.

"Why are you running around so disorganized today?" Rebbe Pinchas demanded. "What happened?"

"Rebbe, I want you to know that the tailor died, and no one wants to go to his funeral."

"The tailor died," repeated the rebbe incredulously. "I loved the tailor so much. I am so sorry to hear this sad news. I will attend his funeral."

The puzzled *shamish* could not understand why Rebbe Pinchas wanted to go to the funeral, so as soon as he left the rebbe's study he retraced his steps through the marketplace. "The rebbe is going to attend the funeral, the rebbe is going to attend the funeral," he called out.

People stopped what they were doing and rushed to join the funeral procession, accompanying the casket all the way to the cemetery.

When the rebbe returned to the *bays midrash* after the funeral, he tried to resume his study, but to no avail, for just then a close friend, Rebbe Yayva, the Maggid Maysharim, burst through the door and shouted, "You can't fool me! The tailor was a social outcast. He was not one of the *lamed-vav tzaddikim*[3] as most people assumed when they heard you were attending the funeral. Why did you go?"

Rebbe Pinchas urged his friend to sit down and calmly said, "I want you to know that there is a special reason why I attended the funeral. Since you are such a close friend, I will tell you who the tailor really was. Do you remember the orphan girl Rachel whom I raised as my own daughter? When she reached

[2]Rebbe Pinchas ben Rebbe Avraham Aba Shapira Koretz (1721–1791) was honored both for his learning and for the humble way he followed the tenets of the newly emerging chasidic movement. He was instrumental in providing a caring community for the downtrodden, helpless Jews who continuously sought his advice. He believed that the only cause for melancholy is lack of desire to visit Eretz Yisrael, so on his seventieth birthday, he decided to realize his lifelong dream. It was never fulfilled, for he died en route, in the *shtetl* of Spitevka.

[3]The *lamed-vav tzaddikim* are the thirty-six holy righteous men (in every generation). It is believed that the world exists because of their meritorious lives. Talmud *Bavli, Succah* 45b.

marriageable age, I arranged a match for her with an orphan boy who had also grown up in this *shtetl*. I wanted them to have a decent start in life, so I made it my business to collect money for her dowry. I planned to use the money to furnish a little house for them with modest necessities: a table, some chairs, beds, pillows, dishes, and pots. I even had enough money left over to pay for a marriage feast. A day before the wedding, I counted the money just to make sure that I had enough. To my horror, I was short twelve rubles, the money I still needed to purchase a new *tallis* for the groom, which is supposed to be a gift from the bride. Everyone in this *shtetl* had already contributed for the bride's dowry, so I did not know where to turn for an additional twelve rubles. I walked through the streets, trying to figure out what to do. I was almost at the outskirts of town when I passed the tailor's shop, for he lived there in a small room in the back. I knocked at his door. I did not have much hope that he would help me, but I thought I would ask anyway. He was very happy to see me. "Rebbe," he said joyfully, "I can't thank you enough for taking the time to come all this way to visit me. No one in this *shtetl* has ever visited me before. What can I do for you?"

"To tell you the truth," I told the tailor, "I am marrying off Rachel, the orphan girl whom I raised as my own daughter. I need twelve more rubles to buy a new *tallis* for her groom."

The tailor ran over to a cabinet, took down a small box, removed one ruble, and handed it to me.

I took the ruble and thanked him, adding that I still needed eleven more.

"Rebbe, I wish I could give you all the rubles you need, but I can't afford any more."

He again expressed his appreciation for my visit and I left. I turned toward the center of the *shtetl*, walking slowly, still sad because I did not know where I could get the additional eleven rubles. I had not walked more than half a kilometer when I heard someone behind me shouting "Rebbe, rebbe, wait, wait!"

I recognized the tailor's voice and stopped short. It did not take long for him to catch up to me. When he came close he asked, "Rebbe, if I give you the other eleven rubles that you need to buy the *tallis*, will you promise me a share in the world to come?"

I promised the tailor a share in the world to come as a reward for the *mitzvah* of providing a dowry for the bride. He looked me straight in the eye and said, "Please, don't move from this spot. I will return in a few moments."

He ran all the way back to his tailor shop and returned in a few minutes. He sheepishly placed eleven more rubles into the palm of my hand.

I repeated my blessing.

In exchange for these twelve rubles, I told the tailor, "I promise you a share in the world to come."

"How could you promise *anyone* a share in the world to come?" Rebbe Yayva scoffed.

"That's why I went to the funeral," Rebbe Pinchas whispered gently. "Even though this was the only charitable act the tailor had done in his life, I felt he merited the world to come. I want you to know that as I followed the coffin to the cemetery, I envisioned the tailor's soul being lifted to heaven wrapped in the *tallis*."

The King Who Loves Righteousness

Rebbe Nachum Tzernobler was visiting in a certain *shtetl*.[1] In the midst of an amiable discussion with the *shtetl* rebbe he suddenly blurted out, "Tell me, if you could improve the spirituality of your people's lives, in which area would you work?"

The rebbe answered unhesitatingly, "We desperately need a *mikveh* in this *shtetl*. However, to finance its building and daily upkeep takes a great deal of money, and," he sighed deeply, "we don't have a group of people who could possibly contribute toward this purpose."

G. Mah-Tov. *Maasayhem shel Tzaddikim*. Jerusalem: Hamesorah Publishers, 1986.

[1]Rebbe Nachum Tzernobler (1730–1798) was born in the Volhynia region of central Poland. Even though he was orphaned at a very young age, he overcame his personal tragedy, became a brilliant yeshiva student, and supported his family as a teacher. He delved into Kabbalah and asceticism as a way to raise himself to a higher level of holiness, hoping that the Jewish people would follow his example. When the chasidic movement emerged after the first third of the 1700s, he followed the path of its founder, the Baal Shem Tov. He traveled continuously all over the region, from *shtetl* to *shtetl*, trying to carry the chasidic message he had learned from the Baal Shem Tov to the people. Wherever he went, he emphasized that the distribution of charity is a major *mitzvah*.

"Isn't there even one person who could be responsible for starting a *mikveh* fund?" prodded Rebbe Nachum.

The rebbe shook his head pensively. Then all of a sudden, as if struck by lightning, he snapped his fingers and whispered, "Yes, there is one very rich man who lives on the far edge of the *shtetl* in a luxurious mansion set far back from the road. His name is Berish. Tall iron fences, huge trees, and high shrubs hide the house from passersby. He is known to be a miser. He has never given one ruble for *any* cause in all the years I have been the rebbe in this *shtetl*. Nothing I have said or done has succeeded in opening his heart or his purse."

"I want you to know," said Rebbe Nachum, "that if you are really earnest in your desire to build a *mikveh*, the Almighty will show you a way to realize your goal. You should know that the Almighty does not demand more from you than you are able to do. You must have faith. Let me think about this for a little while. Perhaps I can think of something to soften the harsh heart of the miser."

He nodded to himself over and over, saying finally, "We have only to find the way to proceed. We have only to find the way to proceed."

Rebbe Nachum took leave of the rebbe, slowly, calmly, so as not to arouse any suspicion that he had already formulated a plan. He set off for a neighboring *shtetl* and sought out two friends, the tailor and the coachman.

"I need a favor," he said to the coachman. "I want you to let me borrow your most beautiful coach for a few hours. I also want you to pretend that you drive exclusively for nobility. I will be your passenger."

This was not the first time that Rebbe Nachum had made a strange request of his friend, so the coachman simply said, "Where do you want to go? When do you want to leave?"

"I want to leave immediately after I visit the tailor. I want to return to the *shtetl* from which I have just come," answered Rebbe Nachum.

He borrowed an elegant silk coat and a big, black, broad-brimmed hat from the tailor, dressed quickly, and told the coachman that he was ready.

The coachman jumped up to his seat just above two magnificent white stallions that took off at a trot. Inside the coach, Rebbe Nachum relaxed. He was completely confident that his plan would reap the desired results. He instructed his friend to drive through the gate, and stop on the path that led to the rich man's mansion.

When the coach faced the house, Rebbe Nachum signaled to his friend to stop. "We'll wait right here," he said.

The rich man, aroused by the sound of horses' hooves, peered out the window from behind velvet brocaded draperies. "I wonder what that coach is doing on my private road," he thought. "Only nobles or the king's royal guard ride up here. Maybe the coachman made a wrong turn. Maybe he is lost!" He watched silently, hidden by the draperies, waiting to see if the coach would leave. He waited and waited and so did the coach and its passenger.

His curiosity was aroused. "I have to see who it is," he decided. He ran out of the mansion, down the path, and stopped in front of the coach window. Peering inside, he saw a passenger dressed in an elegant silk coat with a large, black, broadbrimmed hat.

"He must be a very important person," Berish, the rich miser, thought to himself. "I wonder who he is." He did not recognize the passenger, because he always hid from anyone who might possibly be collecting money for charity.

"Who is your passenger?" Berish called up to the coachman.

"Why, don't you know ?" the coachman replied. "He is no other than Rebbe Nachum Tzernobler."

The rebbe continued to sit quietly inside the coach.

Berish's miserly instincts took over. "Run back to the house. He is after your money! It's a trap. You'll get caught! You've never shown *any* hospitality to *any* stranger. After all these years, you don't want to begin now, do you?"

But some spark of decency hidden in the innermost recesses of his hardened heart awakened Berish. He knocked on the window of the coach and beckoned the passenger to step out. Rebbe Nachum opened the door, alighted from the coach, straightened himself up to his full height and said, "I want you to know, that of all the houses in this entire *shtetl* where I was invited to stay for a few days, I have chosen to stay with you."

Rebbe Nachum's words impressed Berish. Seizing the

opportunity, his good inclination grew. "He's chosen you to be his host for this visit. There must be a special reason why he chose your house for lodging. It is a privilege to be the host to Rebbe Nachum Tzernobler. After all, his reputation is known throughout the entire vicinity. He is such a holy man!" Finally, Berish blurted out, "I am honored to have the rebbe as my guest!"

Rebbe Nachum motioned to the coachman and whispered, "Please come back for me tomorrow!"

Berish showed Rebbe Nachum to the most beautifully furnished, most comfortable room in his entire mansion.

"I need to be alone for a while," the rebbe requested. "Please don't let anyone disturb me until I let you know that I am ready to receive the many people who will assuredly seek an audience with me when they find out I am visiting in this *shtetl*."

The coachman rapidly spread word throughout the *shtetl* that Rebbe Nachum Tzernobler was Berish's guest. Most people could not believe their ears. They streamed forth from every alleyway, from every cobblestoned street, from every crooked, twisting road in a long procession toward Berish's mansion, hoping to see the rebbe.

Berish was astonished at the throngs of people who gathered outside his mansion. They stood patiently in line, hoping for a few precious minutes of conversation with Rebbe Nachum.

He stood behind the velvet brocaded draperies and peered into the distance. He was overwhelmed that he had been selected to be the host and his home had been chosen to be the rebbe's headquarters.

He liked the singsong melody of the words that floated through his mind, "The rebbe has chosen me, Berish. I am so honored. I am so honored!"

Toward evening, Rebbe Nachum raised his head from the book he was studying, stood up slowly from the table, walked to the door of his room, and called out to Berish. Then he returned to the table and continued studying. Berish came immediately, but the rebbe had already returned to the table and had resumed his study. He was so deeply immersed that he did not hear Berish enter the room. He watched the rebbe, bent over his book, and an aura of holiness seemed to hover over the room.

He dared not move for fear of disturbing the rebbe. His heart beat ever faster knowing that he had been chosen to enter the inner circle.

"The whole *shtetl* is waiting in line to see the rebbe, as if he were a king sitting on his throne contemplating the fate of his subjects," he mused. "To think that I am part of all this." He tiptoed across the room and sat down next to the rebbe's table.

It seemed that the rebbe had forgotten that he had called Berish, for he paid no attention to him.

"Who am I that I should be thus privileged?" Berish's thoughts continued. "Certainly, I am wealthy with material possessions, but next to Rebbe Nachum, I am poor indeed and spiritually lacking. If he merits such esteem in this world, can you imagine the honor awaiting him in the world to come?" He closed his eyes and pictured Rebbe Nachum sitting on a silver throne next to the Golden Throne of the Almighty Himself. The *Ofanim* and the *Chayos* flapped their wings as they raised themselves toward the Seraphim, back and forth across the heavens, proclaiming:

Holy, Holy, Holy is the Almighty, Master of the Heavenly Hosts,
The whole world is filled with His glory.[2]

"My wealth is nothing compared to Rebbe Nachum's. I am ready to forego everything for a place next to his in the world to come!" Berish's wandering thoughts returned to the matters of this world when he heard Rebbe Nachum interrupt.

"I think it is time to pray. We will have to postpone our private discussion until later."

Berish blinked, for he had not been aware that Rebbe Nachum wanted a private discussion with him. His curiosity was all the more when Rebbe Nachum asked him to invite all the people inside who had patiently waited outdoors.

"As important as it is to *daven* in *shul*, I should like to have

[2]This passage is found in the daily morning prayer service and is taken from Isaiah 6:3.

the prayer service in this house, if it is all right with you, Berish."

"What honor the rebbe is bestowing upon me!" Berish thought as he joyfully ran to invite the people in.

The people were puzzled. One began whispering to his neighbor, "Berish has welcomed Rebbe Nachum? What happened to him? He's never shown hospitality to anyone before."

"I've known Berish for many years; he always scoffs at rebbes and their *chasidim* . . . and now he is inviting us in to *daven* in his house? Who would believe it?"

"Maybe, having been with Rebbe Nachum for just a few hours has changed his attitude," a third bystander suggested.

In an orderly manner, they followed Berish as he showed the way toward the room where they would *daven*. Their amazement magnified tenfold when they noticed two sets of shining silver candelabra ready on a table that would serve as the *shtender*, the prayer leader's desk.

The commotion quieted when Rebbe Nachum appeared. He moved thoughtfully from one *chasid* to another, extending a warm welcome to each, inquiring about their families, their health, their livelihood. Berish followed the rebbe's footsteps; he glowed when Rebbe Nachum asked him to lead the prayers.

Berish's voice resounded loud and clear. He stood at the *shtender*, his hands gripping the edges, his shoulders enveloped by a large *tallis*, his head bowed, his eyes closed.

He prayed with the deepest emotion, as if his heart had finally been touched. The words came forth with such intense feeling that they reached the hearts of all the other worshipers. He proceeded slowly and only when he reached, "Blessed are You, God, the King Who loves righteousness and judgment,"[3] did he stop short.

"What am I saying?" his conscience demanded. "A King Who loves righteousness and judgment? . . . I have not lived as the Almighty has wished. I never gave charity, I never helped a widow or an orphan, I never considered the needs of the community . . . It is clear to me that I am unloved by my Creator."

[3]The eleventh petition of the silent devotion.

Berish was unable to continue leading the prayers. Intermittent sobs, anguish, contrition . . . "I must change. I must-change. From now on, I promise to lead a life that is loved and respected by both God and man."

The people waited for Berish. They realized that his prayers had purified his soul on their way to the Heavenly Court. Rebbe Nachum had shown Berish how to penetrate the hardened wall around his heart.

When the service ended, the people filed out of the room one by one and let themselves out without having had their long-awaited audience with Rebbe Nachum. Only Berish and the rebbe remained. Rebbe Nachum put his arm around Berish. Together, they found chairs and sat.

"Now it is time for our private discussion," began Rebbe Nachum.

To this day, no one knows what the rebbe and the rich man discussed, but the results were obvious the very next morning.

Diggers, carpenters, bricklayers, and stonemasons waited in an empty parcel of land near the *shul* for instructions to begin a project.

Rumors spread as they usually did throughout the *shtetl*. The scoffers came running.

"If I hadn't seen it with my own eyes, I wouldn't believe it," proclaimed the first.

"Who hired you," demanded the second, "and for what purpose?"

The bricklayer retorted, "Don't you know? Berish hired us to build a *mikveh!*"

"Impossible!" yelled the third. "Leopards don't change their spots. And even if he is paying you to build it, who will be responsible for keeping it up?"

Just then Berish arrived on the scene. "I promise you," he said, "that the entire responsibility will be on my shoulders."

Yossel, another disbeliever asked, "Nu, so Berish, what prompted you to undertake this project?"

Berish took a folded piece of paper from his coat pocket. "Here, you read it aloud," he said as he handed it to Yossel.

Yossel cleared his throat importantly and read in a loud voice, "I, Rebbe Nachum, son of Rebbe Tzvee Tzernobler, sell my share in the world to come to Berish on the condition that he build and provide for the daily upkeep of the *mikveh* in this *shtetl* until the community can maintain it with its own resources.''

A great silence fell on the crowd. No one could believe that Rebbe Nachum Tzernobler would exchange his share in the world to come for anything in this world.

Yossel returned the letter, and Berish smiled a satisfied smile.

Shamefacedly, the scoffers slunk away. When the incident was repeated in Tzernoble, the *chasidim* of Rebbe Nachum whispered amongst themselves, ''We understand our rebbe's devotion to the Jewish people. We also comprehend why he often acts *beyond* the requirements of the law. What we don't understand is why he sold his share of the world to come to Berish, in order that he might build a *mikveh* in that *shtetl*.'' After a few days of conjecture, they decided to go directly to Rebbe Nachum for his explanation.

''I can understand your bewilderment,'' he began, ''but for a long time I have been troubled by the commandment to 'love the Lord your God with all your heart, with all your soul, and with all your might.' ''[4]

''I have been troubled because I learned that the word 'might' means resources and money. Since I haven't any money of my own, I couldn't fulfill this commandment. Even, occasionally, when I was given some, I always distributed it to those who had even less than I, so how could I ever show my love for God? Then this wonderful opportunity came along to prove that I do love the Almighty with all my 'might,' namely with the most precious thing in my possession, which was my share in the world to come. I could not pass up the opportunity. In fact, I actually rejoiced when I signed away my share to Berish, because I knew that I had finally fulfilled that commandment.''

[4]*Sh'ma,* Deuteronomy 6:5.

You Cannot Deprive Me
of This Mitzvah

The stories about Rebbe Layve Yitzchak of Berditchev reveal that he was a man of great compassion and deep emotion.[1] It was generally known that he did not take time to attend funerals, for he thought it more important to minister to the living. Once, however, under mysterious circumstances, Rebbe Layve Yitzchak not only insisted on eulogizing the deceased, he also led the procession following the casket from the center of the *shtetl* to the cemetery. When he returned with the mourners to the house of mourning, Yisrael, one of his loyal disciples, confronted him, "Rebbe, I have a very important question to ask you."

Sayfer Toldos Layve Yitzchak.
[1]Rebbe Layve Yitzchak of Berditchev (1740–1809), descendant of an unbroken chain of twenty-six generations of leading Torah scholars, was one of the most charismatic chasidic rebbes. When the Baal Shem Tov heard of his birth, he commented: "A great and holy soul has been born into this world; he shall be an eloquent advocate for the Jewish people." Rebbe Layve Yitzchak spent his entire life fulfilling that prophecy. People said that he never found fault with any Jew. He loved God and Judaism, but his love for the Jewish people exceeded his love for both God and Judaism. Yitzchak Raphael, *Sayfer Chassidus.*

118

Rebbe Layve Yitzchak signaled Yisrael to lower his voice and beckoned him to follow him to a corner of the room. "Rebbe," said Yisrael, "you rarely attend funerals. This afternoon you not only attended the funeral, but you led the procession to the cemetery. Was there something special about the deceased that made you change your way?"

Rebbe Layve Yitzchak answered softly, patiently, "I want you to know, Yisrael, that Naftali Hertz, the deceased, was a very special Jew. I never revealed to anyone what I knew about him, but now that he is gone, I can tell you. He consulted me three times to settle disputes in which he was involved. I clearly recall each instance, but I can only tell you the first two."

Rebbe Layve Yitzchak paused. A smile gently played around the edges of his mouth as he reminisced. "One day, about two years ago, Naftali Hertz barged into my study. He was clearly agitated and his words were almost incoherent. I asked Naftali Hertz to tell me what he was talking about and why he was so distraught. I listened carefully as he unfolded his story.

* * *

A newly married couple, unknown to me personally, were given 200 rubles as a wedding gift to invest in a business. After

---

He is remembered for the famous soliloquy that showed his truly personal relationship with God:

Good morning to You, Lord of the Universe!
I, Layve Yitzchak, son of Sarah of Berditchev, have come to You to
    complain on behalf of Your people Israel.
You against Your people Israel?
No matter what the outcome, it will always be
My children Israel . . .
Father dear! How many other people are there in the world?
Babylonians, Persians, and Edomites . . . The Germans—
    what do they say?
Our king is a king!
The English—what do they say?
Our sovereign is a sovereign!
And I, Layve Yitzchak, son of Sarah of Berditchev say:
Hallowed and magnified be Your Name, O God, Our Father, Our King!"

(Dr. H. Rabinowicz, *A Guide to Chassidism*. London: Thomas Yoseloff, 1960.)

the week's wedding festivities, the groom put the money in his
jacket pocket and went to the marketplace, searching for a little
shop that he could buy in order to earn a livelihood for himself
and his bride. He thought a little dairy, spice, or fruit and
vegetable shop would be the ideal business for him. As he
walked around the marketplace, he saw more customers going
into the spice shop than any other. "That must be a good
business investment," he mused.

Inquiring, he was told that the shop was owned by a man
who was getting on in years and who found it difficult to run it
by himself. He was looking either for a younger partner or for
someone to buy it from him outright. The groom entered the
shop and received permission from the proprietor to observe the
way he conducted his business.

Near closing time, the groom asked, "Is it true that your
shop is for sale?"

When the proprietor nodded, he asked him how much he
would want for the shop.

The proprietor answered, "I will sell you this shop and the
stock for 200 rubles."

"Why, that is the exact amount of money I have in my
pocket," the groom exclaimed excitedly. "I will buy it." The
groom put his hand into his jacket pocket, expecting to find the
small bundle of rubles, but his pocket was empty. Frantically,
he searched all his pockets, but they were empty. He was
stunned. Tears welled up in his eyes.

"I don't know what happened," he cried. "I had the money
this morning. I had 200 rubles to buy a little business. Please,
give me a chance to find the money."

Sobbing, the groom ran blindly out of the shop, retraced
his steps around the marketplace, searching everywhere for a
bundle of 200 rubles.

"And then he ran right into me," said Naftali Hertz. Before
he could ask if I was hurt, I extended my hand to him and asked,
'Why are you crying? How can I help you? Let's sit down on that
rock and you can tell me what the trouble is.' I put my arm
around his shoulder and guided him toward the rock.

He continued heaving in painful sighs, but gradually
stopped crying. "I had 200 rubles," he stammered. "It was a

wedding present. I was going to buy a little business and decided on that spice shop. I had exactly enough but when I put my hand in my pocket for the money, it was gone."

"That's strange," Hertz answered. "I found a bundle of 200 rubles a little while ago. I took the money to my house for safekeeping. What denominations were the rubles? Can you identify the rubles that way?"

The groom's eyes opened wide. The tears glistened.

"You mean you found my money?" he asked incredulously.

"Yes, it seems so," Hertz answered. "Can you identify the rubles? I want to be sure that the bundle I found is indeed yours."

The groom enumerated, "My bundle had forty five-ruble notes. It was tied with a yellow band."

"Then the money I found must be yours," he said. "Wait here. I will return in a few moments." I ran home, counted out forty five-ruble notes from my strongbox, arranged the money in a neat bundle, fastened it with a yellow band, returned to the rock in the market place and gave it to the groom. Gratefully, he took the money and ran joyfully toward the spice shop.

All this time, I had not noticed a stranger lurking around the marketplace, but apparently he had seen me give the groom the money. The stranger followed me home. No sooner had I entered my house when he began to pound on my door.

"I saw what you did in the marketplace today," said the stranger. "I am the thief who stole the young man's money. I realized that I had done a terrible thing when I picked his pocket so I want to return the money. Please take it." He held out a bundle of five-ruble notes, tied with a yellow band.

"No," Hertz said, "I will not permit you to deprive me of the *mitzvah* of having helped a person in need."

"You see," Rebbe Layve Yitzchak said, pausing to catch his breath, and continuing his story. "Naftali Hertz asked me to arbitrate if he could really keep the *mitzvah*. He felt he was right in not accepting reimbursement from the thief. I agreed with him. I decided that he had acted wisely.

* * *

Rebbe Layve Yitzchak began another story. Last year, he asked me to arbitrate another case. This is what he told me when he came to my study the second time.

"Everyone knows that Berel, the *shtetl shlepper* could not provide for his family. It wasn't that he didn't want to work, or that he put no effort into the jobs he did get. He just had no *mazel*. Anything he tried to do failed. In a state of total despair, he decided to move to a different location, for he had heard that if he changed his place his luck might change.[2]

He considered many places, but South Africa beckoned with adventure. He confided his plans to his wife Chana.

"I am going away to seek my fortune," Berel said. "I promise you that I will return a rich man."

Chana was hysterical. She thought her husband was abandoning her. Wailing, she demanded to know who would provide for her and their ten children.

"You don't understand," Berel told her. "You know Naftali Hertz, the wealthiest man in this *shtetl*? Well, he has a factory in Stuttgart. He offered me a job. He asked me to go there to manage his factory. He told me to tell you to come to his office every Friday afternoon and he will pay you my salary."

Chana breathed a sigh of relief. Berel disappeared.

The following Friday, Chana came to my office to pick up Berel's salary. My foreman had never seen her before. When she told him that she had come to pick up Berel's salary, he laughed.

"Berel who?" he demanded arrogantly. "Naftali Hertz has no factory in Stuttgart, Germany. I know all of his business holdings. He would never keep a business account secret from me. I don't know what you are talking about. You had better leave before I call the constable!"

Faced with real abandonment, Chana started to cry. I heard her piercing wails from behind the closed door of my office. I heard my foreman shouting at her. Hastily, I came out to see the cause of all the commotion.

"What is going on here?" I asked gently. Chana, sensing

---

[2]*M'shane ma-kom, me-shane mazel,* (changing one's place, changes one's luck). Talmud *Bavli, Rosh Hashanah* 16b, *Bava Metziah* 75b.

my concern, gradually stopped crying. Slowly, she stammered out her story. I turned to my foreman and told him firmly:

"I do have business accounts in Stuttgart. You don't know about all my affairs. I did send Berel to manage my factory there. I promised Berel that I would give his salary to his wife. Pay her his wages, 100 rubles, today and every Friday until he returns." Then I apologized for the rudeness of my foreman. Chana took the money and went on her way.

It seems that she was a very clever woman. She came to collect Berel's wages for eight or nine months, then she stopped coming. When I investigated, I found that she lived very frugally, saving every extra ruble. When she had saved enough, she invested in a small tailoring shop, for she was an expert seamstress. People heard about the quality of her sewing and came from the entire surrounding area to give her work. Gradually, she expanded the tailoring shop to include fashionable clothing. The profits of her business have been sustaining her and her ten children since. She has become very comfortable. Her eldest child has just reached marriageable age."

Rebbe Layve Yitzchak interrupted Naftali Hertz's tale.

"I still don't understand what you want me to arbitrate." He prodded him to continue.

"Berel returned recently. What he had heard about moving to a different location to change one's luck was really true, for he had become a very wealthy diamond merchant in South Africa. As soon as he was reunited with Chana, he came to me to repay the money I had given her for those eight or nine months, five years ago. I refused to take his money because I had the mitzvah of supporting his wife, the mother of his ten children, until she was able to support herself."

"Again," Rebbe Layve Yitzchak told Yisrael, "I decided that Naftali Hertz had acted correctly. I decided that he did not have to accept reimbursement from Berel.

"Now you understand, Yisrael, that even though I rarely attend funerals, I could not stay away from this one. I had to honor the man whose acts of kindness exemplified the highest form of *gemilus chasadim*."

Three Conditions

Two tragic encounters changed the lives of Jews in Eastern Europe displacing them from their relatively secure position. Following the horrible Chmielnicki massacres, they realized they were totally helpless from enemy attack.[1] Soon afterward, the revelation that Shabbatai Tzve, the false messiah, was nothing but a hoax challenged their belief in ultimate redemption.[2]

Kuntres Menachem Tzeyon. Pinchas David Weberman. *Sayfer Maaseh Tzadikim im Divray Tzadikim*. Jerusalem: Defus Techeya, 1962.

[1]The Chmielnicki massacres of 1648–1649, known as *Gezayrot Tach V'Tat*, decimated Eastern European Jewry, the largest Jewish community in the world. The survivors fell into a state of total helplessness. Even when Polish King John Casimir regained control of his country ten years later by subduing the marauders, Jewish suffering did not cease. Bandits roamed the countryside, and blood libels, previously unheard of in this part of the world, became commonplace.

[2]This tragedy fostered a messianic movement, led by Shabbatai Tzve, a charlatan who claimed he was the redeemer of Israel. Many Jews uprooted themselves from the lands of exile, sold their property, packed their belongings, and sailed for their ancestral homeland. Only when the false messiah converted

Almost at once, Rebbe Yisrael ben Eliezer, the Baal Shem Tov, founder of the chasidic movement, taught the Jewish people how to change helplessness to helpfulness, hopelessness to hope. He taught them how to serve God with joy, despite their personal suffering. His disciples carried his message of hope throughout the Pale of Settlement, that area of Eastern Europe where the majority of the world's Jewish population lived.

Yoseph Charif, one of the early adherents to this new movement, earned his livelihood by managing an inn for the *poretz*. The inn was in a *shtetl* not far from Austrian-Prussian border. He worked hard, side by side with his wife, devoting his spare time to Torah study. Occasionally, he traveled to Medziboz, home of the chasidic movement, to visit and be part of the circle of disciples that surrounded the Baal Shem Tov.

The *poretz* rarely stopped at the inn, so a visit one day surprised Yoseph Charif.

"I will tell you immediately what is on my mind," declared the *poretz*. "I have decided to move across the border, to Austria and I want to sell all my property because I need money to start all over again. I have seen that you are reliable, you run the inn efficiently, and you always pay your rent on time. I have never heard any of the peasants complain about you, so I would like to propose that you buy my whole estate, with its forests, its lumber mills, and its fisheries. I am only asking you to give me 10 percent of the price as a down payment. I know that you will be able to manage all this property as well as you manage the inn, and I trust you enough to know that you will send me the payments on time every single month. Would you think about my proposal and let me know in a few days?"

Yoseph Charif was flabbergasted.

"I'll think about your offer for a few days," he whispered. "I will come to you on Thursday and let you know my decision."

As soon as the *poretz* had disappeared from the leaf-strewn-path, Yoseph ran to his living quarters, where his wife

---

to Islam did the deluded Jews realize that a cruel hoax had been perpetrated upon them. Hopelessness, the feeling that redemption would never come, overtook them entirely.

was cooking a pot of soup in the kitchen. Excitedly, he shouted, "We have a wonderful opportunity to become rich. . .we have a wonderful opportunity to become rich!"

"What are you babbling about?" she demanded. "Calm down and tell me what you mean."

He took a deep breath. Slowly, he repeated the terms of the *poretz's* offer. "We have the opportunity to become rich," he concluded slowly.

His wife was more practical. "Yes," she said, "the *poretz's* proposal is a wonderful opportunity, but where do you suppose you will raise the money?"

He looked around their rooms, strolled through the front rooms of the inn, and slowly returned to his wife. Excitedly, he blurted, "I know just how we can raise the money. We have accumulated a small amount of silver, we have extra furniture, you brought some family heirlooms with your dowry. . . . I will take all of it to the pawnbroker. . . . He will lend me the money for the down payment. . . . With this vast estate, we should have no trouble redeeming our own things in a short time. . . . We should have no trouble sending the *poretz* the monthly installments!"

On Thursday, Yoseph went to the *poretz* to say that he would accept his offer.

"How long do you think it will take you to raise the down payment?" inquired the *poretz*. "I would like to move by the end of this month." They agreed amicably that all financial arrangements would be completed by the following week.

Yoseph spent the next few days hauling his possessions with his horse and wagon to the pawnbroker. Each day the cash accumulated, until he finally had the required sum. On the appointed day, he joyfully set out with the money for the *poretz's* mansion.

As he rode down the road between the inn and the *poretz's* estate, thinking of all the wonderful opportunities that awaited him, he heard moaning and bitter cries coming from an isolated hut at the side of the road. Turning the horses off the road, he alighted from his wagon and entered the hut. He was horrified to see a middle-aged woman lying huddled in a sickbed with seven emaciated and bedraggled children, aged about 2 to 11, sitting desolately around her bed. Filled with compassion, he said, "I will return in a little while. I will help you."

Jumping into his wagon, he hastily drove to the market-place in the center of the *shtetl*, bought food, drove back to the isolated hut, and fed the starving children and the sick woman. When they had eaten, he emptied the sack in which he carried the money intended for the *poretz* onto a broken and shaky table and said, "I am leaving this money for you. When you feel better, take it to the market and purchase more food and clothing for yourself and your family." Then he departed.

(This incident of self-sacrifice to help others to survive was duly recorded by the Heavenly Court. It decreed that Yoseph Charif merited great reward if he could pass a test administered by the prophet Elyahu *Hanave*.)

Yoseph pulled himself up into his wagon and pointed the horses again toward the center of the *shtetl*, farther and farther from the *poretz's* mansion. Empty-handed, knowing that he had pawned everything he owned, that he had nothing more to live on, he wondered how angry the *poretz* would be, and if at least he would let him keep the inn. Yet, he felt an inner sense of peace and didn't regret for one moment what he had done.

He knew he could not ride around aimlessly, so he reined in the horses, and hitched the wagon to a post. He alighted and walked to the *bays midrash*. He went in and took a volume of the Talmud from its place on the shelf, sat down at a table, and began to study. He sat for a few hours, uninterrupted. Then, an old man entered, greeted him warmly, and sat down. They chatted for a while and Yoseph was completely distracted. The old man commented: "Your face shows such satisfaction. Won't you tell me why?"

Yoseph liked the old man's manner. He thought he could trust him, so he told him what he had done with the money that he was going to give to the *poretz* as a down payment on the estate.

The old man responded, "I am a very wealthy man. I have never been called upon to give away my entire fortune as you have done just a few hours ago. Since you need money for the *poretz*, I would like to propose that you let me repay you all the

money you left with the widow on the condition that I receive
the reward for the *mitzvah* that you did."

For a moment or two, Yoseph was speechless. Then he said
adamantly, "I performed that *mitzvah* because I wanted to. I
did not do it for the reward. Under no conditions will I give up
the *mitzah* for your money!"

The old man did not give up. He insisted on exchanging his
money for the possible reward of the *mitzvah*. "I'll tell you
what," he offered. "Suppose you exchange *half* the reward of
the *mitzvah* for the money."

"I told you once, and I am telling you again," insisted
Yoseph, "I will not barter the reward of the *mitzvah* for your
money, not *one-half* of it, not *one-third*, not even *one-tenth*. I
did the *mitzvah* because I wanted to. I never thought about a
reward. I didn't want it two hours ago, and I don't want it now."

As much as the old man persisted, he could not budge
Yoseph from his position. Finally, he said, "I want you to know
that I am Elyahu *Hanave*. I was sent by the Heavenly Court to
test you, to try to persuade you to accept a financial reward for
your magnificent deed. Since I have been unsuccessful, the
Heavenly Court has authorized me to offer you a choice of three
rewards: you may choose any one of them. First, you and your
wife can have long life; second, you can have position and
honor; or third, you can finally be blessed with a child who will
be a light to all Israel."

"I cannot make this decision without consulting my wife.
Please, can you wait here while I return home and discuss this
with her?"

"I promise I will wait. Remember, don't discuss this with
anyone except your wife!"·

Neither Yoseph nor his wife hesitated in their choice of
reward for one second, for they believed that without children
all other rewards were worthless.

He returned to Elyahu *Hanave* and told him of their
decision. Then the prophet disappeared as mysteriously as he
had come.

It did not take long for it to become obvious that Yoseph
Charif's wife was with child. When the boy was born, they
named him Menachem, "He will bring us comfort," but the

people in the *shtetl* called him Mendel. He studied in *yeshivos* in Koznitz, Lublin, and Nickolsburg, but considered Rebbe Elimelech of Lizensk to be his rebbe.[3]

Rebbe Menachem Mendel (1745–1815) became a great chasidic master, first serving the Jewish community in Pristick, then in Riminov. He is known as the Riminover Rebbe.[4]

---

[3]Before Rebbe Elimelech passed to his eternal rest, it is told that he bequeathed parts of his body to his various disciples. He bequeathed his brain to Menachem Mendel.

His contemporaries believed that Menachem Mendel's soul contained sparks from Rabbi Yitzchak Alfasi, the Rif, one of the principal halachists of the eleventh century, for Menachem Mendel had mastered the Rif's codification of Jewish law.

[4]H. Rabinowicz. *A Guide to Chassidism*. London: Thomas Yoseloff, 1960.

The Rightful Owner

People flocked to the *bays midrash* of Rebbe Avraham Ye-hoshua Heshel of Apt from the surrounding area to seek his advice and to be inspired by his words of wisdom.[1]

One morning, Chaim the tailor cautiously knocked on the door of the rebbe's private room at the rear of the *bays midrash* and waited patiently to be asked in. The rebbe saw from Chaim's red eyes that he had been crying for some time.

The rebbe motioned Chaim to come forward, stretched out his hand in welcome, and tried to soothe the anguished man.

G. Mah-Tov. *Ma-a-say-hem Shel Tzaddikim*, op. cit.

[1]Rebbe Avraham Yehoshua Heshel of Apt (1755–1825) was one of the rebbes affectionately known as "*O-hayv Yisrael*," one who loves all Jews. He was completely devoted to the service of God. Those who knew him said that the *Shechinah*, the Divine Presence, shone from his face. When he recited the *avodah*, the special priestly service on Yom Kippur, he used the first person verb form rather than the third person, believing that in a previous life, he had been the high priest who served in the Holy Temple in Jerusalem. He used to say that the mission of righteous people is to bring joy to the world and *naches* to God by binding love of God with love of mankind.

"What can I do for you?" he murmured.

"Rebbe, poverty is weighing me down like the full water buckets of the *vasser trayger*. I can't stand it anymore. Please pray that a livelihood should be a bit easier to earn!"

The rebbe looked at Chaim and said softly, "I will pray for you, and I will also give you a letter of introduction to Mordechai, one of my *chasidim* who happens to be a very wealthy man. He will give you 200 rubles when he reads my letter. The money will help ease your burden." The rebbe wrote the letter and handed it to Chaim.

The tailor's misery changed to joy. Exultantly, he ran all the way from the *bays midrash* to Mordechai's large, comfortable house on the other side of town. Chaim believed that as soon as Mordechai read the rebbe's letter, his lot in life would improve.

Mordechai welcomed the tailor for he recognized the handwriting on the envelope. He wondered what special favor the rebbe wanted him to do this time. He tried to be polite to his guest, but Chaim impatiently waved the letter, insisting that Mordechai open it at that moment.

"Wait," said Mordechai. "I will open the letter after lunch. First you must rest a bit and refresh yourself. You look like you haven't eaten in a while." He excused himself for a few minutes and instructed his servants to bring his guest some light refreshment and to add another place at the lunch table.

Chaim had never seen such exquisite dishes or glassware with which the table was set. He had never been able to put on his table such generous servings of food. He had never tasted such rich and creamy desserts as were on a silver platter on a serving cart opposite the long table covered with a lace cloth.

Mordechai tried to make Chaim feel at ease. He offered second helpings of everything but didn't even mention the letter during the entire meal. After the meal, he said, "Now that you are rested and relaxed, please explain to me the purpose of your visit."

Chaim cleared his throat, coughed, tried to speak, but words did not come out. His face turned red. Finally, he took the letter he was clutching and silently passed it to his host.

Mordechai's face paled when he read the letter. The words

danced before his eyes. "I want you," the rebbe had written, "to give Chaim, the bearer of this letter, 200 rubles."

"Two hundred rubles!" exclaimed Mordechai. "I can't give one person 200 rubles. If you will settle for fifty rubles, we can call it a deal!"

Chaim stood his ground.

"The rebbe promised me that you would give me 200 rubles. As I ran between the *bays midrash* and this house, I dreamed my troubles would be over. I thought I could buy some extra fabric, needles, and thread. I would be able to prepare garments in a variety of sizes, so that I could attract more customers. I believed it would be easier to earn a livelihood. The rebbe promised. I won't settle for less. If you won't give me all that the rebbe promised, I won't take anything. I will return home empty-handed and forget that I ever delivered this letter to you."

Mordechai struggled with the rebbe's request and his own inner conscience. He had never given *anyone* 200 rubles for *any* cause, ever. Silently he debated whether to share his wealth as the rebbe had requested, or to disregard the rebbe's wishes.

Finally, he shouted angrily, "I can't possibly give you 200 rubles!"

Chaim rose from the chair and, brokenhearted, ran from Mordechai's house.

Tearfully, he returned to town. His shoulders heaved with the pain of a shattered dream. He wandered around the marketplace aimlessly until long after dark not wanting to face his family. When he finally let himself into his dilapidated shack, his wife and children were fast asleep.

The next morning, Chaim returned to the rebbe and told him his disappointing encounter with Mordechai. The rebbe listened sympathetically. Then he said calmly, "I will give you a different letter to Noson, another one of my chasidim. He will not disappoint you."

The rebbe wrote the letter and handed it to Chaim. Bidding him to go in peace, the rebbe pointed the way to his house.

Noson received Chaim graciously.

"What is the reason for your visit? How can I help you?" he

asked as he opened the door wide to welcome him. Sheepishly, Chaim handed him the letter without saying a word. Noson immediately recognized the rebbe's handwriting.

"A letter from the rebbe," he began singing. "What a privilege to receive a letter from the rebbe! It is not every day that I have such joy."

Noson sang and danced as he opened the envelope and read the rebbe's request to give Chaim 100 rubles. Finishing the letter, he said to Chaim, "Sit here until I return. I have to go to the marketplace to do some business. I won't be long. I will have the money for you when I return."

Scooping a few pieces of jewelry into his pocket from the small box in another room, he ran toward the pawnbroker's stall in the marketplace where he pawned them for fifty rubles. Returning home, he added the contents of his cash box into an envelope together with the fifty rubles from the sale of his jewelry and handed the envelope to Chaim.

"Here, this is the money that the rebbe asked me to give you. It is always such a privilege to fulfill the rebbe's wishes. I bless you that this money will help you to prosper, so that soon you will be privileged to give rather than to receive."

In the meantime the wheel of fortune turned, and Mordechai's business investments started to sour. One deal after another turned out badly, very unusual for one whose every business move had been successful.

During the following months, Mordechai became destitute. In gradual stages, he was forced to sell his exquisite dishes and glassware, the silver serving trays, the furniture, the tapestries that hung from the walls of his comfortable home. All these he was forced to sell just to live from hand to mouth, to keep his family from starvation. Finally, there was nothing left to sell. He was forced to knock on the doors of his friends' homes and beg them for food. How he suffered! Mentally anguished, disgraced among his friends, he was humiliated beyond endurance.

Having little strength left to cope with his poverty, he decided to go to the the rebbe for advice. He tried to enter the *bays midrash* through the courtyard, but the *shamish* who sat outside the rebbe's private room refused to allow him to enter, because the rebbe had so instructed him. "Mordechai will come one day to seek my help. I don't want to see him under any circumstances!"

Mordechai sat helplessly in the courtyard, miserably bemoaning his fate, wondering if his pathetic situation was indeed retribution for having turned Chaim away empty-handed. He muttered disconnected phrases.

"I realize this has happened to me because I did not heed the instructions of the rebbe to give Chaim 200 rubles. I know this is why the rebbe doesn't want to see me. I'm so sorry. How can I repent the arrogance of my ways?"

Some of the rebbe's students watched him for a few days, for he refused to move from the courtyard. Finally, one suggested sympathetically, "Instead of crying here in the courtyard, move over and sit under the window of the rebbe's private room. The rebbe is a compassionate man. He will hear your sobs. I am certain that eventually he will listen to you."

Not knowing what else to do, Mordechai decided to heed the advice.

As the student had predicted, Mordechai's weeping disturbed the rebbe.

"Who is that outside my window?" demanded the rebbe.

By this time all the students in the *bays midrash* knew Mordechai's story. As soon as they mentioned his name, the rebbe said:

"It is time for us to talk. Tell him to come in."

Mordechai walked hesitantly into the *bays midrash*, and quietly sat down. He composed himself and the tears stopped. The rebbe emerged from his private room.

"I will appoint three of my most worthy students to act as judges in this case," he announced. So doing, he proceeded to address the court. "Before I was born, the Heavenly Court decreed that I should inherit a fortune. When I became a rebbe I did not want to accept that magnanimous gift, for I had no need of money. Therefore, I proposed that the wealth apportioned to me be divided among my most worthy, devoted, and loyal *chasidim*. The Heavenly Court agreed to my plan and I was permitted to divide that wealth according to the way I saw fit. You, Mordechai, were one of the recipients. Not only that, but you were blessed with a special ability to know how to increase your profits. Your personal fortune was immense. But the moment you refused my instructions to give Chaim 200 rubles, I took back my share of the wealth, and gave it to Noson. You, Mordechai, were not a worthy distributor. I gave your share of the money to Noson who is more compassionate, more understanding of the true meaning of helping one's brother in need.''

Silence spread over the *bays midrash*. Mordechai's tearful, red-eyed face paled. He was shocked to learn that the money he had called his own over the years had not really been his to do with as he pleased. He finally understood that it was a trust that had simply been placed under his control. He raised his eyes and visualized the impoverished plight of his family in the days to come.

Uncontrollably, he began to weep.

The rebbe instructed the judges to consider the facts of the case and render a decision. They conferred for a few minutes and then the eldest spoke.

"Mordechai has no right to demand the return of all his former wealth, for it never belonged to him in the first place. But if the rebbe will forgive him, we suggest that he be permitted once again to earn a livelihood for his family, so that he will not have to beg to survive!''

Mordechai pleaded for the rebbe's forgiveness. Within a few days, he saw a small improvement in his general financial situation. He accepted the fact that he would earn a living, but that he would never again be the wealthiest man in town.

Invite Me to the Wedding

As Mr. Goldman aged, he turned over the management of his thriving timber business to his son. Their unspoiled forestlands extended for kilometers and kilometers, reaching the edge of the gradually ascending slopes of the Carpathian Mountains. It seemed that the ground was covered alternately with evergreen and thick-bark deciduous trees.

Young Eli Goldman could see the 8,000 foot top of the Rysy Peak, the highest elevation in Poland, as he traversed his lands from north to south. On a clear day, he could see the sun-flecked snow-tipped peaks touching the azure blue sky. He loved to listen to the thundering waterfalls rumble down the mountainsides, cascading to the lake below.

Sometimes he rode his horse around the shore of the lake surrounded by the majestic peaks. "I am but a speck in this valley," he thought. "It is obvious that the glory of the Creator fills the world."

Goldman had worked hard to build a reputation as an honest businessman. The lumber and wood products that were

Menachem Mendel. *Sepuray Hacha*. Jerusalem: Defus Hanachal, 1983.

hewn from the Goldman timberlands were much in demand. Fine furniture manufacturers and ship builders with exacting standards used his maple, ash, and oak exclusively. The pines produced resins, tar, turpentine, and varnish; fir and spruce produced cellulose for paper. Its lumber by-products were known all over Galicia, Czechoslovakia, and Prussia, practically from the Baltic to the Black Sea.

The profits from these timberlands provided handsomely for the Goldman family. They lived in a fine mansion near the outskirts of the city of Rukatin. It was beautifully furnished and comfortable.

When Eli Goldman took over his father's business, he built himself a new home in a clearing in the center of the forest, at least fifteen kilometers in every direction from the outskirts of the nearest *shtetl*. The people thought it strange that he chose to live by himself in the heart of his forestlands, but they reasoned that perhaps he had moved to the center of the forest in order to have better control over his workers and the quality of their work.

He furnished his home elaborately. He imported carpets from Paris, furniture from Danzig, tapestries from Brussels. Carrara marble, imported from Tuscany, overlaid the wooden porches and balconies. Gilt-framed paintings adorned the walls and heavy velvet draperies covered the windows.

Occasionally, he traveled to Danzig, Prague, or Frankfurt to collect money from his various enterprises and to keep in touch with business friends. Mostly, he remained in the forest, spending his days overseeing his timberlands and his nights tallying his accounts.

He always welcomed visitors to his home, particularly the charity collectors. No one who made the trip through the forest to seek his aid was ever turned away empty-handed.

One day a group of simple craftsmen came by wagon to his home. Opening the door to their knock, he recognized Berel the tailor, the *shtetl* shoemaker, the blacksmith, and the baker. They were simple, unassuming, humble men, blessed with the deepest faith that the Almighty would provide for all their needs.

"Please come in and sit down," he said, welcoming them and making them comfortable. "It is a long trip through the forest. Let me give you something to eat and drink. How can I help you?" He signaled a servant to bring some refreshments and then sat down facing the four men.

Berel wasted no time in presenting his request.

"We have come to collect money for a bridal dowry. You see, an orphan girl who lives in our *shtetl* has just reached marriageable age. Just recently, we learned that in a neighboring *shtetl* there is an orphan boy, also of marriageable age. Neither have any family whatsoever. They have been raised by the Jewish community. We decided to arrange a match between the two of them. Needless to say, we want to furnish a little house for them, purchase some new clothing, and have enough left over to make a wedding feast to which we can invite the poor of both *shtetlach*."

Eli Goldman raised his hand for Berel to stop talking. "How much do you need to do everything you want to do for the young couple?" he asked.

Without hesitating, Berel answered, "We need 500 rubles."

A smile crossed Eli Goldman's lips. He stood up, walked to a drape-covered wall and drew one of the heavy velvet drapes aside. Behind the drape a wall safe was revealed. Eli turned the lock, opened the door, and removed a strongbox. He opened the box and withdrew 500 rubles, handing them to Berel the tailor.

"I am very glad that you thought of me for this *mitzvah*," he said. "I only want you to promise me one thing: when you are ready to lead the bride and groom to the *chuppah*, come here to the forest to fetch me. I want to be at that wedding."

Berel promised Eli Goldman that the wedding would not begin without him. He took the money, thanked his benefactor, and motioned his friends toward the door, and they all walked joyfully down the path to their wagon. Once they were seated in the wagon, they turned on Berel.

"How could you have asked for so much money?" they demanded. "You know that 400 rubles would have been enough to furnish a little house, buy some new clothes, and make a small wedding!"

Berel only shrugged his shoulders. He wanted the young couple to have a comfortable start in life.

As soon as the men returned to the *shtetl*, they hastened to begin preparations for the wedding.

In the meantime, Eli Goldman decided to take one of his occasional business trips. This time, his itinerary included Leipzig and Danzig. He attended to business matters for two weeks, then decided to return home. He purchased a first-class ticket on a train leaving Germany, traveling southwest from Danzig to Poznan, than east to Ostrow, than south to Krakow. He carried with him a briefcase containing 40,000 rubles.

The first part of the trip was without incident, but as the train crossed the border into Poland, gradually wending its way across vast agricultural plains heavy with ripening corn and wheat, he noticed two men in the corridor staring at him through the window of his compartment. Their stares made him nervous. He turned white and started to perspire. He felt adrenalin surging through his veins. He tried to ignore the stares of the two men, but he was frightened. His heart pounded. As the train inched its way into the station at Ostrow, he decided to hire an armed guard. He descended into the station and walked slowly toward the stationmaster.

"I am Eli Goldman," he explained. "I believe that I am being followed by two suspicious-looking characters. I would like to hire an armed guard to accompany me to my destination near Krakow."

The stationmaster did not think that Eli Goldman's request was unusual, so he appointed two armed guards to accompany him for the remainder of the trip. When the train arrived in Rukatin, he dismissed the armed guard, hired a private carriage, and headed for home. Only after he had locked the 40,000 rubles into the hidden safe did he breathe a sigh of relief. He lay down to rest, clearly exhausted from the harrowing experience. He tried to dismiss the fear of having been followed.

Pounding at the front door interrupted his rest and continued incessantly. He ran down the stairs from his bedroom to see who was making the commotion. Just as his feet touched the last step, he heard the crash of glass from his sitting-room window. He froze, for there were the same two men who had been on the train. One carried an ax, the other a heavy stick.

"Quickly, the money," they shouted. "We want all you brought from Danzig! Your money or your life!"

One of the robbers lunged toward him, grabbing the collar of his coat, dragging him toward his accomplice, who stood brandishing the ax. Unbeknownst to him, Eli Goldman realized now that they had followed him from the train. He wondered if he would live if he turned over all the money to the robbers.

They were impatient. They pushed him and pummeled him. "Hurry, where did you hide the money?" they demanded.

They pulled him in the direction of the sitting room. He realized that he had no choice. He stumbled slowly over to the drapery-covered wall and drew the heavy velvet drape, revealing the safe to the intruders. He fiddled with the lock, opened the metal door, and withdrew the strongbox.

He had just opened the box and was about to hand the money over to the robbers, when suddenly, the sounds of song and dance echoed through the forest, approaching closer and closer to the house. The rhythm of the drummer kept pace with the pounding of Eli Goldman's heart. The sweet notes of the flute floated through the tops of the trees. The rumbling wagon wheels rolled over the underbrush on the forest floor. The sounds of joy drew closer and closer.

"Who are these musicians?" wondered Eli Goldman. "I can't believe this! First I am being attacked by merciless robbers, now musicians are descending upon my home!"

"Mr. Goldman, Mr. Goldman," called out Berel the tailor. Mr. Goldman did not answer.

As the singing troubadors approached the house, Berel noticed the broken glass and the open door. "Something must be wrong," he realized.

He was not polite this time. He called to his friends and they stormed the house. The sudden intrusion stunned the thieves. Berel lunged for the ax, knocking over one thief. The others jumped the second one, throwing him to the ground. The drummer ran to the window, pulled the drapery cord from its valance, and tied up both thieves. Carrying them like sacks, they threw them into the wagon.

"Mr. Goldman," Berel whispered. "The bride and groom are waiting for you by the *chuppah*. We must hurry, but first we must make a short stop at the police station!"

Hachnasas Orchim–

HOSPITALITY

achnasas *orchim* (hospitality), within Jewish tradition is characterized by our patriarch Abraham. On the third day, following his circumcision, he sat outside the open doors of his four-sided tent watching for passersby. He saw three strangers (disguised angels) approaching and "he ran from the door of his tent to meet them and bowed to the ground. He said to their leader, 'My lord, if I am worthy of your favor, do not pass by me. Some water will be brought, you will wash your feet and rest under the tree. And I will bring some bread that you may refresh yourself . . . (and partake of my hospitality). . .'"

—Genesis 18:1–3

Abraham had been conversing with the Almighty Who had appeared to him, to visit him, to heal him after his circumcision. Rashi, the greatest of our biblical commentators, explains that the word "lord" has two meanings: the first ordinarily is addressed to a high ranking individual, the second refers to the Almighty. By interpreting the verse as Abraham's conversation with the Almighty, it characterizes hospitality, for then the verse reads: "I beg You, Almighty, please wait for me to return until after I have attended to the needs of my guests."

—Genesis 18:3

Rav Judah therefore commented in the name of Rav: "Hospitality is greater than welcoming the Divine Presence."

—Talmud *Bavli, Shabbos* 127a

Abraham attracted people to the service of God through hospitality. To assure them that they were welcome, he planted groves of *ayshel* trees throughout the length and breadth of Eretz Yisrael, wherever he set up his tent from north to south, east to west. *Ayshel* is an acronym for the Hebrew words *achelah*, food, *shteyah*, drink, *lenah*, rest.

—Genesis 21:33, Rashi

143

He wanted the wayfarers to know that the symbol of welcome was the *ayshel* tree, where they would receive both physical and spiritual comfort, food and drink for their famished and parched bodies and kind words for their souls.[1]

[1]Rebbe Yehuda Layb Ayger. *Imray Emes, B'rayshis*. Originally printed in Lublin, 1902. Reprinted in Jerusalem, 1973.

Torah Thoughts

Hospitality

Rabbi Eliezer Hagadol wrote a special ethical will for his son:

"My son, take care to show respect to the poor. Speak gently to the poor man and commiserate with him in his troubles. Give him alms privately. Feed him in your own home. Do not watch him while he eats, lest, if he is famished, you might embarrass him.

"Teach your household humility, so that if a poor man stands at the door and asks: 'Is the father in?' they will respond, 'Yes, come in.' As soon as the man enters, let the table be set for him."

—Avos d'Rabi Nasan. Chapter 7

Shammai said: "Greet all persons cordially." He explained that the most expensive gift given morosely is insignificant compared with a pleasant greeting without a gift.

—Avos d'Rabi Nasan. Chapter 13

When Ezra the Scribe returned with many Jews Eretz of Israel from the Babylonian exile, he decreed certain laws which he hoped would revitalize the spiritual level of the Jewish people in their land. Among these laws was: "Bake bread

on Friday for the whole week, that there may be bread for the poor."
—Talmud *Yerushalmi, Megilla* 4

Rav Huna opened the door of his house at mealtime and called, "Anyone who is hungry, come and eat."
—Talmud *Bavli, Taanis* 20b

And the woman said to her husband, "I perceive that this holy man is a man of God. He passes our way often. Let us build a little attic and furnish it with a bed, a table, a chair and a lantern, so that when he visits, he will be comfortable among us."

Rabbi Yossi ben Chanina said, "We learn from this that a woman detects the needs of another human being more readily than does a man."
—2 Kings 4:9 and Talmud *Bavli, Berachos* 10b

"When a poor man visits you at home, receive him cordially. Serve him food at once, for he may not have eaten for a long time and may be ashamed to ask. Console and encourage him. Attend to his needs yourself, even if you have many servants. Are you superior to Abraham, who himself served the disguised angels?"
—Rabbenu Yonah

Why is Abraham the model of hospitality?

Abraham had such unmitigating love for God that he wanted mankind to recognize Him. He was convinced that God provides unconditionally for mankind. Therefore, he devoted much energy emulating God through hospitality. He invited wayfarers to his home and personally attended to their every need. He diverted their thanks away from himself toward God. Abraham originated the first Jewish outreach program; through hospitality, he brought people closer to God.
—Rebbe Yerachmiel Yisrael Yitzchak Me-Aleksander,
Yismach Yisrael, Parshas Va'yay-ra

It is preferable to share a meal at one's own table with the poor than to give money. The first is a personal act, the second, an impersonal one. A meal is of immediate benefit; giving money delays the poor man's benefit until he is able to buy something.
—Ellyahu Ki Tov, *The Jew and His Home.*
New York: Shengold Publisher, 1963

Stories

The Amazing Mirror

One day Yechiel Michel appeared at the door of a modest one-room inn located at the edge of an isolated *shtetl.*[1] Inside, a bar and counter stocked with liquor stood at the far end of the room. Separating the counter and the family's living quarters were some rickety chairs and tables that accommodated the

Mordechai ben Yechezkel. *Sayfer Hamaseyos*, op. cit.

Rabbi Mayer Shapira (1887–1934) was a prominent *rosh yeshiva* and communal leader in Lublin, Poland. He is remembered for two innovations. He conceived the idea of Jews all over the world studying a *daf yomi*, the same page of Talmud daily at the same time, and he insisted that his Yeshiva Chachmay Lublin provide students with dormitory facilities so the students would not have to board in individual homes. He was fond of telling this story to his students to mold their character.

[1]Rebbe Yechiel Michel ben Rebbe Yitzchak (1726–1786) was born in Brody in the Volhynia region of Poland. He studied under Rebbe Yisrael ben Eliezer, the Baal Shem Tov, founder of the chasidic movement and developed his talents as a fiery speaker, a moral preacher, and a storyteller during the years that he wandered before settling down in the *shtetl* of Zlotochov. He left few of his writings to posterity. People said that each of his five sons represented a book of the Torah and they were his immortality.

area's peasants when they stopped in for a drink on their way from the fields to the ramshackle huts that were their homes.

Anshil the innkeeper and his family were about to sit down to a meager dinner of black bread, borscht, and potatoes. He welcomed his guest enthusiastically and insisted that he share their meal. The innkeeper hovered over him making certain he had enough water to wash his hands ritually before eating bread. He served him before the other members of his family and honored him by asking him to lead the blessing following the meal. He truly imitated every aspect of the patriarch Abraham's hospitality to the three angels who came to visit him as he sat outside his tent in Mamre.[2]

After the meal, Anshil personally set up a bed for his guest against one wall of the inn. Yechiel Michal stood at the opposite side of the room praying. All the time he prayed, he heard Anshil sighing and muttering. When he had finished praying, Yechiel Michel asked the innkeeper, "Why are you sighing so? You know that hospitality has much reward both in this world and in the world to come!"

"You don't understand," responded Anshil. "I am sighing because I have only very modest means to fulfill this *mitzvah* properly. You see, few peasants patronize my inn. I barely earn a livelihood for my family. Occasionally, when a passerby stops, as you did tonight, I share our meager meal and sleeping quarters. I learned a long time ago that providing hospitality is greater than receiving the Divine Presence, but I wonder if I will ever be able to fulfill this *mitzvah* properly."[3]

He sighed again with great feeling and continued, "It must be that I am not worthy, for if I were, then at least I would build a small, separate room for my guests and furnish it with a bed, a table, a chair, and a lantern.[4] Then I would be able to fulfill the *mitzvah* of my Creator." As he finished, he began to sob.

Yechiel Michal realized the sincerity of the humble inn-

---

[2] Genesis 18:1–3. See detailed explanation on p. 143.

[3] Talmud *Bavli, Shabbos* 127a.

[4] 2 Kings 4:10. The passage describes the Shunamite woman who built a special room for the prophet Elisha, so that he would be comfortable when he passed through that town. It contained a bed, a table, a chair, and a lantern.

keeper's words. "Since you mentioned our patriarch Abraham's hospitality, I will bless you with the same blessing with which he was blessed. Blessed be Anshil, representative of the Most High God, Creator of Heaven and Earth.[5] May the Almighty bless you, Anshil, with abundant wealth, so that you will be privileged to sustain the poor and extend hospitality to both the needy and the passersby."

Then he turned to the bed that Anshil had made up for him. He lay down and fell fast asleep.

In the morning, after he had prayed and eaten the small breakfast Anshil had provided, he departed with the words, "May the Almighty fulfill the innermost desires of your heart, and may abundant blessings be upon you and your household."

Soon afterward, the innkeeper noticed that more and more peasants were coming to the inn. At the end of the second month, his business had increased to such an extent that he tithed his income and set the money aside to purchase extra food for both the needy and the passersby. He graciously received the many guests who now frequented his inn, hovering over them as a mother bird hovers over her young.

After six months, he built an addition to the inn, the small guest room he had always thought about. In it, he placed a bed, a table, a chair, and a lantern. Six months later, he added another room. Both guest rooms were always occupied.

One good year followed another. He leased a flour mill from the *poretz* and hired people to bake bread and pastry from his flour. He bought forest lands and employed loggers. The wood was sold for building or for fuel, but always profitably. He had become a very wealthy man and people began talking about him.

"Did you hear," they gossiped in the marketplace, "that Anshil the innkeeper, the one who always sighed that he could never fulfill the *mitzvah* of hospitality properly because he had such limited means, the one who was so compassionate, well, he has hired a guard to stand at the iron gate of his new mansion. If a needy person or a shabbily-dressed person passes by begging for money, the guard has instructions to send that

[5] Genesis 14:20, paraphrased.

person away. It seems that his compassionate heart has turned to stone."[6]

People whom Anshil had previously helped could not believe the change in him. One of the poor people whom he had helped tried to stop the idle chatter. "I will go to see him. I will tell you if what you hear is true or false."

The guard refused to let him pass, for he was dressed like a beggar. "My master told me to tell you and every other beggar," he shouted at the poor man, "that he will give you a job if you want to work! Charity only encourages people to remain idle. He will not hand out money anymore!" The guard acted far beyond what he had been hired to do; elderly people who had depended on Anshil's charity were now deprived of the barest necessities.

In the meantime, Yechiel Michel had become renowned as the rebbe of Zlotochov. People came from all over the area to seek his advice or to spend a *Shabbos* or holy day in his *bays midrash* and at his *tish*.[7]

From these people, he heard how Anshil the innkeeper had completely changed. "I don't understand how it is possible for such a compassionate man to change character so completely. I don't believe it." But he heard the story more than once.

"I will visit him," he decided. Before he set out the next day, he changed his garb to that of a prosperous merchant. When he arrived at the gate of Anshil's mansion, he had to contend with the guard who repeatedly told him that his master was too busy to receive guests.

"Tell your master," Rebbe Yechiel Michel said firmly, "that a long lost friend, a friend he hasn't seen in many years, has come especially to see him."

The guard stared at the rebbe's fashionable clothing. Finally, he stepped aside, opened the gate and showed the rebbe in.

Rebbe Yechiel Michel found Anshil sitting at a long table in

---

[6] "It is true that there are stones that melt like a human heart, but there are human hearts that are as hard as stone." Rabbi Avraham Yitzchak HaKohen Kook's reference to the *Kotel*, the western wall of the Holy Temple.

[7] The rebbes of chasidic communities conducted a special *tish* during *Shabbos* and holy days. A *tish* is a table, and it was here that Torah was studied and melodies were sung, in addition to the meal that was served.

a room decorated luxuriously with rich tapestries, magnificent paintings, and comfortable couches. Anshil raised his head from his ledgers at the sound of Rebbe Yechiel Michel's footsteps, but when he saw who had intruded upon his privacy, he pretended he did not recognize him and lowered his head.

Being ignored did not bother Rebbe Yechiel Michel. He strode noisily back and forth across the room, snapping his fingers and clearing his throat.

Anshil could not concentrate. The commotion clearly upset him. Finally, he shouted, "How dare you barge in here . . . under false pretenses. . . . Look at the way you are dressed. . . My guard would never have admitted you had he known you were a rebbe, not a prosperous merchant. What do you want from me?"

"What do I want from you?" repeated Rebbe Yechiel Michel angrily. "What has become of you! I have heard that your heart has turned to stone!" He continued pacing. Suddenly, a mirror on top of a bookcase caught his attention. He strode over to the bookcase and took down the mirror. He continued to pace back and forth the length of the room, the mirror clutched in his hands. Finally, he stopped before Anshil, placed the mirror on the table and demanded, "What is the difference between this mirror and that glass window? Quickly, stand up, and go to the window, so that you will be able to see what I see."

Anshil rose, went to the window and peered out at the street.

"I see people walking, some quickly, toward the marketplace, some slowly, ambling leisurely; I see children chasing each other, playing games, enjoying themselves."

"Now, look into this mirror," urged Rebbe Yechiel Michel. "Tell me what you see."

Anshil picked up the mirror. "I see my own reflection," he responded. "You are telling me," whispered the rebbe, "that you see no one else in the mirror?" He took the mirror from Anshil's hand. He resumed striding back and forth, this time talking to himself.

"What is the difference between a window and a mirror?" he muttered, loudly enough for Anshil to hear. "Why can a person see other people through a window, but only his own reflection in a mirror? It must be that the silver that covers the back of the mirror creates a separation between the person who sees only his own reflection and the rest of the world. How sad it is for people to have ears that do not hear, eyes that do not see, hands that cannot reach out to other human beings. Their idols are silver and gold . . . ."[8]

Total silence pervaded the room. Slowly, slowly, Rebbe Yechiel Michel peeled the silver backing from the mirror. The fragments fluttered to the ground, scattering across the floor.

"I understand what you are telling me," sobbed Anshil. "I confess that I have misused all the abundant wealth that came to me as a result of your blessing. I will dismiss the gatekeeper immediately. I will personally take charge of hospitality for the needy and the passersby. I will provide them with food, drink, and a place to rest, as I used to do. I will never again hide myself from the needs of other human beings."

Rebbe Yechiel Michel replaced the mirror on the shelf, bid farewell to Anshil, and returned to his home. Anshil immediately ordered his carpenter to build a special frame for the mirror, to protect it from damage, and placed it at the center of the long table.

When he reached his 70th birthday, he wrote an ethical will. In it, he repeated the story of how he had been blessed by Rebbe Yechiel Michel to fulfill the *mitzvah* of hospitality; how abundance of wealth had temporarily blinded him to the needs of the poor, and how he had repented his ways. The mirror was to remind his descendants of the importance of *hachnasas orchim*. He instructed his children to read his ethical will every week, just before *Shabbos*.

The mirror was the most precious possession in that family, more than the money, jewels, and land holdings that Anshil's children inherited. When the Russian government decreed that every family adopt a surname, they chose the name, *R'ee-el*, the Hebrew equivalent for "the mirror that belongs to God."

[8] Psalms 115:4, 5, paraphrased.

Chanukah in the Month
of May

The twisting road was barely touched by the last glow of daylight. The winter sun slowly set behind the frozen branches of the trees, shorn bare by winter's frost. A white blanket of freshly fallen snow, untouched by human or animal tracks, unmarred by carriage wheels, lay for miles ahead. Two horses trotted cautiously trying to keep to the road, trying not to throw the carriage they pulled into the drifts on either side of the road.

Inside the carriage, a rebbe and his *shamish* sat huddled together, wrapped in fur pelts from neck to feet. Only the rebbe's hand, clutching a *sayfer*, a holy book, extended from under the warm protection of the fur pelts. The rebbe peered intently at the words. He strained to decipher the last letters before darkness enveloped him. The *shamish's* teeth chattered.

"Rebbe," he asked, "don't you think we have travelled far enough today? Since we are near Ellick, why don't we stay in the inn that is just down the road. Don't you think we should stop there for the night?"

R. Friedman. *Matbayos shel Esh*. Jerusalem: Hamesorah, 1986.

The rebbe lifted his eyes from his *sayfer*, struggling to return to the realities of the world of frost and biting wind that howled around the carriage and through it.

"Feivel," said the rebbe, "that's a wonderful idea! We will not be able to travel any further tonight. Why don't you tell the coachman to turn off the road into that inn? I know it is owned by one of our fellow Jews."

When the innkeeper heard the crunch of the coach's wheels on the ice-covered path to his door, he threw a fur coat over his shoulders, grabbed a lantern, and rushed outdoors to welcome his guests. He had not seen a traveler for many days, since the bitter winds of winter had been blowing from the nearby mountains.

"Hurry, please come in," he sputtered, trying to catch his breath through the howling wind. "I have a warm fire and I will make you comfortable."

The rebbe and his *shamish* alighted from the coach and entered the inn. The innkeeper seated his guests in comfortable chairs in the sitting room and ran to the kitchen to bring them hot soup and tea. While they warmed themselves, the innkeeper went to prepare a room for his guests.

The rebbe finished eating, opened his *sayfer* and continued studying. When the innkeeper returned to the sitting room, the rebbe excused himself and retired for the night. The *shamish* remained to chat with the innkeeper.

The innkeeper thought that his guests might be important people, but he wanted to know for sure, so without wasting time, he came directly to the point.

"What is your rebbe's name?" he asked.

"The rebbe," replied the *shamish*, "is the *tzaddik*, Rebbe Avraham of Stretin."[1]

---

[1] A friend asked Rebbe Avraham Stretin (second half of the nineteenth century) to provide him with an amulet that would enhance his fear of God.

"I have no such amulet," he said. "However, I do have one for the love of God."

"That is even better," responded his friend. "Love of God is much higher than fear of God."

"In that case, let me tell you the secret of this amulet. The only way you come to love God is through love of every Jew. When you love every Jew, it is simple to achieve love of God."

"Is that so?" murmured the innkeeper. "I thought that he lived in Eretz Yisrael, in Safed, the city of the Kabbalists."

His voice trailed off. He closed his eyes and imagined the holy sites of Eretz Yisrael: Jerusalem, the ruins of the Holy Temple, the wall surrounding the old city, the mountains surrounding Safed, the graves of Rabbi Akiva, Rabbi Mayer, and Maimonides on the outskirts of Tiberias. How he wanted to see these places for himself!

"No, it's not a mistake," answered Feivel, swallowing the last drop of tea in his glass. He stood and moved near the hearth, holding his hands close to the open fire and sighing deeply. "You're quite right," he repeated. "It is true that a Stretiner rebbe lives in Eretz Yisrael. His name is Rebbe Ahron and he made *aliyah* in his old age. The rebbe whom I accompanied on this trip is his son Avraham. He remains in Galicia to visit the graves of his ancestors on their *yahrzeits*. Actually, the reason we were traveling in this blizzard is because one of the *yahrzeits* he observes is rapidly approaching. We were traveling toward the cemetery when the night and the storm forced us to stop." Both men sighed deeply, then retired for the night.

The storm had not subsided the next day. The fields looked like ice hills, gradually increasing in bulk from the swirling sleet. Rebbe Avraham decided there was no choice but to remain at the inn in Ellick.

A few hours before nightfall on the twenty-fourth day of Kislev, the Jews of Ellick gathered in the *bays midrash* in anticipation of kindling the first Chanukah light. They sat around long tables, some studying, some singing, some chatting. A joyous mood permeated the room as they awaited darkness in order to pray. As soon as the service concluded, they streamed out of the *bays midrash*, eagerly heading toward home, to their wives and children who waited to kindle the Chanukah lights. The sounds of Chanukah echoed throughout the *shtetl* and intensified as people in fur coats and oversized shawls emerged from warm houses and returned to dance in the courtyard of the *bays midrash*.

Rebbe Avraham, a stranger in Ellick, decided to go to the *bays midrash* on this first night of Chanukah.

"As long as I can't be with my own *chasidim*," he thought,

"I might as well join the people of this *shtetl* in their celebration." He stood near the edge of the circle of the dancers for a while, then followed them indoors.

Hopping, jumping, leaping, the dancers rejoiced in the Chanukah festival. Suddenly, one of the dancers signaled for silence, for he recognized the rebbe. Leaning over, he extended his hand and said, "Shalom aleichem, Rebbe Avraham. It is a great privilege to have you visit us. To what do we owe this honor?"

Rebbe Avraham answered softly, "I am on my way to the graves of my ancestors in Stretin. The storm interfered with my journey. It was impossible to travel, so I stopped in the local inn."

"Wait a minute," called out an old man with deep penetrating eyes and shaky hands. "Might you not be the Rebbe of Stretin himself?"

"I am the *son* of Rebbe Ahron of Stretin who made *aliyah* to Eretz Yisrael in his old age," he answered.

Stunned silence fell over the study hall.

The old man turned toward the dancers and continued, "Since the Almighty sent us this holy man, we need to receive him in a fitting manner!"

Instantly, the circle of dancers separated. Some men ran to the wall to pull additional benches toward the tables that were already standing, others spread white tablecloths, and others ran home to fetch cakes and schnapps.

The food and drink warmed both body and soul. Rebbe Avraham rose to the occasion from his honored place at the head of the table that he transformed into his *tish* with his special melodies and Torah thoughts.

Seated near him was one of the community's recognized leaders. His name was Michel, and he seemed a bit nervous. His hands twisted and untwisted the edges of the tablecloth; beads of perspiration stood out on his brow, his eyes darted back and forth among the *chasidim* seated around the tables.

He hesitated a long time before he stood up. The eyes of all the *chasidim* turned toward Michel. The words tumbled forth from his lips. "Rebbe, please listen to me. I have a very special connection to the House of Stretin. I am an only child. It was due to the blessing of your holy father that I was born. . . ." He lowered his voice. The *chasidim* stared intently at him.

The rebbe smiled before he spoke. "It is important to retell stories of miraculous occurrences on Chanukah. Why don't you tell us your story?"

* * *

Michel cleared his throat and began to speak softly. "My father, Rebbe Zalman, was considered the genius of Tzchelik, the Ukrainian *shtetl* where he lived with his family. Many wealthy Jews wanted him for a son-in-law. He married Leah, the daughter of Shimon Ber, one of the leaders of the community. She wanted only to build a home filled with kindness and traditional Jewish values. Her father promised to support the newlyweds so that Zalman might sit in the yeshiva and learn uninterruptedly, without worrying about earning a livelihood.

"On the surface, life was perfect for the young couple, but days followed months, and months turned into years. Zalman and Leah were childless. It was apparent that the cause of Leah's red eyes were the tears she shed while she prayed.

"She busied herself helping the other women in the *shtetl*; she prepared food for the poor, attended the ill, mothered the orphans, nursed the women after childbirth, looked after their older children. She did all this with a smile on her face but her heart was breaking.

"Zalman spent his time in the *bays midrash*, trying to drown his pain in the joy of study, but reality always evoked anguish each evening as he returned home.

"Winter arrived early in Tzchelik that year. Chazkel the *shamish* cleaned the furnace, stacked the firewood, and shuttered the windows. He wanted the people who devoted their lives to the study of the Almighty's word to be comfortable and warm. He had just finished his morning chores when Zalman arrived.

" 'Good morning, good morning,' he called out cheerily. 'May this *bays midrash* be filled with more like you!'

"After the morning prayer service, Zalman sat in his accustomed place, opened the volume of Maimonides' *Mishneh*

Torah dealing with the laws of the sanctification of the new month that he had been studying the evening before, a text whose meaning evaded him. He pored over the text for hours, trying to understand it and finally grasped the underlying principles.

"Suddenly, the words on the page started to swim before his eyes. He lowered his head, trying to control the dizziness. He tried to stand, but found that his knees trembled, and he was shivering in the warm *bays midrash*! He had never paid much attention to his physical being. What were these sharp pains that pierced his shoulders and ribs? He bit his lips, felt the color leave his face.

"He struggled to unwrap the roll that Leah had sent with him that morning, crept to the wash basin to wash his hands, raised the roll to his lips and bit into it. 'Maybe the pain is from hunger,' he thought. 'It seems to be near midday and I haven't yet eaten a morsel of food. I've been so immersed in studying.'

"But the pain did not subside. He could not concentrate. He closed the volume of the *Mishneh Torah*, threw his coat over his shoulders, dragged himself down the path from the *bays midrash* toward the street, knees knocking together as he exerted every last ounce of strength to reach home.

"Leah was alarmed that he had returned home during the day. She tried to make him comfortable, but nothing she did could ease his pain. He lay down on his bed and fell into a troubled sleep.

"Toward evening, Shimon Ber returned from his business. He was terrified when he saw his son-in-law doubled over in pain, his face white and drawn. He tried to remain calm. 'Don't worry, my children, this illness will pass. Zalman will be better tomorrow!' But deep inside, he was very frightened.

"He instructed a servant to fetch the doctor. When the doctor arrived, he looked at Zalman's tongue, tapped at his back and knees, took his temperature. Then, as he returned his instruments to his case, he said, 'This is nothing more than a cold. He will be fine in a week's time.' He gave Zalman a powder to dilute with water to gargle and a salve to rub into his chest. Leah's father breathed a sigh of relief, finally assured that Zalman would recover. As he paid the doctor, he thanked him for coming out on such a cold night.

"A week passed and the patient did not improve. The pain was still as intense as it had been the week before. Leah's father sent for other doctors from surrounding *shtetlach*. All were perplexed with Zalman's illness. Each one had a different opinion how to treat him; each one prescribed a different cure. Nothing seemed to help.

"One day a friend stopped by to visit the family. Seeing that Zalman was still ill, he demanded of Shimon Ber, 'Why are you spending so much time and money with these small-town doctors? I know of a wonderful doctor in Lemberg, a Herr Professor. Certainly, he has had experience with this type of illness before. He most assuredly will know a cure.'

" 'Lemberg?' responded Shimon Ber. 'Do you know how far Lemberg is from here? And it is so cold now! How could a man as sick as Zalman possibly make such a long and arduous trip?' He discarded the idea, but he had no peace, for Zalman's health deteriorated.

" 'Maybe I have no choice,' Shimon Ber finally realized. 'I will make arrangements for Zalman to go to Lemberg. I will make an appointment for him with the Herr Professor. Maybe he will know a cure for his strange malady.'

"Zalman refused to permit anyone to accompany him. He lay in the carriage, wrapped in fur and many blankets. Only his head could be seen. The coachman took the road for Lemberg.

"Immediately upon arrival, Zalman went to see the Herr Professor. He examined Zalman thoroughly and took notes as he checked all his vital organs. Sitting at his desk, he reviewed those notes. He raised his hand to his forehead, mulling over various diagnostic possibilities. Finally, he turned to Zalman and said, 'I don't think that you are seriously ill. Indeed, I am puzzled by your pain. I do not know the cause, but I think that if you go to the hot springs in Carlsbad, you will find them beneficial.'

"Zalman returned to the inn. He did not know what to do about the Herr Professor's prescription for his eventual cure. He weighed all the possibilities. 'The hot springs are open only in the spring and summer, five months from now. It is the month of Chanukah, barely the beginning of winter. What could I do until the beginning of May? To return to Tzchelik and then set out on another journey in May is ridiculous, for Carlsbad is double the distance from Tzchelik as from Lemberg. It will be so lonely for me if I remain here for the duration of the winter months. I don't know anyone in this city. What could I do to pass the time? I don't even know if I will have enough strength to sit in the study hall here since I haven't had a moment's relief from the constant pain. Master of the World,' Zalman sobbed, 'only You can help me. I don't see any solution to my problem, but You are the Master of all Solutions. Help me! Help me!'

"He sat shivering in a chair, covered with blankets, tears streaming from his eyes. His thoughts changed. 'Tonight is the first night of Chanukah. I will be alone in this room. I will pray by myself and kindle the menorah without my wife who is very far from here.' Memories of home and holiday flooded his mind. Suddenly he pulled himself up from his chair.

" 'No, I will not be alone this first night of Chanukah. Even though I am in such pain, I will go to find a *minyan*. It is not permitted to be sad on this holiday of light and joy! I will go out to search for some friends!'

"He put on his coat and stepped out the door of his room, went down the stairs, and into the street. He walked slowly, not knowing exactly where he was going. Snow fluttered through the air. He noticed a man dressed in chasidic garb a few feet in front of him and hastened to catch up.

" 'Do you perhaps know where I can find a *minyan*?' he asked.

" 'Come with me, I am headed that way,' the man answered.

"They entered a warm *shtibel*. *Chasidim* were preparing to pray. At least ten people rushed over to Zalman.

" '*Shalom aleichem*,' they said, welcoming him to their midst. After the prayer service, the *chasidim* jubilantly danced to 'Maoz Tzur' ('Rock of Ages,' a well-known Chanukah hymn).[2] Zalman sat gloomily along the edges of the circle, not being able to forget his pain, trying to remember that this was the first

---

[2]"Maoz Tzur" was composed in the mid-thirteenth century. The author's name, Mordechai, appears in the acrostic signature of the initial letters of the first five stanzas. The verses recall the various exiles the Jewish people have endured throughout the ages. Rabbi Nosson Scherman, Rabbi Meir Zlotowitz, eds. *Chanukah*. Artscroll Mesorah Series, 1981.

night of Chanukah. Then, he felt himself being pulled along by the dancers. They lifted his hands to their shoulders and carried his weight with the rhythm of their steps.

"When the dancing ended, the *chasidim* departed, one by one, to their own homes to kindle their menorahs. Only the stranger, who had showed Zalman the *shtibel* remained with him.

" 'Where are you from?' he queried.

"Zalman desperately needed to tell someone his story. It seemed to him that the stranger was ready to listen. Zalman detailed everything that had happened to him, from the moment he had his first pains that day in the study hall in Tzchelick to the remedy suggested by the Herr Professor to visit the hot springs in Carlsbad in May. The stranger listened attentively as they walked in the direction of the inn.

"When Zalman finished, the stranger said, 'Why don't you join us this *Shabbos* of Chanukah in Stretin? A group of us is going to spend *Shabbos* Chanukah with Rebbe Ahron.'

" 'I don't know who he is,' answered Zalman. 'Why should I go with you? I've never gone to a chasidic rebbe before!'

"The stranger laughed. 'Just because you never did something before doesn't mean you can't do it. You are a Jew. You need help. Stretin is very close by. We will make room for you in our wagon. Maybe the rebbe can help you. What do you have to lose?'

"By the time the stranger had asked his question, they had reached the inn. Zalman agreed to spend *Shabbos* Chanukah with Rebbe Ahron Stretin.

"*Chasidim* streamed toward Stretin from the surrounding area. Zalman watched from the sidelines of the study hall as the rebbe kindled the Chanukah lights, led the prayer service, taught Torah, recited *Kiddush*, passed pieces of *challah* to all who sat at his table.

"He was aware that he had no pain for the many hours that he had immersed himself in the celebration of *Shabbos* Chanukah. 'Strange,' he thought, 'my pain seems to have eased. This is the first time in many days that I am fairly comfortable. I wonder if I am getting better? Or is the relief only temporary?'

"After *Shabbos*, Zalman's stranger-friend hinted that it was now a propitious time to talk to the rebbe. For the second time, Zalman detailed his story. He emphasized that his mental pain at not being able to learn was as great as his physical pain. He even told the rebbe that the Herr Professor had suggested a visit to the Carlsbad hot springs in May.

"The rebbe responded 'The Herr Professor told you to visit the Carlsbad hot springs in May. I am telling you, in the name of our talmudic sages,[3] that "Mai Chanukah!" You don't have to wait until the month of May. Chanukah is May. This day was meant to heal you.'

"The rebbe finished speaking. Zalman looked puzzled. He did not understand. He wanted to ask questions, but the *shamish* escorted him out the door.

"He felt wonderful when he awoke the next morning in the inn. He had no pain, no fear, no weakness, no depression. He couldn't believe what his heart was singing: cured, cured, cured! He heard a voice whisper within him, 'the Almighty has led you into the presence of a righteous man. Stay here a few more days, until the end of Chanukah. Don't run away.'

"On the last night of Chanukah, after the rebbe kindled the lights, a trembling Zalman slipped a *kvittel* into Rebbe Ahron's hand. The rebbe read it and whispered, 'Next year at this time you will be the father of a son.' "

* * *

His story told, Michel wiped his forehead. His voice faltered. The *chasidim* stared intently at him. He breathed slowly and deeply, regained his composure and smiled gently. "I want you to know," he concluded, "that I am the son of Rebbe Zalman and Leah who Rebbe Ahron Stretin, your father blessed." Michel sat down slowly. Rebbe Avraham raised his glass and motioned to the *chasidim* to join him. They drank and raised their voices in joyous song.

The sound of "*L'Chayim*" reverberated throughout the room. Hope and joy rang forth from the lips of the *chasidim*.

---

[3]Chanukah is discussed in the Talmud with the words beginning "Mai Chanukah," meaning, what is the reason for Chanukah? (Talmud *Bavli, Shabbos* 21b). The rebbe's interpretation is a play on the Aramaic word *Mai* and the German word for May.

"What a story!" they shouted, almost in unison. "What a joyous way to relive another miracle!"

Rebbe Avraham had known that story, but he was happy that Michel had shared it with the others. He secretly wondered if his unexpected stop in Ellick was for the purpose of Michel repeating the story of a modern miracle.

A Chair, a Table, and Something to Eat

Many holy masters, before they became rebbes, traveled incognito around the *shtetlach* of the Pale of Settlement, investigating the conditions under which Jews lived, how they earned a livelihood, how much Torah they studied, if they truly fulfilled the commandment of loving kindness.

Mendele, destined to become the Rebbe of Vishnitz,[1] started traveling from his father's house in Kosov when he was 13 years old. He traveled for two years throughout the Podolia region of Poland, making his rounds in the vicinity of the *shtetlach* of Kitov, Vishnitz, Horodenko, Okup, Kamenetz, Sadiger, Mohilev, and returning to his native Kosov for the holy days.

As he approached one of these *shtetlach*, a small 8-year-old girl always came out to greet him. She would run to

Rabbi Shlomo Carlebach. Ruach tape. Recorded at the Berkshire Mountains Retreat Center, Massachusetts.

[1]Because Rebbe Mendele Vishnitz (1830–1885) personified *middos tovos*, character traits that reflect God, he had tremendous influence on those people who yearned to be part of his inner circle.

welcome him, beckon him to follow her home, and bring out a little table and a little chair, some cake, and a bottle of wine. She would sing, "Sit down in the shade of my house, and eat some cake and drink some wine."

He would always rest on the little chair outside the girl's house. While he ate and drank, she sang and danced. She was so happy to feed him. He began to depend on her hospitality, and she waited eagerly for his visits.

One day, amidst the dancing and singing, he called to her, "What is your name, sweet child?"

She answered, "My name is Rivkele. What is your name?"

"My name is Mendele."

Rivkele continued, "Promise me, Mendele, that whenever you pass this way, you will stop for some cake and wine."

Mendele promised her that he would not forget and Rivkele looked forward to his visits.

Mendele returned to Kosov, to the house of his father Rebbe Chaim. A match was arranged between him and Miriam, the daughter of Rebbe Yisrael of Rizhin, on condition that he commit himself to studying for the next ten years. When he was 25 years old, he was invited to take over the chasidic leadership in Vishnitz.

As the years passed, Rebbe Mendele of Vishnitz became famous the world over. His followers believed that his prayers cured the ill, that his caring concern mended broken souls. People streamed to Vishnitz from all over the area to seek his advice and to receive his blessing.

When Rivkele turned 18, she was afflicted with a disease that paralyzed her completely. Her joyous song ceased. Her parents sought the help of the most eminent doctors, but they were unable to suggest a remedy for her ailment.

Rivkele refused to give up hope that she would dance again. She lay on her bed recalling how, as a child, she used to dance and sing for an itinerant stranger, how she used to bring him some cake to eat and a bottle of wine to drink. People who passed through her *shtetl* spoke enthusiastically of a certain Rebbe Mendele of Vishnitz, whose prayers cured the ill. She remembered that her friendly stranger's name was Mendele. Rivkele imagined that he had become the famous Rebbe Mendele.

She pleaded for her parents to take her to Rebbe Mendele for a blessing. "I have this feeling that the itinerant stranger who used to stop by this house on his travels, the one to whom I used to serve cake and wine when I was a small child, the one for whom I danced and sang, is Rebbe Mendele. Please, please, take me to see him."

Rivkele's parents scoffed at her. "How do you know that the itinerant stranger is Rebbe Mendele? Even if it is how do you know he will have time to see you? How do you know that he can cure you? Do you think he could possibly remember a small child for more than ten years?" They refused to consider the possibility that Rebbe Mendele of Vishnitz could help their daughter.

Years passed. Rivkele yearned to see her special friend. Her parents remained skeptical that any cure could be found.

One day, Rivkele spoke to her parents in a very gentle but adamant voice. "I know that Rebbe Mendele was the itinerant stranger for whom I danced and sang when I was a child. He promised that he would never forget me. I know that he can help me. Since I have been lying on my back for so many years, I think it is worth the effort to visit him. I am determined to make the trip. If you will not take me to see Rebbe Mendele, I will find another way to get to Vishnitz on my own, even if I have to crawl all the way by myself. I have a feeling that he can cure me."

Rivkele's parents finally gave in to her plea. The next day, they carried her onto the wagon, harnessed the horses, and set off for Vishnitz. However, they really didn't understand their daughter's faith in the curative powers of Rebbe Mendele and ridiculed her the entire length of the trip. They took turns chanting "Don't put your faith in a rebbe! Don't raise your hopes that you will ever walk again! He might not even have time to see you!"

Rivkele held on to her faith. She was finally on the way to visit her special friend. She recalled the melody that she used to sing for the itinerant stranger and began to hum it. They traveled late into the night.

That night, Rebbe Mendele emerged from his private room at the back of the *bays midrash* to prepare for Rivkele's arrival. The night shift of students was studying Torah and Talmud, for

Rebbe Mendele insisted that learning continue twenty-four hours a day.

He approached two students and whispered to them: "I am expecting a special friend in a few moments. Hurry, bring me a little table and a little chair and place it where I sit. Put a bottle of wine and some cake on it. Then light all the extra candles and place them around the *bays midrash*. I want her to feel welcome. Call me the minute my special friend arrives."

When Rivkele's wagon finally arrived, two disciples ran to call the rebbe, and two others ran to greet the rebbe's special friend. They called cheerfully, "Do you see all the light in the *bays midrash*? It is all in your honor. Rebbe Mendele is waiting for you!"

Rivkele smiled happily. Her parents lifted her from the back of the wagon and carried her into the *bays midrash*, laying her gently on the floor.

Rebbe Mendele hadn't seen his special friend for more than ten years. Slowly, he rose from his seat to acknowledge her presence, then he lowered himself to the floor and began to chant solemnly: "Rivkele, my special friend. I am so happy to see you. I have never forgotten for one moment how you used to dance and sing for me. I have never forgotten for one moment how you used to bring me some cake and a bottle of wine. I have never forgotten for one moment your kindness, your hospitality." Tears welled up in his eyes and coursed down his cheeks as he rocked on the floor, staring at his paralyzed friend.

Suddenly, Rebbe Mendele turned away from Rivkele. He called, "*Ribbono Shel Olam*, Master of the Universe! I can't stand Rivkele's pain any longer! Do You see how she is suffering? Do You remember how she used to dance and sing, how she used to bring me a bottle of wine and some cake?"

Rebbe Mendele prayed. He sobbed and shuddered. He screamed in anguish for the Master of the Universe to heal her.

He remained on the floor near Rivkele for a long time. The disciples were silent. They watched their rebbe intently. Rivkele's parents were silent. They were still skeptical. Only the pleading voice of Rebbe Mendele's tortured prayer was heard in the *bays midrash* that night. Finally, Rebbe Mendele whispered gently, "Rivkele, do you remember how you used to meet me at the edge of the *shtetl*, how you used to beckon me to come to your house, how you used to run to set a little table, a little chair, some cake, and a bottle of wine, how you used to dance and sing while I refreshed myself? Rivkele, do you remember?"

He paused for a few moments, then continued, "Rivkele, you can do it again now. I want you to bring me that little table and that little chair. I want you to serve me a drink of wine and some cake. I want you to do it now."

Rivkele struggled to raise her shoulders from the floor. Slowly, she bent her knees and pulled herself up. Cautiously, she walked over to the little table and the little chair, and placed them before Rebbe Mendele. He raised himself from the floor and sat down on the little chair. Then Rivkele served the cake and the wine. Then she danced around him while he ate. She danced and she sang.

Rebbe Mendele's shining eyes revealed to Rivkele that God had never forgotten her hospitality to a stranger.

The Mysterious Guest

Wandering around the world, I heard of a man who had an unbelievable reputation for hospitality.[1] I couldn't believe that his kindness had no bounds, no limits. Investigating, I found out that he searched not only the immediate vicinity of his own *shtetl* for guests, but the entire surrounding area. People said that when he found a traveler or a person in need of any kind of help whatsoever, he went out of his way to treat him as a

---

[1]Elyahu *Hanave* lived during the reign of Achav, King of Israel (1 Kings 17, 2 Kings 2).

Many miracles are attributed to him. In addition, he was a fiery orator in his efforts to persuade the Jewish people not to worship pagan images or forsake the ways of Torah. According to the text, Elyahu *Hanave* did not die; rather, he ascended to heaven in a flaming chariot. Therefore, many legends arose around him. It is widely believed that he appears as the "helper" of Jews who are in trouble because of the most unusual circumstances. We welcome him to our homes at the Pesach *seder*, at *havdalah*, and at the circumcision ritual.

One of the sources of legends about Elyahu *Hanave* is the midrash *Tana Devay Elyahu*, which is divided into two sections, *Sayder Elyahu Raba* and *Sayder Elyahu Zuta*. The following was adapted from *Sayder Elyahu Zuta*. Mordechai ben Yechezkel. *Sayfer Hamaseyos*. Vol. I, op. cit.

member of his own family. He never sat down to a weekday meal, let alone a *Shabbos* or holy day meal, without guests gracing his table. I was so awed by what I heard that I decided to see if it were true.

I disguised myself as a beggar, making certain that my clothes were tattered and torn, that I appeared dirty and unkempt. I placed myself in his *shtetl* of Gustinin, in the shul and sat on a corner of the bench, opposite the eastern wall,[2] to rest and warm myself near the stove.

I dozed while I was waiting. It did not take long for me to be awakened by a man tapping me on the shoulder.

Before the Almighty created man, He consulted with Elyahu *Hanave*. "Shall I create man?" He queried.

Elyahu answered, "Master of the World: I cannot answer Your question, but if You decide to create man, I will go into the world and teach him Torah, so that he may serve You."

And so, Elyahu descended into the world as an emissary of the Almighty, teaching Torah wherever he roamed, to whoever would listen. Once when he was walking along the banks of a river, he saw a man standing on the nearby wharf. Elyahu approached and asked, "How do you earn your living?"

The man answered, "I am a fisherman. In fact, I am the greatest fisherman on this wharf."

Elyahu continued to probe: "What else do you do in addition to fishing?"

The fisherman arrogantly replied, "Nothing."

Elyahu persisted. "Do you study Torah?"

The fisherman shuddered. "I was never given the opportunity to study Torah. I don't know how to begin. I don't think I would be able to understand it even if I had a teacher."

Elyahu continued gently. "How did you become the greatest fisherman on this wharf?"

The fisherman did not hesitate. "I became the greatest fisherman on this wharf because I spent all my waking hours, all of my strength, fishing. I spend so much time fishing because I know that my life depends upon it."

Elyahu cried out. "Oh, fisherman, if only you knew that there is more to life than fishing. . .that real life depends on studying the mysteries of God's Torah. . . . If only you spent one-tenth of the time studying God's laws as you do fishing, you could become the greatest scholar in the world."

The fisherman nodded his head, vowing to follow Elyahu's advice.

Elyahu left the inspired fisherman and continued on his mission, roaming the world, searching for people to whom he could teach Torah.

[2] The wall facing east in the direction of Eretz Yisrael in most synagogues, is generally the wall into which the holy ark is built.

"Please wake up," he said. "You can't spend *Shabbos* here alone. You must come home with me where there is a delicious meal and a warm bed awaiting you."

He helped me to my feet, put his arm under mine to steady me and guided me the short distance to his home.

I entered a room that had truly been prepared to greet the *Shabbos* Queen. Two tables covered with festive white cloths stood perpendicular to each other in the center of a large dining room. Many pairs of candles sparkled in silver candlesticks; delicately embroidered cloths covered the golden twisted *challos* that were at the place of the head of each family. I saw his children and grandchildren waiting around the *Shabbos* table for him. When he entered the room, he greeted everyone with a warm "Good *Shabbos*," pointed to a chair on his right side, and motioned for me to sit down. His wife sat on his left. No one sitting at the table expressed surprise at my presence or at my appearance.

After singing "*Shalom Aleichem*," all rose to their feet. My host lifted the wine bottle, poured some wine into his goblet, raised it, and chanted the *kiddush*. He poured some wine into another goblet for his wife. When he finished, each of his sons and his son-in-law chanted the *Kiddush* and passed their goblets to their wives and children. Then my host turned to me and inquired gently, "Would you like to chant the *Kiddush*?"

"I'm not familiar with the words," I responded sheepishly.

"Then I will fetch you a *siddur*." He walked over to the bookcase, removed a *siddur* from a shelf, and returned to the table. Flipping through the pages, he located the *Kiddush* and placed it in front of me.

"I can't read the words," I muttered. "Then I shall help you," he said. He pronounced one word and I repeated it. His family waited patiently while I stammered away at the words.

He didn't even ask me if I knew the blessing for ritual hand washing; he assumed that I needed help. I permitted him to wash my hands for me, then I threw the towel on the floor. I suspected that what I heard was true. Not one family member acted dismayed at my uncouthness. I realized that they were used to their father bringing home all kind of strangers.

Each family had two *challos* of their own. My host placed a very large slice in front of me. In an unmannerly fashion, I gobbled it down and motioned to him for another slice. I alternated a piece of *challah* and a gulp of wine until I had finished the entire *challah* and had emptied the *Kiddush* goblet in front of me. Unperturbed, my host went into the kitchen to fetch another *challah*, which I ate hungrily. I was served two portions of fish and I proceeded to scatter the bones all around my plate on the white tablecloth. I ate three portions of soup and four portions of pot roast, *tzimmes*, and *kugel*. I burped loudly twice.

"Are you still hungry?" my host asked me lovingly.

"Yes, I could still eat more," I muttered. He rose, went into the kitchen, removed the *cholent*[3] pot from the stove and brought it into the dining room and set it in front of me. I finished the whole thing with great gusto. He never said one angry word either about my disgusting table manners or the amount of food I had consumed.

After the meal, my host asked me to hum along the *Shabbos zemiros*, but instead my head began to nod and I pretended to snore. In the middle of the grace after meals, I suddenly pulled myself up from my chair and stumbled over to an ivory and gold colored brocaded sofa, throwing my full weight and my muddy shoes across it with a resounding thud.

I noticed that my host didn't blink an eyelid, although the womenfolk looked at each other nervously. Thinking I might be cold, he covered me with three blankets as soon as he finished chanting the grace after meals.

While I pretended to sleep, the children and grandchildren returned to their own nearby homes, the tables were cleared, and the house became shrouded in deep darkness for the candles had burned down. I folded the blankets neatly, replaced them in the cupboard and disappeared from sight, satisfied that what I had heard about this man who practiced exemplary hospitality was true.

I hid behind a thick-barked, lush-foliaged, broad-branched oak tree near the fence of his property to see his reaction when he discovered that I had disappeared. He arose at daybreak.

---

[3]*Cholent* is a seasoned dish of barley, beans, potatoes, and meat that simmers all Friday night. It is served at the end of *shul* (shul-end) for the *Shabbos* lunch.

When he discovered that I was not on the sofa, he shouted, "Where are you? Where are you?"

A few minutes later, he left and ran in the direction of the *shul*, apparently thinking that I had returned to my corner on the bench near the stove, but soon I saw him returning slowly, sadly, to his home without me. Then I heard him call to his wife that he was going to search for me at the marketplace. I waited. Again, I saw him run, again he returned without me. I knew he was clearly puzzled, but I could not reveal my true identity to him.

Finally, I left my watching post behind the tree, knowing that I had never met such a gracious host[4] before. I wondered if, in my future travels, I would meet anyone who would surpass his kindness.

---

[4] The host was Rebbe Yechiel Mayer Lifshitz, the Yehude Hatov, the Good Jew of Gustinin (1817–1888) noted for his meticulous observance of the *middah* of hospitality. He was also called the *Tehillim Yid*, the Psalm Jew. During his lifetime, the Jewish people suffered terrible hardships at the hands of the tzarist government. People came to him from the surrounding area, not only to sit at his *Shabbos* or holy day *tish*, but for advice on dealing with their problems, both with the government and the neighboring peasants. He would inevitably advise, "Recite *Tehillim*." He wrote down their problem, the numbers of the chapters of *tehillim* he had instructed them to recite, and he would recite them as well. People said, "Even though King David composed *Tehillim*, Rebbe Yechiel Mayer recited them with more fervor. . . ." He went out of his way to guide his people in the ways of peaceful living, always mediating between antagonists. He wrote his ethical will eight years before he died. In it, he instructed his children to, "Always distance yourselves from arrogance . . . and even if you should become very wealthy, know that money is a blessing from the Almighty. . . . All mankind was created from the same mold, the people who suffer and the people who enjoy comfort. . . . Know that my reprimands were only meant to direct you toward specific goals." Rabbi Avraham Yitzchak Bromberg. *Hayehudi Hatov MeGustinin*. Jerusalem: Bays Hillel Publishing. Lichtenstein and Holder, 1982.

Emunah—
FAITH

munah (faith), denotes absolute belief in Divine Providence, in God's control and guidance of the universe, in God's unfailing goodness. Judaism does not separate belief from the performance of *mitzvos*. There is no difference between the *mitzvah* to believe and the *mitzvah* to honor parents, give charity, or observe holy days. One's actions show the measure of his or her faith.

Rabbi Akiva declared, "Everything is foreseen by God, yet free will is granted to man."

—*Avos* 3:19

This means that an omniscient God does not predetermine man's actions, whether for good or evil, but man has free choice. With faith, man is better able to overcome the obstacles put in his path, thereby drawing closer to the service of God.

Maimonides, in the "Thirteen Principles of Faith," defined the basic principles of Judaism.[1] They fall into three categories: the nature of belief in God, the authenticity of Torah and its validity, and man's responsibility and ultimate reward.

1. I believe with perfect faith that the Creator, Blessed is His Name, creates and guides all creatures, and that He alone made, makes, and will make everything.

2. I believe with perfect faith that the Creator, Blessed is His Name, is a Unity and there is no uniqueness like His in any way, and that He alone is our God, Who was, Who is, and Who always will be.

[1]Rabbi Moshe ben Maimon Maimonides (Rambam) (1135–1204). Codifier of Jewish law, halachist, philosopher, physician, he is considered the luminary of medieval Sephardic Jewry. His *Mishneh Torah (Yad HaChazakah)* covers every facet of Jewish law in lucid language. His gravestone in Tiberias, Eretz Israel is inscribed "From Moshe to Moshe, there arose none like Moshe." (The first Moshe refers to Moshe Rabaynu, our teacher, who led Israel from Egyptian bondage.)

3. I believe with perfect faith that the Creator, Blessed is His Name, is not physical and is not affected by physical phenomena, and that there is no comparison whatsoever to Him.

4. I believe with perfect faith that the Creator, Blessed is His Name, is the very first and the very last.

5. I believe with perfect faith that to the Creator, Blessed is His Name and to Him alone is it proper to pray, and it is not proper to pray to any other.

6. I believe with perfect faith that all the words of the prophets are true.

7. I believe with perfect faith that the prophecy of Moses our teacher, peace upon him, was true, and that he was the father of the prophets, both those who preceded him and those who followed him.

8. I believe with perfect faith that the entire Torah now in our hands is the same one that was given to Moses, our teacher, peace be upon him.

9. I believe with perfect faith that this Torah will not be changed nor will there be another Torah from the Creator, Blessed is His Name.

10. I believe with perfect faith that the Creator, Blessed is His Name knows all the deeds of human beings and their thoughts, as it is said: He fashions their hearts all together, He comprehends all their deeds.

11. I believe with perfect faith that the Creator, Blessed is His Name, rewards with good those who observe His commandments, and punishes those who violate His commandments.

12. I believe with perfect faith in the coming of the Messiah, and even though He may delay, nevertheless, I anticipate every day that He will come.

13. I believe with perfect faith there will be a resurrection of the dead whenever the wish emanates from the Creator, Blessed is His Name and exalted is His Fame, forever and for all eternity.

"The Thirteen Principles of Faith" are based upon the commentary of Maimonides at the end of Talmud *Bavli, Sanhedrin.*

Torah Thoughts

Faith

Faith, the yearning to believe in God, is intrinsic to man's nature. How is faith deepened?

Everyone that is thirsty (for the word of God)
Come, refresh yourself with water (Torah is likened to
        water).

> —Isaiah 55:1, Talmud *Bavli, Baba Kama* 17a

Based upon the quoted verse, we learn that just as one waters seedlings, causing them to grow, so studying Torah nourishes one's faith.[1]

"And when you go forth to war against your enemies, the Almighty will deliver them into your hands."

> —Deuteronomy 21:10

The phrase, "your enemies," means your evil inclination. The lesson that having faith teaches us is that if we are attached to the ways of the Almighty and reach out for His help, then,

---

[1]Rebbe Aharon Yosef Luria Slonim. *Avodas P'nim.* Yerushalayim: Privately printed by his children and grandchildren, 1974.

even though we struggle with our evil inclination and err, we will find the way to return.

—*Avodas P'nim*

"The Almighty takes pride in those of His children who possess these three character traits: the person who controls his temper, the person who does not become intoxicated, and the person who does not retaliate."

—Talmud *Bavli, Pesachim* 113b

There are many who become intoxicated to ease their loneliness, their unwarranted fears, and guilt. True believers know that since God is always with them, they are never alone (for You are with me), that their fears are many times unwarranted (I will fear no evil), Psalm 23:4, that their irrational guilt is unnecessary because God forgives (He, the Merciful One is forgiving).

—Psalms 78:38. Rebbe Gershon Chanoch Henich Ishbitz–Radzin, *May Hashiloach, Parshas Noach*

A person's belief in God should come from faith, not from experiencing miracles.

Faith has the ability to draw people closer to God, just as trust brings husband and wife closer. Without faith, there is no true understanding of God.

Studying Torah erases doubts; ridiculing Torah increases doubts.

There is no true understanding of God without faith. Rebbe Nachman of Bratslav.

—*Sayfer Hamidos*

Historically, people who did not succumb to assimilation were those who served God with unquestioning faith, knowing that their observance was the "decree of the King." For the person of faith, God's gift to the Jewish people of His Torah and His command to study and observe it is a privilege, even if one does not completely understand the rationale of each commandment.

—*Tiferes Shmuel*

Look up towards the heavens and count the stars . . .
Just as you are unable to count the stars, so you will be
   unable to count your children. . . .
And he (Abraham) will believe in God's (promise).
—Genesis 15:5–6

At a very young age, Abraham recognized that God was
master and creator of the world.
—*Midrash Rabbah,* Genesis 39:1

The language of Torah is exact, therefore, we must understand why the verb for *believe* is in the future tense, when in
reality, it should have been in the present tense.

The future tense signifies that Abraham transmitted to
Isaac, his son, and his descendants that the essence of holiness
is faith in God. It was as if Abraham molded genes of faith which
were infused into every Jewish generation. It is for this reason
that it is also said of the children of Abraham, "They are
believers and the descendants of believers."
— Talmud *Bavli, Shabbos* 97a

Stories

You'll Get What Is Coming to You

The sun's rays danced on the Moldau (Ultava) River, reflecting the amber and ochre bricks of the houses that glowed along the river's edge. Spires could be seen in the distance over the closely built buildings that followed the curve and bend of the narrow cobblestoned streets. The ghetto was located at the north and west edges of the river. Nearby, the Charles bridge spanned the river, connecting the ghetto with the remainder of the city on the opposite bank. Nestled in the center of the ghetto, the low arches and brick gables of the Gothic-style *Alt-neu shul* gleamed in the shimmering radiance of a warm summer day, the court-yard of the *shul* separating it from other buildings.

Prague was the center of intense learning in those days.

The Maharal, Rabbi Yehuda Loew ben Bezalel[1] was bent over the wrought iron-railed *almemar* (pulpit) in the center of the *shul*, deeply engrossed in talmudic study. Matching

---

This story was told to us by Rabbi Shlomo Carlebach.

[1]Rabbi Yehuda Loew ben Bezalel, the Maharal of Prague (1515–1609), was a noted authority on Jewish law, a profound thinker, a commentator on Torah, and a Kabbalist.

straight-backed wooden chairs lined the sides of the wall; only the Maharal's chair was taller. The holy ark glowed on the east side of the *shul* from the sun's rays piercing the gabled windows.

The Maharal was the acknowledged rabbinic leader of Prague Jewry. His contemporaries compared his scholastic achievement to the vitality of mighty cedar trees,[2] for they believed that his explanation of Rashi commentaries, his clarification of obscure aggadic passages, his responsa, and his knowledge of Kabbalah would endure. By interpreting the mysteries of Kabbalah and combining them with divine inspiration, with which he was blessed, the Maharal created the *Golem* that saved the Jewish community of Prague from a blood libel.[3]

Not only did he serve as the head of the Jewish court, but he was an exemplary communal leader, guiding his people with love, patience, and devotion.

The Maharal picked the best and the brightest from among all of the young men as his disciples. He studied with them day and night.[4] It was his custom, immediately after morning prayers before formal classes began, to preach a special, inspirational Torah thought that related to the needs of their individual lives.

One morning, the Maharal said, "As simple as my Torah thought for today sounds, I want you to know that whatever is meant for you from Heaven, you will eventually receive. Don't despair! Be patient! Persevere!"

This statement had very little effect upon Asya, the best of all the Maharal's students. He did not relate to the thought for

---

[2] Cedar trees are often used as a metaphor for strength and durability.

[3] One of the most infamous blood libels took place in the Prague ghetto. There, the Maharal is said to have created a Golem, a clay, human-shaped form. The Golem responded to the Maharal's command when a piece of parchment inscribed with the Holy Letters of the Almighty's Name was placed into its mouth. The Maharal commanded the Golem to find the murderer. This accomplished, the Jewish community was saved from destruction. The Golem solved many more crimes that were concocted by their neighbors and blamed upon the Jews. According to tradition, the remains of the Golem were hidden in the attic of the *Alt-neu shul,* where an aura of mysterious holiness still envelops it. See Glossary.

[4] Day and night is a metaphor for "unending study "(Joshua 1:8).

the day, for he did not think that the statement had anything to do with him, since he had his own way of dealing with the problem of survival. Although Asya was very poor he was too shy to ask for food. When anyone asked him, "Asya, are you hungry?" he would shake his head and respond politely, "No, thank you, I've already eaten."

Actually, Asya had his own ways of obtaining food. He mentally divided the narrow streets of the Prague ghetto into six zones, and each night, after he was certain that the evening meal was over, he stole into the kitchen of house one in zone one and took the leftovers. He never took much, only what he needed to survive. Usually, a piece of bread, an apple, and a little kasha made up his meal. Some nights he was actually able to find a piece of chicken or meat. He went methodically from house to house, house two, zone one, house three, zone four, a different house each night. It took many months until he returned to the first house in zone one. Asya thought he was justified in taking leftover food, because he needed to have strength to learn. Besides, most people could ignore the fact when food was missing once in a while. That night, Asya again helped himself to leftovers. His one meal for that day consisted of a slice of black bread spread with white cheese.

The next morning, the Maharal said, "If only that thief would be patient, if only he would hold on, he will get everything from Heaven that is coming to him." He lowered his voice and whispered: "I know that it takes a lot of strength to hold on."

Amazed expressions crossed the students' faces. This was the second day in a row that the Maharal had spoken about stealing, about patience, about persevering. It was so unlike him to repeat a Torah thought two days in a row.

The Maharal was interrupted in his learning that day by Anschil, the richest man in the ghetto. "Something very important must be on your mind," said the Maharal in greeting, "that you took time from your business day to visit me. How can I help you?"

"You must know," Anschil replied, "that my only daughter has reached marriageable age. I want to arrange a match for her with the best student in your yeshiva."

The Maharal did not have to think very long which student

would be the best match. "I have just the right young man for your daughter. His name is Asya. This is what you must do. Tell your cook to prepare a big feast tomorrow night. I will bring the young man to your house for dinner so that you may meet him."

The same night, a starving Asya found his way into Anschil's house. He could not hold out, for he had not eaten a morsel since his meager meal the previous evening. Knowing his way around the house, for he had been there before, he took the lit candle from the kitchen table and tiptoed into the pantry. From the soft light of the glowing candle, he noticed that the cook had prepared a grand feast. Roast turkeys and smoked beef cooled on elaborately decorated platters on the top shelf. Delectable pastries were arranged on silver trays on the tables below. Freshly baked bread and small *challos* were piled in overflowing baskets. Brightly colored vegetables and fruits peeped out at him from crates on the floor. He inhaled the fragrance of the food and his salivary glands testified to his hunger. Asya was ready for his evening meal.

"I have never seen so much food in all my life," thought Asya. "I am *so* hungry. With all this food, I'm sure no one will miss a turkey leg or a small *challah*. Maybe I can even sneak a piece of cake for dessert."

He raised his hand to pull a leg off the turkey when, suddenly, he understood the meaning of the Maharal's words. "Asya," his conscience called, "Asya, what are you doing? Your rabbi told you this morning that you must be strong, that you must be patient, that you must persevere, that you will get everything from Heaven that is coming to you."

Allowing his conscience to get the upper hand, he tiptoed back to the kitchen, replaced the candle, and left the house with empty hands and an even emptier stomach.

The next morning after the Maharal delivered his Torah thought for the day, he called Asya to his side, put his arm around him, and said, "Tonight, we have been invited to have dinner with Anschil, the richest man in the Prague ghetto. After we finish our studies for the day, I want you to go to my house and wash up. My wife will give you a clean shirt. We will go to dinner together."

When the Maharal and Asya walked into Anschil's house, Asya anticipated all the food that would be served, for had he not been in the pantry the night before?

All the important people of the Prague Jewish community sat at the festive tables, eagerly awaiting their host's explanation for having invited them to this feast. When he explained that the feast was to celebrate the betrothal of his daughter Channah to Asya, the Maharal put his arm around Asya and whispered quietly, "Nu, Asya, now do you understand the meaning of my Torah thought?"

Missing Rubles

Rebbe Zusia's two sons, Yisrael Avraham and Tzve Menachem Mendel had reached marriageable age.[1] "Master of the World!" he prayed. "I am so very poor. I can accept your decree that I should not have any money, but how will I be able to arrange marriages for my two sons?"

This problem plagued Rebbe Zusia for a long time, and he found no solution. He did not know how Rebbe Dov Ber found out about his problem, but on his next visit to Mezeritch, the Maggid said, "Zusia, I know that you have to arrange marriages for your sons. I also know that you don't have the money you need to do so. Please take these 300 rubles."

"I can't take," whispered Rebbe Zusia.

"I order you to take it," persisted the Maggid.

Zusia knew that he had to obey his rebbe, that it would be disrespectful to argue, so he reluctantly took the money and started for home on foot.

Walking from Mezeritch to Anipoli, he had to pass

G. Mah Tov. *Ma-a-say-hem shel Tzaddikim*, op. cit.
[1]For a biography of Rebbe Zusia of Anipoli, see footnote 1, page 18.

through a number of *shtetlach.* The world temporarily appeared more beautiful than it had for a long time. He meditated, laughed, sang, praised God. Suddenly a shrill shriek interrupted his soliloquy. He ran rapidly toward the ruckus and collided head first with the *shtetl*'s tailor. "What's happened?" he cried. "Please, tell me what's happened."

The tailor muttered sadly, "The baker's widow had arranged for her daughter's marriage this evening. After her husband died, she scrimped and saved kopek upon kopek for her daughter's dowry, accumulating 300 rubles by doing all kinds of menial work. Finally, when she had saved enough money, she made a match with a suitable young man. They were on their way to the wedding hall. She had the bag of money in her hand, and she lost it. The groom says he will not marry the widow's daughter unless he receives the money promised."

Rebbe Zusia asked, "Where is the widow now?"

The tailor pointed in the direction of the shrieking and pathetic sobbing. Rebbe Zusia found the widow, unable to control herself, the bride weeping by her side. "How long will it take me to save another 300 rubles? What am I to do?" she sighed. "Who will then want to marry my daughter?"

"Excuse me," interrupted Rebbe Zusia. He had to speak quickly when the widow gasped for breath. "I found a large amount of money, but before I return it to you, you will have to describe some identification marks on the bag since I want to return it to its proper owner."

"You found 300 rubles," she asked incredulously, "and you think it is mine? And if I can identify it, will you really return it to me? Where did you find the money?"

"I was passing through this *shtetl,* searching for the inn in order to make arrangements with the innkeeper to stay over the night. I found a bag nearby. Tell me what the bag looked like," said Rebbe Zusia. "Tell me the denominations of the bills."

The widow stopped crying. "My 300 rubles were divided this way: five bank notes were for twenty rubles each, and four bank notes were for fifty rubles each, a total of nine bank notes worth 300 rubles. All the bank notes were tied together with a thin string and were in a flower-embroidered bag."

"That's exactly what I found," shouted Rebbe Zusia excitedly. "Wait right here. I will run to the inn, fetch the bag, and return in a few moments." The widow smiled; the bride's eyes radiated joy.

Rebbe Zusia ran to the inn. "Here," he said to the inn-keeper, "is 300 rubles. Change them over into the following denominations: five twenty-ruble bank notes and four fifty-ruble bank notes." He took the money that the Maggid of Mezeritch had given him for his own children's weddings, gave it to the innkeeper and waited for him to exchange it. Then he went to the market, asked one of the merchants for a thin string, and bought a small flower-embroidered bag. He tied the ruble notes, put them into the bag, and ran back to the widow and the bride.

As he approached, he saw that preparations for the wedding were proceeding. The musicians were playing joyful tunes, the family and friends had begun to gather near the wedding hall.

Everyone was chattering excitedly about the fact that Rebbe Zusia found the money and was returning it.

Walking over to the widow, he said:

"I am returning 280 rubles. I have decided to keep twenty rubles for my trouble."

"What, you, Rebbe Zusia? How can you do such a thing? You did such a big *mitzvah* by returning my lost money. How can you possibly keep the twenty rubles that are rightfully mine?" demanded the widow.

"Nevertheless," insisted Rebbe Zusia stubbornly, "I will keep twenty rubles for my trouble."

The widow persisted, "You do *mitzvos* for heavenly reward, not for earthly reward!"

Rebbe Zusia was adamant.

The music stopped, the laughter, the celebration ceased. Family and friends took up her cause.

"Rebbe, the widow worked very hard to save the money. Twenty rubles is too much for you to keep for your trouble. Five rubles is a more reasonable reward!"

When the widow saw that patient pleading did not change Rebbe Zusia's mind, she began screaming at the top of her lungs. "Blackmailer! Extortionist! Thief!"

Mayhem ensued instead of joy. "If you don't return the

money, we will take you to the rabbinical court!'' shouted the uncle of the bride.

They surrounded Rebbe Zusia and carried him through the streets of the *shetl* to the rebbe's house where they deposited him in front of the rebbe.

He listened carefully to both sides of the story, then he said pensively, ''These are very serious complaints against you. According to the facts as I understand them, you, Rebbe Zusia, must return all of the money to the mother of the bride.''

But even after the rebbe rendered his decision, Rebbe Zusia refused to return the twenty ruble note.

The widow, the bride, the uncle, the guests were so angry that they forcibly pulled him outside and began to beat him. The uncle grabbed the twenty ruble note from Rebbe Zusia's pocket, then lifted him high into the air, and dropped him to the ground. Then he signaled everyone to follow him. He led them back to the wedding hall, righteously indignant. Rebbe Zusia lay alone.

''They think they have shamed me,'' he chuckled, ''but I am so happy.''

A few weeks later, the rebbe of the *shtetl* met the Maggid of Mezeritch. The rebbe brought up the story again. ''Do you know what your disciple, Rebbe Zusia, did in my *shtetl* a little while ago? He tried to steal the dowry money that belonged to the poor, unfortunate widow of the baker.''

The Maggid of Mezeritch looked him squarely in the eye.

''Let me tell you something,'' he began. ''You owe Rebbe Zusia an apology. That money he returned to the widow was not really her money. He gave the widow the money that I had given him that morning in order to arrange marriages for his two sons. He never found the widow's money.''

''Then why did he insist on keeping the twenty rubles for his trouble?'' demanded the rebbe.

''You don't know Rebbe Zusia like I do. Can't you understand that he didn't want all the people to honor him for doing a *mitzvah*? He must have found it very distasteful to hear people praising him for returning the money when his intent was altruistic. Therefore, he kept the twenty rubles, so they would humiliate him!''

The rebbe could not respond. Immediately, he ordered his

wagon driver to hitch the horses. They set out for Anipoli in search of Rebbe Zusia.

"I beg your forgiveness," pleaded the rebbe of the *shtetl* when he found Rebbe Zusia. "I committed a terrible wrong by embarrassing you in public."

"No," smiled Rebbe Zusia. "You did what you had to do and I did what I had to do. I sincerely forgive you. Promise me one thing: you will never reveal to the widow the secret of how her money was found, or the secret of the missing twenty rubles."

"Mine Is the Silver,
Mine Is the Gold"

Eliezer, known as the *shlepper* of Rimanov, had a daughter of marriageable age. He knew that the only way he could find a proper match for her was if he had 1,000 rubles for a dowry. He realized that no one would lend him money. In desperation, he decided to approach Zundel, the richest man in the *shtetl,* for a loan.

He knocked timidly on the door of Zundel's beautiful house. Zundel, taken by surprise at Eliezer's sudden visit, invited him in. "What is it that you want?" he asked.

"I'll tell you the truth," Eliezer began haltingly. "You must know my daughter. You will agree that she is very pretty. I realize that I will never be able to find her a proper husband unless I have a proper dowry. I have come to ask you to lend me 1,000 rubles. I will pay you back."

Zundel listened incredulously. He knew that Eliezer had no money, no job, and certainly no way of paying back a loan for the enormous sum of 1,000 rubles, so he laughed.

The Holy Beggar's Gazette. Vol. 2, No. 1, San Francisco, CA, 1973.

"How do you ever expect to pay back such a loan?"

Then he realized that Eliezer, who had come with downcast eyes, had lowered his gaze still further, totally demoralized. Zundel regretted his words, so he said, "I'll tell you what I'll do! Take this contract. Find another rich man to guarantee the loan. Bring it back to me with his signature. Then I will gladly give you the money you need."

Eliezer smiled weakly. He lifted his head slightly, stuck out his hand, took the contract, put it into his pocket, and slumped out of Zundel's house. He trudged toward the *bays midrash.* Stepping up to the holy ark, he opened it and laid his head on the inside ledge. Eliezer poured out his heart and soul. When he finished praying, he stepped back three steps, moved over to a table, withdrew the contract from his pocket, and filled in the required information. On the blank line reserved for the guarantor of the loan, he wrote:

"Mine is the silver, Mine is the gold, signed the Lord."[1]

Eliezer returned to Zundel's house, entered timidly, and handed him the signed contract.

Zundel was surprised that Eliezer had returned so soon. He was shocked when he looked at the contract and read the signature of the guarantor that Eliezer had written. Then he said:

"When you first asked me for the loan, I laughed. I knew you could never repay it. Had you asked me for charity, I certainly would have given you a large sum toward your daughter's dowry. But a loan? I really thought it was funny, so I made life a little difficult for you. I never expected you to find a guarantor. I see by the contract that you were unsuccessful, but I admire your resourcefulness, so I am nevertheless going to lend you all the money you need."

Thirty days later, a stranger knocked on Zundel's door.[2] A servant opened it. The stranger said to the servant:

---

[1]*Chaggai* 2:8. Rashi, greatest of biblical commentators, explains this verse to mean that all worldly wealth is in the hands of God, and it is He Who distributes it to whomever He wishes. Further, the Hebrew word *neum* used in this verse means both *to say* and *to sign.* Eliezer had been taught the latter definition.

[2]"If a person lends his friend some money without specifying a date for repayment, it is payable after thirty days" (Talmud *Bavli, Makkos* 3b).

"Eliezer sent me to deliver this envelope to your master, Zundel. It will repay the money he borrowed." He handed the envelope to the servant and left.

Zundel was sitting in his study. His servant handed him the envelope saying, "A messenger brought this from Eliezer for you. He said to tell you that it would repay the money he borrowed."

"Oh," he thought to himself, "I never believed that Eliezer would repay the loan. I don't see how he could possible have saved enough money to repay it. I'm sure he must have gone to another rich man to borrow 1,000 rubles so he could repay me." Zundel felt very ashamed of his actions. He picked up the ruble notes and put them in the envelope. He then ran to the stable, hastily harnessed his horse to his carriage, and rode through the *shtetl* searching for Eliezer. When he saw him in the distance, he called:

"Eliezer, Eliezer, wait for me. I have to talk to you."

The two men stood face to face. "Listen," began Zundel, sheepishly. "I am really sorry that I hurt your feelings. I don't know if you can ever forgive me. You really didn't have to borrow money from someone else to return my money to me. I would like you to take the 1,000 rubles and return it to the other rich man who lent you the money to pay me back."

Eliezer sputtered, "I don't know what you are talking about. I didn't borrow money from anyone else."

Zundel showed him the envelope that the messenger had given him. "Then how can you explain this envelope that a messenger left with my servant a short while ago? He said that the contents of the envelope would repay the money that I had lent you."

"I can't explain it," said Eliezer. "Why don't we go to our rebbe, Menachem Mendel Rimanover.[3] He might have an explanation."

Eliezer jumped into Zundel's carriage and the two curious men rode to the *bays midrash* of the Rimanover Rebbe.

The rebbe took the envelope. He turned it over in his hand a few times, then he took out the money, looked it over

[3]For biographical information about Rebbe Menachem Mendel Rimanover, see pp. 124–129.

carefully, and reinserted it into the envelope. It took a long time before he whispered, "Don't you recognize that this envelope and the money inside is a gift from Heaven? I want you to know that when Eliezer signed God's Name to that contract, he really believed that the Almighty would repay the loan, if he were not able to do so himself. When he signed God's Name, there was *such* commotion before the Heavenly Court. The Heavenly Court had finally found a Jew who truly believed that God is the real guarantor of all . . . that God would repay the loan. All of our patriarchs and matriarchs argued over who would be privileged to be the messenger to repay the loan. But Elyahu *Hanave*, the prophet of peace, persevered and he was chosen to be the debt-repaying messenger. It was he who knocked on your door. Had *you* believed that God would repay the loan like Eliezer, *you* would have been privileged to see Elyahu. Since you did not believe, since you mocked Eliezer's faith, your money was repaid, but you did not merit seeing Elyahu."

"Rebbe, I can never use this money, it is too holy. Take it and use it as dowry money for other poor brides."

You Could Wear These
Pants Even in Jerusalem

Rebbe Aryeh Layb Sarah's rushed breathlessly into the *shul*.[1] The morning service had just ended and the people stood around chatting, delaying for a few moments their departure for their jobs. When they saw him, the chatting stopped, for they

Shmonih Seforim. Bulgaria, Bays Pinchas, 1913. Reprinted in New York, 1983.

[1]Rebbe Aryeh Layb Sarah's (1730–1791) was a disciple of the Baal Shem Tov, the founder of the chasidic movement. The Baal Shem Tov placed upon his shoulders the responsibility of supporting the *lamed vav tzaddikim*, the thirty-six hidden holy righteous people, who by their merit sustain the existence of the world. To fulfill this responsibility, he constantly travelled from *shtetl* to *shtetl*, raising money to provide for them. Many stories are told about him.

Once, he forced his way into the palace of Joseph II of Austria, son of Maria Theresa to demand that he rescind the law forcing Jewish children to attend public schools. He knew that public education would deemphasize Jewish identity and learning in eighteenth-century Vienna, which was devoted to promoting literature, art, and music, rather than religion.

At another time he was asked why he went to see the Maggid of Mezeritch (successor to the Baal Shem Tov) so often. He replied, "I do not travel to the maggid to listen to him teach Torah, rather I visit him to see how he puts his shoes on. A true *tzaddik* is not only a leader when he teaches Torah in public. A true *tzaddik* shows by his every action how a Jew should behave."

knew, since he was breathless, something important had happened.

"Quick," he explained to the group, "I need to borrow 300 rubles. The situation is desperate." The people loved Rebbe Aryeh Layb Sarah's and trusted him implicitly. They knew that every kopek he collected for the poor was distributed fairly. He had barely finished his sentence when a prosperous businessman stepped forward and said, "I was on my way to the marketplace to purchase some merchandise. I happen to have 300 rubles in my pocket, but I will give them to you." And so saying, he took out the money and handed it to Rebbe Aryeh Layb Sarah's.

"Thank you for your trust," responded the rebbe. "I bless you that from this day on you will have much more than the money you are lending me."

From the tone of the rebbe's voice, the businessman perceived that he could ask for anything he wanted, so he whispered, "Rebbe, could you introduce me to one of the *lamed vav tzaddikim*[2]?"

Rebbe Aryeh Layb Sarah's shook his head. "Right now, I must take care of this emergency, but I promise to introduce you to one of the *lamed vav tzaddikim* the next time I pass this way."

The businessman was satisfied. Many years elapsed before Rebbe Aryeh Layb Sarah's passed through that *shtetl* again. In the meantime, his blessing was fulfilled. The businessman prospered more than he had ever dreamed possible. Every investment turned out profitably. He thought about fulfilling a lifelong yearning—to sell his holdings in the Diaspora and settle in Eretz Yisrael where he knew he could live comfortably on his accumulated wealth for the remainder of his life. He decided to wait for Rebbe Aryeh Layb's next visit to seek his advice.

When the rebbe passed through the *shtetl*, the businessman rushed over to see him. "Rebbe, I need your advice. Your blessing was fulfilled a hundredfold. I have enough money to live comfortably the rest of my life, so I want to know if I should sell my business investments here and settle in Eretz Yisrael." He dropped his voice and whispered as an after-

[2]See footnote 3, p. 107.

thought, "And you have not yet introduced me to a *lamed vav tzaddik*."

Rebbe Aryeh Layb Sarah's responded, "This is what you have to do. After *Shabbos,* saddle your horse and ride toward the outskirts of this *shtetl.* Then, keep following the road. Eventually, you will find a little hut. The hut belongs to a tailor. Go into the hut and talk to the tailor. Watch his actions. You will know whether to settle in Eretz Yisrael or not. He will guide you in what to do with the rest of your life."

The businessman could not wait for *Shabbos* to end. As soon as he had made *havdalah,* he saddled his horse and set out for the tailor's hut. By the time he reached his destination, the hour was late. He felt a little embarrassed to intrude without an excuse, so he tore his pants and knocked on the door. When the tailor opened the door, he stammered, "I was passing this way, and I saw your light. Back there on the road, my horse brushed too close to a low-hanging branch. My leg caught on the branch, and my pants ripped. I was wondering if you could mend them."

The tailor asked the businessman to enter and held his hands out for the pants.

"Stand behind the curtain," he said. "I will mend your pants while you wait."

The tailor started to mend the pants. As he inserted the needle into the fabric, the businessman squirmed uncomfortably. The tailor pierced the fabric with the needle again, and this time the businessman felt as if the needle had pierced his soul. As the tailor pulled the needle out of the fabric, the businessman felt relieved. The tailor sewed. With each consecutive stitch, the businessman sensed that his soul was being repaired. When the tailor finished and handed the businessman his pants, he perceived that his soul had been redeemed. However, the questions still remained: whether to go to Eretz Yisrael, whether he had really met a *lamed vav tzaddik.*

While the businessman pondered these questions, standing behind the curtain, Rebbe Nachum Tzernobler, a disciple of the Baal Shem Tov, entered the hut.[3] He had with him a torn pair of pants that needed mending. The busi-

[3]See footnote 1, p. 110.

nessman observed Rebbe Nachum's reaction as the tailor sewed his pants. With each stitch of the tailor's needle into the fabric of the pants, Rebbe Nachum squirmed. He cried with pain when the needle pierced the fabric, and sighed with relief when the tailor pulled the needle through. Comparing his own actions of a few minutes earlier with Rebbe Nachum's, he realized that, indeed, the tailor must be one of the *lamed vav tzaddikim*. He listened carefully as the tailor and Rebbe Nachum exchanged a few words. "I want you to know, Rebbe Nachum, that I mended your pants so carefully, that you can wear them even in the streets of Jerusalem."

The businessman felt faint. He realized that he had an answer to his questions. He knew that the *lamed vav tzaddik* was telling him that the time had come for him to settle in Eretz Yisrael. He sold his business holdings and spent the remainder of his life in Jerusalem.

From Where Will My Help Come?

In the nineteenth century, the majority of world Jewry lived in Poland/Russia, in the areas comprising Volhynia, Podolia, the Ukraine, and Belorussia (White Russia).

In Dobromysl, one of the towns in Belorussia, in the county of Mogilev, near the Dnieper River, a God-fearing Jew named Meshullam earned his living distilling liquor. The Russian government had decreed that the owners of liquor distilleries pay a tax on each bottle of liquor sold. To make sure that factory owners complied with the law, the town constable attached a meter to the spout of every barrel to measure the liquor as it trickled from the barrels into the bottles.

Many people worked in Meshullam's distillery, among them a dishonest man named Boris who thought he could help himself to liquor without paying for it. With a nail, he punctured a hole in some of the barrels on the side opposite the spout and the meter. He placed bottles under the small holes to collect the dripping liquor. When the bottles were filled, he replaced them with others. Soon Boris had enough bottles to open his own

G. Mah Tov. *Ma-a-say-hem shel Tzaddikim*, op. cit.

private liquor business. He believed that neither Meshullam nor the Russian government would ever discover his deceit.

One day, unbeknownst to Boris, another worker watched from a distance as he removed one full bottle and replaced it with an empty one. Just as Boris stepped away from the barrel, the evidence clearly in hand, his co-worker Vladimir stepped into his path, slapped him on the back, and challenged him.

"What do you think you're doing?" he demanded. Without waiting for an answer, he concluded, "You are stealing liquor from Meshullam, our employer!"

Boris raised his finger to his lips. "Sh, sh," he whispered. "If you keep my secret, we can become business partners. We will divide the profits equally!"

Vladimir, equally dishonest, agreed to Boris's scheme. The partners carried on their own private enterprise for months. Neither Meshullam nor the constable were the wiser.

However, the partners didn't trust each other completely, and after about six months, Boris and Vladimir began to fight over the profits, each suspecting the other of taking extra bottles of liquor. Finally Vladimir alerted the police.

When the constable and two policemen arrived at the distillery to arrest Boris, he blurted out, "You have the wrong man. I am not the thief. Meshullam, the owner of this distillery instructed us to siphon off some of the liquor in order to avoid paying taxes. He puts the profit in his pocket. He doesn't even give us our share for remaining silent."

The constable and the two policemen didn't hesitate to accept Boris's words at face value. Since they had been indoctrinated into hating Jews, they chose to arrest Meshullam rather than investigate Boris's accusations. They rushed toward Meshullam's office, breaking down the door as they shoved their way in.

"You are under arrest for cheating the government of its rightful taxes!" shouted the constable. "Take him away," he ordered the two policemen.

They seized Meshullam, dragged him out of the distillery and through the town, and threw him into a cell at the jail. "You will remain here until you are turned over to the proper government authorities for trial," thundered the constable.

Word spread rapidly through the town that Meshullam, the wealthy distiller, was guilty of withholding taxes from the Russian government. People could be heard chattering in the marketplace: "I hope he'll be punished with an enormous fine," one peasant said.

The second peasant sneered, "The government ought to confiscate his business. Let him beg in the streets, together with all the members of his family!"

The third muttered, "They should sentence him to hard labor in Siberia."[1]

Meshullam's family knew that he was not guilty. They contacted some of his most influential friends and explained what had happened. They pleaded with them to intervene on Meshullam's behalf. The friends agreed that Meshullam could not possibly be guilty of the crime of which he was accused. They pressured the constable to release him on his own recognizance until the trial. The constable demanded an exorbitant sum of money for Meshullam's release.

As soon as he was freed, Meshullam saddled his fastest horse and headed toward Lubavitch[2] to consult with Rebbe Shmuel,[3] the Maharash.

[1]Siberia was used as a penal colony and a place of exile for political prisoners from the early seventeenth century on.

[2]Luba means *love* in both the Polish and Russian languages. Lubavitch means the town of brotherly love.

[3]Rebbe Shmuel (1834–1882) was a direct descendant of the founder of Lubavitch, Rebbe Shneur Zalman of Liadi. He engaged in "communal activities to improve the spiritual and material conditions of the Jewish masses within and beyond the ranks of the chasidic movement."

He traveled extensively to meet and influence both Russian and Jewish leaders. The confidence he inspired in his many friends was of great help to the Jewish people in later years.

His leadership of *Chabad Chasidim* (1866–1882) coincided with one of the stormiest periods of anti-Semitism in Russian-Jewish history. It was a time when nobles schemed to harass Jewish communities, resulting in sanctioned government pogroms. He was the "moving spirit" of the Council of Elders, whose task it was to be on constant alert in the defense of Jewish interests.

He ministered to the individual needs of his *chasidim,* strengthening their devotion to Torah study and their commitment to faith. *Biography of Rebbe Shmuel, Hamaharash, The Fourth Lubavitcher Rebbe.* Challenge. London: Lubavitch Foundation of Great Britain, 1970.

He urged the horse forward, faster and faster, and only permitted it to slow its gait as it trotted up Brom Street. He marveled at the serene beauty of this secluded town surrounded by huge forests. It was not much larger than one square mile, with a marketplace in the center.

Meshullam turned his horse in the direction of Benjamin's House of Prayer, the community *bays midrash.* When he entered, the *shamish* informed him that he would have to wait a few days to see the rebbe.

"So many people come to seek the rebbe's advice," Meshullam marveled. He whispered to the *shamish* his urgent need to see the rebbe immediately. His words touched the heart of the *shamish,* who replied, "Don't despair. I will make time for the rebbe to see you early tomorrow morning."

Meshullam walked to the back of the *bays midrash,* found a vacant place at a long, book-laden table, opened his book of Psalms and began reciting in a broken, almost inaudible voice. Sighing deeply, he poured out the pain in his heart for many hours, remaining in the *bays midrash* the rest of the day and the entire night.

When he finally stood before the rebbe, he was weak from lack of sleep and lack of food. It was difficult for him to speak. Slowly, he laid out the reasons for his visit to Lubavitch.

"I have been arrested on trumped-up charges. When my case is brought before the authorities, I will certainly receive a harsh punishment. How can I fight against lying witnesses?

The Lubavitcher Rebbes are:

Rebbe Shneur Zalman of Liadi (founder of Chabad) (1745–1812)

Rebbe Dov Ber ben Rebbe Shneur Zalman (1773–1827)

Rebbe Menachem Mendel, grandson of Rebbe Shneur Zalman, son-in-law of Rebbe Dov Ber (the Tzemach Tzedek) (1789–1866)

Rebbe Shmuel ben Rebbe Menachem Mendel (1834–1882)

Rebbe Sholom Dov Ber ben Rebbe Shmuel (1860–1920)

Rebbe Joseph Isaac Schneersohn, son of Rebbe Sholom Dov Ber (1880–1950)

Rebbe Menachem Mendel Schneersohn, son-in-law of Rebbe Joseph Isaac (sixth in direct paternal descent from Rebbe Menachem Mendel) (1902–   ). (Excerpted from *The Memoirs of Rebbe Joseph I. Schneersohn.* Brooklyn, New York: Otzar Hachassidim, 1961.)

What shall I do? From where will my help come?"[4]

Meshullam's body shook, his voice trembled. Hot tears flowed down his cheeks.

The rebbe listened attentively to Meshullam's pathetic story without saying a word. When he finished, the rebbe said gently, "This is what you must do. Wait until a Jew comes to you and asks you, 'from where will my help come?' Help him immediately. When you fulfill his need, the Almighty will fulfill your need as well."

The rebbe's words lifted Meshullam's spirits. He took leave and returned home, confident that the Almighty would send him a Jew that *he* could help.

Upon his return, Meshullam's family greeted him joyfully, for they perceived a certain confidence in his smile. Two days later, Mendel rushed into Meshullam's office at the distillery.

"Did you hear what happened to Chaim?" he asked.

When Meshullam shook his head, Mendel continued, "His business has been destroyed by fire. An enormous blaze broke out in his restaurant. It burned everything—the restaurant, his house and all his possessions. He doesn't even have a roof over his head. He is sitting forlornly on a tree stump near the river. He looks like a beaten man."

Meshullam grabbed his coat. He ran out of the distillery, through the town to the edge of the river, passing the charred ruins of Chaim's restaurant and home. He found Chaim, dejected, sitting on the river's bank. Chaim lifted his head. "Meshullam, I'm so glad to see you. I'm so happy that you have been released from jail!"

"Chaim," Meshullam interrupted. "I ran over here just as soon as I heard about your terrible misfortune. Tell me, how much will you need to rebuild your house and restaurant? I will give it to you."

Chaim refused to tell him. "I can't take any money from you, because I don't know if I will ever be able to repay you.

[4]"From where will my help come? My help will come from the Almighty, Creator of heaven and earth" (Psalms 121:1) is interpreted to mean that man must look to the Almighty for assistance in both his physical existence and spiritual well-being. Commentary of Rabbi Shimshon Raphael Hirsch.

Furthermore, you can't afford to give your money away. I know your troubles are not yet over. What if you are found guilty? What if the judge fines you an exorbitant sum? Suppose he sends you to Siberia? Your family will need money to live on. No, I can't take it. The Almighty will help me. I believe that verse 'from where will my help come, from the Almighty who created heaven and earth,' will be fulfilled for me."

"Chaim," said Meshullam adamantly, "I'm pleading with you to take this money to rebuild your house and your restaurant!" They argued for a long time.

Finally, Chaim consented to accept the money, but only as a loan. When Meshullam brought it to him a few hours later, his face glowed with new hope.

"Meshullam," Chaim called after him as they parted, "just as you have fulfilled for me 'from where will my help come,' so I bless you that the Almighty will help you when the time of your judgment comes."

On the day of the trial, Meshullam found himself face to face with Vladimir and Boris, his unfaithful workers. They were asked to repeat their accusation to the judge.

"Our employer, Meshullam, ordered us to make holes in the barrels. He showed us how to siphon off the liquor so that it would not register on the meter. He warned us that if we told the inspector, he would fire us!"

The prosecuting attorney rose. His face was clouded with assured righteous indignation.

"That man," he sputtered with rage, pointing his finger at Meshullam, "made criminals out of innocent workers by ordering them to deceive the government. I demand that he be punished to the fullest extent of the law!"

Vladimir and Boris whispered to each other gleefully. The prosecuting attorney glared at Meshullam, confident that he would be found guilty.

The judge tried to maintain order in the disorderly courtroom. He turned to Meshullam and said firmly, "It is your turn to speak. What do you have to say in your own behalf?"

Meshullam could hardly pull himself to a standing position. He clutched the railing of the prisoner's box tightly. His face was ashen, his shoulders stooped. He whispered, "I can only say that I am innocent of all these charges. I fell into a trap.

Vladimir and Boris are accusing me of something that I did not do. I have never stolen from any man. I have never knowingly hurt another human being." Meshullam breathed heavily and sat down.

The judge rose to speak. "The time has come for me to decide the guilt or innocence of the accused. Before I render my decision, I would like to tell the people in this courtroom a short story."

* * *

A young man, descendant of a long line of wealthy nobles, traveled to a distant city during a vacation from his university. When he reached his destination, he realized that all his luggage, money, traveling permits, and return-train ticket had been stolen. In despair he left the train, not knowing which way to turn, stranded in a place where he did not know a living soul.

He wandered around the city during the daylight hours, trying to find a way out of his dilemma, but to no avail. No one paid attention to him. Hungry and tired, he returned to the train station to spend the night sleeping on a bench.

When he awoke the next morning, he decided to beg for money in order to be able to buy some food. Many people crossed through the train station, ignoring him. Only one passenger, a merchant, noticed him and touching him on the shoulder said, "By your appearance, it seems strange to me that you are begging. How is it that a person dressed in such expensive clothing has to beg for money? Let me buy you some food."

The merchant led him to a nearby cafe. "Please order anything you like," he said gently. As he watched him eat ravenously, the merchant asked, "Please tell me how it is that you are in such a predicament?"

"I was on holiday from my university studies. I wanted to travel a little. This city was my destination. When I realized that all my belongings had been stolen, I left the train and wandered around the city, not knowing what to do. I haven't any idea how I will return home."

The merchant didn't hesitate. He purchased a train ticket for the student to return home, and placed enough spending money in his palm to take care of his personal needs.

The young man asked for the merchant's name and address, so that he could return the money. However, the merchant refused to tell him. "Have a pleasant journey." he waved, and then he disappeared from sight.

* * *

"Many years passed," the judge said, lowering his voice. "I'm sure that all of you in this courtroom would like to know why I chose to tell this story at this particular time. Let me first tell you the end of the story. The young man returned home, continued his university studies and became a judge. I am that judge.

"During those intervening years, I searched all over for the man who helped me. I wanted in some way to repay my debt. However I never found the merchant who so graciously helped me, until I entered my courtroom this morning.

"He is in this courtroom, and he is the accused, Meshullam. When Meshullam stood to speak on his own behalf, something connected in my head. I knew he was the merchant for whom I had been searching. It is said that truth is recognizable. Because of what Meshullam did for me, I'm certain that he is telling the truth. I believe he is innocent of the charges."

Meshullam sat on the chair in the prisoner's box, his face wet with tears. His mind heard again the words of the Lubavitcher Rebbe:

"When you fulfill the 'from where will my help come' of another person in need, the Almighty will fulfill your needs also!"

Tefillah—
PRAYER

efillah (prayer) is man's connection with God. It is the natural expression of man's religious feelings consisting of an outpouring of the deepest thoughts and emotions of his mind and his soul.

The root of the Hebrew word for prayer means "to judge, to praise, to think, to meditate, to beg," teaching us the manifold aspects of prayer. Of the different categories of prayer, four exemplify the relationship between God and man: thanksgiving, praise, confession, and pleading.

Maimonides explains that the verse in the Torah, "And you shall serve Him with all your heart and all your soul" (Deuteronomy 11:13), begs the question—what is service of the heart? He answers that service of the heart is prayer.

"Before engaging in prayer, the worshiper ought to bring himself into a devotional frame of mind by visualizing that he is standing in the Divine Presence. Praying without devotion is not prayer. . . . He whose thoughts are wandering or occupied with other things ought not to pray."

— Maimonides, *Yad Hachazakah, Tefillah* 4:16

Torah Thoughts

Prayer

Prayer is first found in the Torah when Abraham prays for the people of Sodom, pleading with God to nullify His decree to destroy the city. "And Abraham drew near [to pray]."[1]

Until that time, man could not conceive that his prayer could change God's decree, for Noah did not pray to God to rescind the decree of a destructive flood upon the world nor did Adam pray to nullify God's decree of expulsion from the Garden of Eden.

Abraham's prayer was answered in that Lot and some of his family were saved from the destruction of Sodom.

Lot was the ancestor of King David, *Neim Zemiros Yisrael* (the Sweet Singer, the Poet Laureate of Israel), who refers to himself with the words "As for me, I am a prayer." (Psalms 69:14). King David personified prayer.

We learn from Abraham that there is no such thing as a totally unanswered prayer, for although the city of Sodom was destroyed, his prayer gave birth to King David.[2]

[1]Rashi, Genesis 18:23.
[2]Rebbe Zadok Hakohen. *Pree Tzadik*, Vol. I, Originally printed in Lublin, 1922.

Why did Moshe Rabaynu, Moses our Teacher, mandate that the Jewish people pray three times each day?[3]

The Almighty showed Moshe Rabaynu a prophetic vision of all that would befall his people in the future. He wanted to instill faith in their hearts, no matter what the future would bring. Therefore, he mandated prayer three times each day, since prayer is the acting out of the *mitzvah* to believe in God and to serve Him with "all your heart, and all your soul."[4] If we did not believe that God answers prayer, we would not pray. Prayer affirms our faith.[5]

A farmer can be symbolically compared to a person who prays. Just as the farmer works his field, first he plows, then he sows, then he waters and fertilizes, then he stands back and watches his produce grow; so the person who prays must plow by opening his heart, he must sow by slowly uttering words of thanksgiving, then he waters by pouring out his heart before the Holy One, Blessed Be He, waiting for salvation.[6]

Many people yearn to be in the Divine Presence, closer to the spiritual world. They prepare themselves for one hour before prayer, then they pray for one hour, and are uplifted for at least an hour afterward. Repeating this three times each day enables them to spend nine out of twenty-four hours in the Divine Presence.[7]

Man feels inadequate to overcome his evil inclination alone. When he prays, he pleads with God to help him succeed in this endeavor.[8]

---

[3] The origin of the morning, afternoon, and evening prayer service is the following: "Rabbi Jose, son of Rabbi Hanina said: Prayer was conceived by the patriarchs: Abraham conceived the morning prayer, Isaac, the afternoon prayer, and Jacob, the evening prayer" (Talmud *Bavli, Berachos* 26b).

[4] Deuteronomy 11:13.

[5] *Tiferes Shmuel*, ibid.

[6] *Netivos Shalom*, ibid.

[7] *Netivos Shalom*, ibid.

[8] Rebbe Ahron Yosef Luria. *Avodas P'nim*. Slonim: Tiberias, 1974.

Prayer, communion with God, elevates and exalts the soul.

The gates of Heaven are opened with the keys of devotional prayer. Just as a lowly thief knows how to enter the gates, so man must learn to humble himself as if he were a thief for his prayers to enter the gates of Heaven. A humble heart removes the barriers between man and God.[9]

Pray with outstretched hands, thereby symbolizing that you are ready to receive that which God will certainly give you.[10]

If you are not at peace with mankind, your prayer will not be heard.[11]

While you pray, forget everybody and everything.[12]

There is a lush, verdant field; majestic trees, tall grass, bushy scrub, and colorful, radiant wildflowers dot the landscape. Holy souls, waiting to be mended, to be uplifted, to be bathed in the bliss of praising the Creator walk through the field picking at the foliage. Each leaf, each blade of grass, each petal of each flower is a letter, a word, a song. He who prays walks through the garden of words, picking flowers one by one, twining a wreath of phrases, weaving the phrases into sentences, forming the sentences into prayer bouquets. Gently, he lays the bouquet on the path, retraces his steps, gathers more leaves, more branches, more buds, more radiant wildflowers, adds them to his blossoming bouquet. This is the way he prays: he says each letter, he carries it on his tongue, swirls its sound in his mouth, listens to its melody with his heart and ear, utters another letter and combines it with the first. He joins the letters until they form words, slowly, slowly, tasting the flavor of each syllable, combining the syllables until the words form a complete prayer. Who can measure the heights that kind of prayer can reach? That kind of prayer is the deepest expression of the soul and pleads for it, never separating from it. Love, prayer,

[9] M. Meisels. *Judaism: Thought and Legend*, op. cit.
[10-12] Rebbe Nachman of Bratzlav. *Sayfer Hamidos.*

and the soul are woven together like newly picked flowers into bouquets. This prayer does not part from the soul, it is never forgotten. It crowds upon the heels of an earlier prayer, following it, binding itself to it, forming one complete, whole, perfect prayer. When the prayer is ended, the very first petal and the very last petal are attached to the very first letter and the very last letter in perfect harmony.[13]

Follow this advice and you will be granted the strength needed to overcome any obstacle, to conquer all sadness. Take time each day to speak with the Lord of the Universe. Talk to Him in the language you are most familiar with, for He understand all words. Place your burden upon the Lord and He will carry it for you. Thank Him for the many good things He has done for you. Ask His forgiveness for any disrespect you may have shown Him. Pray for His help in all that you need. Pour out your heart to Him as though you were talking things over with a truly good friend. Always remember that there is no request too great for God to grant and no prayer too small for Him to hear.[14]

My soul! Always remember that God created us and placed us in this world. Remember everything that He did for us, from the moment of conception until birth. As much as He took care of us in the womb, so He continues to care for us, every day, every minute, every hour. He only wants us to remember Him, to follow His ways, to accept the Yoke of Heaven and to serve Him truthfully.

Remember, my soul, to have been born a Jew is a precious gift. It is a crown of holiness upon our head. Every holy thought, every compassionate deed lifts the crown higher and higher to the place of Heavenly Bliss.

I cannot think of the void, the meaningless, when I am attached to Heavenly bliss.

Remember who we are, my soul. We come from the Source of all Happiness. The moment we are sad, we are capable of

---

[13] Rebbe Nachman of Bratzlav. *Likutay Maharan.*
[14] Rebbe Nachman of Bratslav.

doing evil. By trusting in Him, the Source of all Happiness who makes us joyous, we can achieve so much more with our life.

My soul! Stand before Him, and let us tell Him what we need. Ask Him how we can serve Him. He will carry our burden and we will rejoice by placing our trust in Him.[15]

[15]Rebbe Arele Roth.

Stories

I Will Die a Jew

Mainz was one of the cities located in the Rhine river valley that had a large Jewish population and a fine yeshiva. Rabbi Amnon, a man of wealth and distinguished ancestry, was the religious leader of the Jews of this city in the first third of the eleventh century.

He was friendly with the bishop of Mainz, which helped further the "relatively secure" relationship between the two religious communities.[1] The two men enjoyed each other's company, and they spent many hours discussing intellectual matters. Usually, as they parted company, the bishop would say, "Rabbi Amnon, it's time for a man of your intelligence and stature to adopt the *true religion*. When will you set the example for your people and convert?"[2]

Elyahu Ki Tov. *Sayfer Hatodaah*. Jerusalem: Yeshurun Publishers, 1966.

[1]"Relatively secure" means that the fate of Jewish communities during the Middle Ages depended upon the whim of either the feudal lord or the bishop.

[2]During the Middle Ages, leaders of the Catholic church preached that Christianity is a religion of love, the *true religion*. Priests and feudal masters, seeking to attain salvation for their Jewish subjects, tortured and forcefully converted them to Christianity.

Needless to say, Rabbi Amnon always refused to answer.

At one point the bishop put so much pressure upon Rabbi Amnon that he perceived his request to be more than the habitual closing words of a usually friendly visit.

To put him off, Rabbi Amnon countered, "Give me three days to consider your request!" The bishop agreed to wait for Rabbi Amnon's answer.

As soon as he left the bishop's mansion, Rabbi Amnon realized his error. "What did I do?" he cried desperately. "How could I ever utter those words? No matter the consequences, I would never consider conversion. I could no longer bear the pressure! I only wanted to put him off!"

When Rabbi Amnon did not appear on the third day, the bishop sent soldiers to Amnon's house to remind him of their appointment. Rabbi Amnon refused to return to the mansion with the soldiers.

The bishop was infuriated. "Return to his house," he ordered, "and drag him here to me."

The soldiers dragged Rabbi Amnon through the streets of Mainz and stood him before the furious bishop. "For refusing to come as you agreed," thundered the bishop, "you will suffer an agonizing death."

Rabbi Amnon pleaded, "Allow me one last request: let me decree my own fate. Let the tongue that dared mention conversion be cut from my mouth."

"No," shouted the bishop. "I will order the legs that did not come to keep their appointment to be cut off. I will order that your fingers be dismembered. I will order salt to be poured onto your wounds to increase your suffering!"

The bishop's sentence was carried out on Rosh Hashanah. Rabbi Amnon begged his faithful followers to carry him, bleeding and dismembered into the synagogue and on to the *bimah*.

He interrupted the *chazan* who was chanting the *musaf* prayers, the additional prayer service for holy days. Writhing in pain, he affirmed his faith in God with these words:

U'nesaneh tokef kedushas hayom,
May our sanctification of Your name ascend,
For You are our God and our King.
Let us observe the holiness of this day.
This is the day Your Kingdom is exalted,
It is established in mercy and truth.
You are the Judge of mankind . . .
And You hold each man accountable for his deeds . . .
On Rosh Hashanah day man's destiny is inscribed
And on Yom Kippur his fate is sealed. . .
Who will live and who will die. . .
But repentance, prayer and charity avert an evil
    decree . . .
And You are Our God, Our Living King.[3]

As Rabbi Amnon uttered these holy words, his soul ascended heavenward. Three days later, Rabbi Kalonymus ben Meshullam dreamed that Rabbi Amnon was teaching him the words of *U'nesaneh Tokef.* In the dream, Rabbi Amnon commanded him to travel throughout the Jewish communities and teach the people this prayer.[4]

Rabbi Kalonymus followed the command in the dream and traveled to many Jewish communities, teaching the prayer wherever he went.

[3]*Machzor: High Holiday Prayer Book.*
[4]To this day, Ashkenazic communities recite this prayer on both days of Rosh Hashanah and on Yom Kippur.

Kaddish after Kol Nidre

A peaceful calm had descended upon the Prague ghetto that Friday night between Rosh Hashanah and Yom Kippur in the year 5337 (1577). The houses in the ghetto were crowded together, one story built upon another so that very little sunlight penetrated the cobblestoned, crooked streets. Some of the streets led to the ancient cemetery, some led to the Moldau (Ultava) River that surrounded the area on three sides, and some ended at the wall that divided the Jewish community from the rest of Prague.

In a small, second-floor apartment, furnished with the barest necessities—an unsteady chipped table and two straight-backed wooden chairs—the last glimmer of the seventh candle flickered from the *Shabbos* candlesticks and shed a tiny ray of light through the shabby dwelling. On a rumpled bed lay a young woman, writhing in acute labor pains for the second day in anticipation of the birth of her first child. Mordechai, her

Menachem Mendel. *Otzar Hachag, Yom Kippur*, op. cit.
Sippurim Prager Sammlung: Judisher Legenden. Wien and Leipzig: R. Lowit Verlag, 1921.

frightened husband, stood nearby, wiping her forehead. The midwife tried to calm them both.

Suddenly, an eerie wind rustled through the apartment, extinguishing the one remaining ray of light. "I must have some light," whispered the midwife. "She is about to give birth. Light another candle."

"But, I can't. It is *Shabbos*," moaned Mordechai pathetically.

"You know as well as I do that saving life is more important," said the midwife. "Even when I worked at the rabbi's house, he . . .

"Quiet, woman, I will figure something out," he shouted.

Mordechai's wife began to cry. He grabbed his threadbare coat and rushed out of the apartment, slamming the door behind him.

He walked around the streets, not knowing exactly what to do. The rustling breeze turned into gusty squalls, threatening a violent storm. Mordechai found himself standing in front of the gate to the ghetto wall. A lieutenant had stopped in the small guardhouse, to rest from overseeing the safety of the Jews who at that time were living in the ghetto in relative security.

"Please, sir, I need your help," gulped Mordechai. "You see, my wife is about to give birth. The wind blew out the last candle. Our dwelling is completely dark. Tonight is *Shabbos*. I am not permitted to light a fire. Could you please come with me? Could you please light another candle for me?"

The lieutenant awoke the soldier sleeping peacefully on a chair. "Go with this man and do as he tells you," he ordered.

The soldier struggled to his feet and followed Mordechai back to his apartment.

After the soldier had lit a few candles, Mordechai served him a portion of fish and a piece of *challah*. "I am so grateful to you," he murmured. "Because you helped me in this emergency, I did not have to desecrate my *Shabbos*."

The soldier left. Soon afterward, Mordechai heard the first cries of his newborn daughter.

The midwife made Mordechai's wife comfortable, then, leaving, she said, "I must go home to rest. These two days have been very difficult for all of us. Your wife is sleeping, and the baby is fine. I will return in a few hours."

Some time after midnight, she reappeared breathless at the doorway of Mordechai's apartment. "You don't know what I saw on my way here," she blurted out. She was obviously agitated, frightened, confused.

"By the dim light of the moon I recognized the soldier that came with you to kindle the candle. He was lying in the street, not too far from here . . . dead. What shall we do?"

Mordechai knew that the unexplained death of a soldier lying so near to his house would be blamed on him. Terrified, he ran as quickly as he could to the house of the *parnas*, the president of the community, for advice.

"Hurry, wake up!" he shouted, pounding on the door.

Eventually, the sleep-eyed *parnas* appeared and calmed Mordechai down. "This is more than I can handle," he admitted. "We have a very serious problem on our hands. Let's go to talk to the Maharal."[1]

The Maharal listened attentively as Mordechai repeated the story from the beginning. When he finished, the Maharal responded angrily, "You acted foolishly, without thinking! You surely know that you are permitted to do anything to save life. Under the circumstances, you were permitted to kindle more candles so that the midwife would have light to deliver your baby. By your zealousness to keep yourself from desecrating *Shabbos*, you have endangered all of us. If the people outside the ghetto find out what happened, they will use the incident as a pretext for a blood libel.[2] No one must ever know what happened here tonight. Now, you must act quickly, before the sun rises. Find the lieutenant and repeat to him, in all confidence, the same thing you told me. Ask him what to do. He will know how to protect the Jewish community from harm."

The *parnas* and Mordechai ran in search of the lieutenant. They found him making rounds along the outside of the ghetto wall.

"We have to talk to you," they pleaded. They pulled him inside the gate of the ghetto.

---

[1]Rabbi Yehuda Loew ben Bezalel, the Maharal of Prague (1515–1609). (See footnote 1 on p. 191.)
[2]See footnote 3 on p. 192.

"Calm down, calm down," the lieutenant urged. "How can I help you?"

Again, Mordechai repeated the story.

"This is what you have to do," responded the lieutenant. "Put an empty liquor bottle into his left hand. Drag the body outside the gates of the ghetto. Do it now, before sunrise, before people begin to come out of doors. When his body is found, it will be obvious that he drank himself to death."

Mordechai and the *parnas* followed the lieutenant's instructions. When they finished, they returned to their homes, thinking that the incident was over.

The Maharal could not sleep. He dressed and went to the *Alt-neu shul*,[3] waiting to see what would happen. He did not have to wait very long. In a few minutes the lieutenant stood in the doorway. The Maharal beckoned him to enter. The lieutenant entered hesitantly.

"I will not waste words," he began. "You no doubt know what happened to the soldier."

"The Jewish people are forever in your debt," interrupted the Maharal. "What can we do to repay you for your quick thinking, for your kindness?"

"Before I tell you that, let me tell you a story."

The Maharal pointed to a chair. The lieutenant sat down and began to speak softly, "I did not always wear this uniform. I was born into a wealthy, Polish Jewish family. When I was 14, as was the custom, I was married, to the lovely young daughter of a scholarly Jew. It was arranged that I should continue studying in a *yeshiva* for a few years. My father took upon himself the obligation to support us. We had a few very joyous years together, especially after the birth of our son.

"My father had an older brother who lived in Amsterdam. At that time, the Jews who lived there were permitted to engage in any business enterprise, and my uncle tripled his share of the family fortune by accumulating vast land holdings.

"One day, my father received the sad news that his brother had passed away. The lawyer who wrote the letter stated that since the deceased had no children, he had instructed him,

[3]See glossary, p. 283.

prior to his death, to make me his beneficiary. My father asked me to go to Amsterdam to settle my uncle's estate. I was 20 years old at the time.

"I arrived in Amsterdam after a long, weary trip. Not knowing anyone in the city, I stayed at an inn. I planned to contact the lawyer after I had rested for a day. That night, a fire spread through the inn. To save my life, I jumped from a room on the second floor without thinking about identity papers or personal possessions. I did not know that everything had burned to ashes in the fire.

"When I regained consciousness, I found that a man named Moshe Tauber had saved my life and had carried me to his house. He personally attended to me, solicitous for my well-being, never asking one question about my identity, the reason for my visit to Amsterdam, or how long I planned on staying in his house. I trusted him and told him everything. Then he offered to advise me how to best invest my inheritance. He even volunteered to send to Poland for new identity papers, so that I could conduct my business. In the meantime, he undertook to solve all the legal problems of settling my uncle's estate. When all the property had been sold, I asked Moshe Tauber to invest my money in a business that did not demand my living in Amsterdam. I wanted to return to Poland and to my wife and my child. Much to my dismay, Moshe Tauber disappeared with all my money. I remained alone in his house. I waited for his return, but I never saw him again.

"Finally, I pretended that I was the owner of the house and sold it. I felt under the circumstances that the proceeds of the sale were rightfully mine. I used the money to return to Poland.

"These were the years of turmoil preceding the Thirty Years War[4] and intermittent fighting made crossing borders very difficult. On many nights, I slept in open fields. It took me two years to reach my town.

"You can't imagine my joy when I reached home late one night. I pulled myself up the steps, walked around to reacquaint myself with the surroundings, located the bedroom, and gently

---

[4]The Thirty Years War (1618–1648) was fought for territorial, dynastic, and religious issues. Shifting alliances and local peace treaties fueled the struggle between Protestantism and Catholicism.

pushed the door ajar, hoping to find my wife sleeping. I bent over to kiss her forehead. My joy was shortlived. From behind a tapestry two soldiers pounced upon me and tied me hand and foot. I demanded to know why I was being treated this way and I was told that I had fallen into a trap.

" 'That woman is not your wife, and you know it,' they shouted gleefully. 'You have been carrying on with the wife of a Polish nobleman. He suspected his wife of infidelity, and you have been caught in the act.'

"I protested my innocence, to no avail. I could not prove my identity. There was no way that I could convince my captors that I had once lived in this house, that I had made a mistake thinking the lady was my wife.

"They took me to a secluded room in the back of the house. There, a priest waited to interrogate me. He told me that if I would confess to my crime and convert, he would turn me free, otherwise, he would hand me over to the nobleman who would probably behead me for my indiscretion.

"During the course of the interrogation, I found out that the priest had lived in the area for many years, so I begged him to tell me what had happened to my wife and my son.

" 'Your wife is dead, and your son is dead,' he sneered.

"I did not believe him, so I consented to baptism in order that I might live to search for them. The priest and my captors escorted me to the church, baptized me, then released me into the hands of a coachman headed for Prague. He instructed him to abandon me at the gates of the city.

"I knew that I would devote the rest of my life trying to find the whereabouts of my wife and my baby. To do that, I needed money. The only job that I could find was the job of a soldier, so I volunteered to serve. I have done well in the army. Yesterday, I was promoted to the post of lieutenant. I was assigned the task of guarding the ghetto. You asked what you could do to repay me for saving the entire Jewish community. I want you to promise me that you will recite *kaddish*[5] for me. You see, I don't

---

[5]*Kaddish* is a prayer praising God, recited with congregational responses at the close of individual sections of a prayer service. It is also recited by a mourner following the study of Torah, Psalms, or Talmud, or after specified prayers during the prayer service.

know if I will ever find my wife and my son. I don't know if there will be anyone to say *kaddish* for me. Therefore, I am asking you to make this promise."

The Maharal sat quietly for some time. When he spoke, his voice was filled with emotion:

"I will do more than promise you to recite *kaddish*. I assure you that the recitation of *kaddish* in your memory will become part of the *Kol Nidre* service in the *Alt-neu shul* each year. I also want to bless you. Wherever you travel, I pray that you will be privileged to save life!" And so they parted.

Fifty years later, on the eve of Yom Kippur, as the *Kol Nidre* service was about to commence, Rabbi Naftali Cohen, the grandson of the Maharal, noticed an old and bent army general hobble into the back of the *Alt-Neu* shul. Many medals were pinned to his uniform. At the conclusion of the *Kol Nidre*, the rabbi recited the *kaddish*. Suddenly he heard a heartbreaking cry from where the general sat.

He sent his *shamish* to find out who the general was and instructed him to ask him to wait at the conclusion of the service.

The general waited in his seat. Before the rabbi had a chance to great him, he spoke. "Since you still recite the *kaddish* after *Kol Nidre*, I see that the promise that the Maharal made to me is being honored. I was the lieutenant to whom he made that promise and his blessing was fullfilled. As a soldier, I had the opportunity to save many lives. I have spent many years searching for my wife and son. A few days ago, I found their graves. I have a premonition that this is my last Yom Kippur. I am going to live my remaining days in the village where they are buried, so that I may be buried next to them. Please promise me that you will continue the tradition of reciting *kaddish* after *Kol Nidre* in my memory."

To this day, *kaddish* is still recited after *Kol Nidre* in the *Alt-neu shul* in Prague.

The mourner, through the recitation of *kaddish*, declares his faith after the anguishing pain of losing a loved one. He also affirms his faith in God and in the eternity of the Jewish people. The mourner who recites the *kaddish* reaches out to God for strength and consolation, knowing that the memory of his loved one crosses the span of time.

Prayers Must Ascend

At the start of a glorious spring day, the Baal Shem Tov[1] walked with a group of students toward the *shul*.

The sun was ascending in the heavens as a whirling wind gusted through the treetops. The Baal Shem Tov's *tallis* flapped wildly, sometimes almost covering the two students who walked on either side of him.

When they reached the *shul*, Baruch hastened to open the door so that his rebbe could enter first. But the Baal Shem Tov stood at the doorway, as if glued to the spot.

"Rebbe," Baruch spoke gently, "I have opened the door for you. Please, won't you enter the *shul*?"

"I can't go in there," whispered the Baal Shem Tov. "It is too crowded inside!"

Baruch peered over the Baal Shem Tov's shoulder. He knew they were the first to arrive for morning prayers. He

D. H. Rabinowicz. *A Guide to Chassidism*. London: Thomas Yoseloff, 1960.

[1]For a biography of Rebbe Yisrael ben Eliezer, the Baal Shem Tov, founder of the chasidic movement, see footnote 3, page 60.

hadn't noticed any other worshipers inside. He didn't understand, so he repeated:

"Rebbe, the door is open. Won't you please enter?"

Once again the Baal Shem Tov shook his head. He stood
quietly, refusing to move. All the students were clearly puzzled
by his actions and asked:

"Rebbe, we still don't understand; we can't see anyone
inside the shul."

Thereupon, the Baal Shem Tov answered "The *shul* is
crowded, but not with people. All of yesterday's *tefillos* have
remained on the benches because they were not offered with the
proper devotion. When Baruch opened the door, I could not
enter because yesterday's prayers blocked the way. That's why
I said the *shul* was too crowded. I am waiting for yesterday's
tefillos to ascend. In the meantime, I am certain that if we pray
today with fervent devotion, as we should at all times, then
yesterday's *tefillos* will ascend together with today's."

It Will Outweigh Them All

Rebbe Layve Yitzchak of Berditchev[1] pondered over the letter he had received a few days before from Rebbe Boruch of Medziboz.[2]

He sat on a low chair in his *bays midrash*, shoulders stooped, head resting in his hands, trying to decipher the message. He turned the paper over and over, hoping the message would become clearer. True, he understood the words, but he could not understand the real intent of the letter.

"I want to warn you," Rebbe Boruch had written, "that the prosecuting angel is doing everything possible to indict the Jewish people before the Master of the World. He is building a wall to block their prayers from ascending before the Throne of

---

Menachem Mendel. *Sepuray Hachag. Rosh Hashanah.* Defus Hanachal. op. cit.

[1]A detailed biography of Rebbe Layve Yitzchak of Berdichev may be found in footnote 1, p. 118.

[2]Rebbe Boruch of Medziboz (1757–1811),the son of Udel, daughter of the Baal Shem Tov, continued spreading the tenets of the chasidic movement started by his grandfather.

243

Glory so they will not be able to nullify his indictment. I beseech you to find a way to stop him.''

Rebbe Layve Yitzchak sat disheartened for a long time. ''What special powers does Rebbe Boruch think I have? What can I possibly do to outmaneuver the prosecuting angel?'' he cried.

Mentally, he reviewed his normal preparations for the coming Holy Days, beginning with the recitation of *selichos*.[3]

''I always prepare with such careful intent,'' he pondered. ''How can I change my actions to have an impact on the prosecuting angel? What must I do differently this year than I do normally? It is only a few days until *selichos*, and I have already started reviewing the talmudic tractate of Rosh Hashanah. On *selichos* night I will immerse myself forty-two times in the *mikveh*. Then I will recite prayers lamenting the destruction of the Holy Temple. I will fervently beseech the Almighty for the redemption of His people from this bitter exile. What more can I do to fight the prosecuting angel, to make certain that he does not block our prayers from ascending to the Throne of Glory?''

He was deeply disturbed. He felt that Rebbe Boruch had placed an awesome burden of responsibility upon his shoulders.

Suddenly, a passage from the Rashi commentary on the Jacob and Esau story flashed before his mind. ''I know what I must do. I must do what our patriarch Jacob did when he met his adversary.[4] I will pray, fight, or give a present. One of these will surely help. It must help!''

Early on *selichos* night, Rebbe Layve Yitzchak immersed himself forty-two times in the *mikveh*, donned a white *kittel*, and walked slowly, painfully to the empty *shul*. He entered, lit a few candles and placed them on a bench. Then he sat down on the floor, opened his prayer book, and started reciting the prayers lamenting the destruction of the Holy Temple. He

---

[3]*Selichos*, special prayers of forgiveness, are recited for a minimum of four days before Rosh Hashanah.

[4]Jacob prepared himself in three ways to meet with Esau: He would offer presents, he would pray, and if these failed, as a last resort, he was prepared to fight. Rashi, Genesis 32:8.

formed the words with his lips and uttered the sounds, but the prayers he uttered were lifeless, spiritless, like a body without a soul.

"I have to break the barrier between me and the Holy One, Blessed Be He!" he cried out. "I have to, I have to do it before all the worshipers arrive!" He pulled himself up to his full height, lifted his head heavenward and shouted, "Master of the World! Listen to me! At least You can act toward us like an ordinary Jew acts toward You in the marketplace. If, Heaven forbid, the *tefillin* of an ordinary Jew fall to the ground, You know that he bends down, picks them up and kisses them. We, the Jewish people are your *tefillin*. We have been living in this bitter exile for so long, persecuted and oppressed. We, Your *tefillin* are lying on the ground. Why don't You bend down and lift us up closer to You?" He waited, silently. He felt a little better, but he was still not certain that he had defeated the prosecuting angel.

When the people arrived for *selichos*, he ascended the *bimah*, but stood bent over the *shtender*, grasping its sides for support, waiting patiently for the opportune moment to begin in a fighting mood. He wanted to make certain that his prayers would reach the Throne of Glory without the prosecuting angel suspecting his intentions and interfering with their flight.

Finally, Rebbe Layve Yitzchak lifted his arms and cried out "You are the righteous One, and we are ashamed of our deeds."[5] Before the worshipers had a chance to understand, he stopped short, realizing that his words were appropriate for fighting with the Almighty, which was his second plan of action.

"What do we mean, 'You are the righteous One, and we are ashamed of our deeds.' Master of the World. Is it not enough that we are slain and slaughtered for Your Holy Name, only because we recite '*Sh'ma Yisrael*, Hear O Israel!' twice each day? Are we the ones who have to hide our faces in the dust, are we the ones who should be ashamed? On the contrary! Why aren't the people who persecute us ashamed of their deeds? Because of You, we have been exiled among the nations of the world! You must immediately declare that we are righteous and

[5]Introduction to *selichos*.

that You forgive all our sins. You must renew for us a blessed New Year, and only then will we consider that You are righteous!''

He stopped, gasping. The worshipers were stunned. Rebbe Layve Yitzchak did not move. He was watching the *selichos* prayers ascend. He followed their flight, higher and higher, but they stopped short of the Throne of Glory. It was as if the prayers were tapping gently at the Gates of Heaven but did not have the power to enter.

He knew that he had not won the battle with the prosecuting angel. Sadly, he trudged out of the *shul* and wandered aimlessly through the dark streets and deserted alleyways of the poor section of Berdichev, searching for a present that he could bring to the Almighty.

At the last dilapidated hut on the outskirts of the *shtetl*, he knocked on the door, and gently pushed it ajar. A young woman sat on a broken chair whispering the words of the psalms from a tattered prayer book. When she recognized Rebbe Layve Yitzchak, she stammered agitatedly. "Rebbe, what are you doing here on this *selichos* night? You usually visit sinners at this time, trying to show them the way to repent. You must think I sinned. I did sin, but it was such a long time ago, I thought that I had done everything to cleanse myself."

"Yes, your repentance was accepted," Rebbe Layve Yitzchak said soothingly. "I know that it is difficult to talk about the past, but could you please tell me again what happened? I have to know. I have a special reason for asking you to repeat the story."

Brokenly, the young woman spoke. "I was 17 years old when my parents died. They had earned their living by supplying the *poretz* with dairy products. I knew how to milk the cows, how to make the butter and cheese. I wanted to continue their business, so I could care for myself. I went to the manor house to speak to the *poretz*. I begged him not to evict me from the land that my parents had leased from him. Before I could finish, he grabbed me. I wriggled free of his grasp and ran. He shouted after me, "Wait! Don't run! I won't hurt you! I will not evict you. You may continue bringing milk and cheese to the manor."

He caught up with me and whispered, 'Before you leave, please let me touch your long blond braids just once.'

He reached for them and stroked them before I could run away. When I returned here, I tried to find some peace for myself, but I could not rest. All night I was plagued with disgust that he had touched my braids. I felt defiled. In the morning, I took a knife and cut them off."

"Where are the braids?" gently prodded Rebbe Layve Yitzchak.

"Rebbe, do you really need them?" she asked.

"Please, give them to me," he urged.

She went to a small chest, took out the braids and handed them to the rebbe.

The first day of Rosh Hashanah, the worshipers waited for Rebbe Layve Yitzchak to return from the *mikveh* to sound the *shofar*. There was a hush of expectancy in the air, as if they anticipated something unusual. He rushed into the *shul*, carrying a small package. He ran up to the pulpit, removed his *tallis*, laid it on the *shtender*, and placed the package on top of it. Then he stood for a few moments, breathing deeply.

The eyes of the worshipers were fixed on him. Opening the package, he lifted out the braids, raised them above his head, and called out, "Master of the Universe! If you place all our wrongdoings on one side of the scale of judgment and these braids on the other side, You know that these braids will outweigh them all!"

Suddenly, a wild commotion reverberated throughout the Heavenly Court. And the people of Berditchev were convinced that they heard a Voice call out, "My children! The Gates of Heaven are open to receive your prayers."

Daven First

Among the *chasidim* who bade farewell to Rebbe Mordechai Tzernobler[1] after having spent *Shabbos* with him was a simple but honest merchant. Rebbe Mordechai singled him out from the group. "Tell me," he inquired, "how do you spend your days?"

"Well, Rebbe," he responded, "I rise very early in the morning. Immediately, I wash my hands, I dress, and I go directly to the marketplace to buy whatever I need for that day from the farmers who come into town to sell their merchandise. When I finish there, I return home and I *daven*."

"You should not delay *davening*," said Rebbe Mordechai. "First, you should *daven*, then you should conduct your business."

"But," said the merchant, "you don't understand. "If I

G. Mah-Tov. *Ma-a-say-hem shel Tzaddikim*, op. cit.
[1] Mordechai the son of Rebbe Nachum Tzernobler (1770–1836), the son of Rebbe Nachum Tzernobler, inherited all his father's qualities. However, unlike his father who lived in poverty all his life, Rebbe Mordechai's disciples supported him in comfort.

take the time to *daven* first, all the farmers will have sold their merchandise to other merchants who arrive earlier, and there will be nothing left for me to buy."

"Let me tell you a story," said Rebbe Mordechai.

"Once there was a very resourceful traveling salesman who had amassed a fortune. At the end of a very successful business trip, he found that he had earned twelve gold coins and one copper coin. He had reached the end of his usual route and was ready to return home, but being very tired he decided to remain in that *shtetl* until after *Shabbos*. Knowing that his coins were very valuable, he wanted to leave them locked up over *Shabbos* with someone he trusted. On inquiring he was assured that the innkeeper was honest, so he made arrangements to stay there and leave his coins locked in the innkeeper's strongbox.

"All of the twenty-five hours of *Shabbos*, he was plagued with doubt. Could he depend on the innkeeper's honesty? What if he refused to return his gold coins to him? What if he ran off with his money? The merchant did not enjoy the *Shabbos* food, he could not concentrate on the *Shabbos* prayers, nor could he sleep *Shabbos* night.

"As soon as *Shabbos* was over, the merchant ran to the innkeeper and asked him to return the bag of coins that he had locked in his strongbox. Seeing his guest so agitated, the innkeeper stopped what he was doing, went to the room where he had locked up the valuable coins, and retrieved them. The merchant opened the small bag and counted the gold coins. He breathed a sigh of relief when he found all twelve. Then he remembered that he had not seen the copper coin. Even before he looked, he suspected that the innkeeper had taken his copper coin. How foolish he felt when he removed the gold coins and found the copper coin at the bottom of the bag."

"Now," Rebbe Mordechai lowered his voice, "do you see how foolishly the merchant acted? If he counted the twelve gold coins and found them all, why would he suspect that the innkeeper had taken the least precious coin?

"I need to teach you the lesson of this story. You entrust your soul to the Hands of your Creator every night. It is your most precious possession, like the gold coins that belonged to the merchant. Yet, when you arise each morning, and you realize that your most precious possession has been returned to you in purity and in holiness, you doubt that you'll be able to make a living; your sustenance, your copper coin, will be denied you. You run off to the marketplace and delay thanking God for returning to you your most precious possession. If you really believed that your soul was more precious, you would not delay *davening*. You would thank your Creator first, and trust that He would see to your sustenance."

The merchant understood his rebbe's parable. From then on, he rose, washed his hands, *davened*, and *then* went to the marketplace to attend to business matters.

Rebbe Zev Tzve's Tefillin

Growing up in the *shtetl* demanded conformity to a religious way of life, especially if your father happened to be Rebbe Yechiel Michel of Zlotchov,[1] a descendant of a long line of rabbis, and more especially if he were known as the maggid of all the Jewish communities in the area, and still more especially if he had already raised four scholarly sons who were following in his footsteps.

But Zev Tzve, the fifth son, was different. He liked to play rather than study, and it seemed that he would never be as scholarly as his brothers. The *bahelfer* escorted him to the *cheder*, but he ran off into the woods when the *melamed* was not looking. Then he ran around, playing hide-and-seek among the trees. Sometimes, he signaled to a comrade in the *cheder* that he was about to sneak away, and thus assured himself of another companion.

This story was told by Rabbi Shlomo Carlebach at the Rainbow Conference in Pasadena, California, in 1979.

[1]See the biography of Rebbe Yechiel Michel of Zlotchov in footnote 1, p. 151.

When his father asked him what he had learned in *cheder* that day, he had no answer. Years passed. Zev Tzve played while his contemporaries learned.

His mischievousness grieved his parents. They scolded and lectured, they punished, but nothing seemed to change Zev Tzve's behavior. Rebbe Yechiel Michel was at his wit's end.

Zev Tzve's *bar mitzvah* day approached and Rebbe Yechiel Michel did not know how to make his son understand that he would soon be responsible for his actions, that he had to be serious about his religious studies, that playtime was over.

According to tradition, one month before a boy's *bar mitzvah*, he begins donning his *tefillin*, a *mitzvah* that he commits himself to observe for the rest of his life. Rebbe Yechiel Michel had commissioned the *shtetl sofer*,[2] to write a special pair of *tefillin* for Zev Tzve.

The day before Zev Tzve was to begin donning his *tefillin*, Rebbe Yechiel Michel sat in his study, inspecting the *sofer*'s work. He carefully read the sections of the Torah that the *sofer* had written to place into the black boxes. When he reached the verse: "And you shall teach them to your children and speak about them when you sit in your house and when you walk by the way, when you lie down and when you rise up. . ."[3] He completely lost control of his emotions. Tears welled up in his eyes. He sighed and shuddered, alternately hitting the table with his hands and raising them toward Heaven in prayer, tormented by his son's behavior.

At that moment, Zev Tzve was chasing a companion through the house. They had moved their hide-and-seek game indoors. As he passed the open door of his father's study, he saw him weeping. He stood silently, hiding behind the open door, watching his father. The tears ran down his father's cheeks onto the parchment of the *tefillin*. Still shaking, Rebbe Yechiel Michel placed the wet parchment into the black boxes. Zev Tzve stood silently, watching the pain on his father's face as he prepared the *tefillin* for the next day. His father's tears left an indelible impression on him. "I never understood before now how much pain I've caused my parents," he thought.

[2]The *sofer* (scribe) writes Torah scrolls, *tefillin*, *mezuzos*, and *megillos* on parchment with special pen and ink.
[3]Deuteronomy 6:7.

That moment was the turning point in his life, and he later became Rebbe Zev Tzve of Zabarz. People referred to him and his four older brothers as cedar trees, a metaphor for righteousness, scholarship, and physical strength, each one representing one of the five holy books of the Torah.

Shvartze Wolf

The Rebbe of Tzeznikov, after eighteen years of marriage, was still childless. He had heard that the blessings of the Koshnitzer Maggid[1] were fulfilled, so in desperation, he sought his help.

Facing the maggid, the Rebbe of Tzeznikov pleaded "Please, holy master, bless my wife and me with children. We have been married for eighteen years and we will soon be too old to have children. We don't want to die without leaving children to follow us."

The maggid listened quietly; then he said softly, "I want you to know that all the gates of heaven are closed to my prayers on your behalf."

Tears welled up in the eyes of the Rebbe of Tzeznikov. Bitterly, he cried out, "Do you know what it means to leave this

Rabbi Shlomo Carlebach told this story at a concert in Jerusalem.

[1]Rebbe Yisrael Haupstein, the Maggid of Koshnitz (1737–1815), was known not only as a talmudic scholar, but also as a mystic and a miracle worker. He was greatly influenced by the kabbalistic writings of the Maharal, Rabbi Yehuda Loew ben Bezalel, creator of the Golem. For almost fifty years, the Koshnitzer Maggid lovingly served his people, bringing them closer to the service of the Almighty.

world childless? I refuse to accept that you can't open the gates of heaven for my prayers. Nobody in this world can open the gates of heaven like you. Nobody in this world can bless us with children like you. Please, please, bless us with children."

His shoulders shook, his entire body shuddered, his moans rent the air. He fell to the ground in a faint. After a long while, he looked at the Maggid and pleaded again:

"Please, please, bless us with children!"

The Maggid sat silently, deep in thought.

Finally, he said, "By any chance, do you know a Jew by the name of Shvartze Wolf who lives in the forest near your *shtetl*?"

The rebbe calmed himself in order to answer the question. "Yes, I know a Jew named Shvartze Wolf," he said. "People say that he is a woodcutter. He rarely comes to *shul*. When he does, the people run and hide from him. No one wants to have anything to do with him, and he doesn't want to have anything to do with anyone in the *shtetl*, either. He is repulsive."

The Maggid whispered, "That is the person I mean. I want you to know that he is one of the hidden *lamed vav tzaddikim*.[2] In fact, he is their leader. Try to have him invite you to his home one *Shabbos*. He is the only one that I know that can open the gates of heaven on your behalf. He is the only one that can bless you."

The Rebbe of Tzeznikov left in a state of shock. Not knowing exactly how to proceed, he nonetheless formulated a plan that he thought would yield the desired result, to spend *Shabbos* with Shvartze Wolf. First, he recited all 150 psalms with great intent, then he deliberated how he could improve his deeds to be more pleasing to God and to man. He set aside 10 percent of everything he owned for charity, immersed himself in the *mikveh*, prayed that if the Almighty would bless him with children, he would do anything the Almighty demanded of him in return, said goodbye to his wife, and set off for the forest.

It was well known that no one had ever been invited to the house of Shvartze Wolf, not for a meal, not for a holy day, certainly not for *Shabbos*. The Rebbe of Tzeznikov decided that

[2]The *lamed vav tzaddikim* are the hidden thirty-six righteous people in every generation who, it is believed, sustain the world because of their meritorious lives. Talmud *Bavli, Succah* 45b.

the only way he could possibly achieve his goal was to pretend that he was lost in the forest. He thought, "Maybe, Shvartze Wolf will have compassion on me and invite me for *Shabbos.*"

He waited until two minutes before *Shabbos* to rap on the door of the woodcutter's cottage. The door was opened by a very ugly woman demanding to know what he wanted. "What are you doing here two minutes before *Shabbos*?" she sneered.

Trembling, he replied, "I am lost in the forest. I need a place to spend *Shabbos.* Would you please let me spend *Shabbos* in your house?"

She tried to slam the door in his face, but he reacted quickly. Pushing himself against the door, he stuck his foot into the opening. The door moved inward a bit. He looked inside the cottage and saw the ugliest children, dressed in the most mismatched clothing he had ever seen, sitting on the bare floor, waiting for their mother to kindle the *Shabbos* candles.

Knowing that he had never seen ugly children, he felt that there was some character flaw within himself that made them appear that way. He had learned once that if the *lamed vav tzaddik* or his family appear ugly, then the person who sees them sees an exact reflection of his own soul. Therefore, he was more determined than ever to spend *Shabbos* in that cottage, for he wanted to heal himself. He repeated his request more firmly. "Please, I have lost my way in the forest. I need to have a place to spend *Shabbos*, for I am sure that I will be unable to find my way back to the *shtetl* before nightfall."

Finally, his plea struck a compassionate chord in her soul.

She pointed to a weather-beaten stable in a small clearing among the trees. "Do you see that stable?"

He nodded.

"Well, there is a horse in that stable and a pile of hay. You will be out of danger for the night if you stay there. Make sure you don't do anything to arouse my husband's suspicions because he would be very angry if he found you."

The Rebbe of Tzeznikov removed his foot from the doorway and sadly walked toward the stable. He knew he had lost his attempt to spend *Shabbos* with Shvartze Wolf. He entered and saw the last rays of light through a slit in the roof and sat down on the hay strewn earthen floor. He withdrew two small candlesticks and two candles from his knapsack, two small *challos*, a bottle of wine, and a small package of chicken that his wife had given him before he left.

He placed the candles where their soft glow might not be noticed by Shvartze Wolf. He chose a wall where he could pray. He leaned against the wall, and buried his head in the crook of one elbow. And he wept.

The sun was no longer to be seen. Night had fallen. The Rebbe of Tzeznikov had no idea how much time had passed. He knew only that when he heard plodding steps approaching, it was completely dark.

Shvartze Wolf opened the door and shouted into the stable, "I know you are in there. Whoever you are, you'd better not come near my house tomorrow, the entire day of *Shabbos*. And as soon as you see three stars in the sky, as soon as *Shabbos* is over, you'd better leave. I mean it. Don't let me catch you around here after *Shabbos!*"

Shvartze Wolf's shouts terrorized the Rebbe of Tzeznikov. His heart fluttered, he crouched in a corner of the stable, intimidated, despairing that he would ever be able to approach him for a blessing.

As Shvartze Wolf slammed the door, the Rebbe of Tzeznikov imagined that he had seen a gruesome human form resembling a witch.

When he had calmed down, he stretched out on the hay going over what had happened.

"Imagine," he thought, "I am so close to Shvartze Wolf's house and all I need is one blessing. My life is passing so rapidly. I don't know what to do any more. The blessing seems beyond my grasp." Despondently, he fell into a deep sleep.

The next morning he was overpowered with the same depression that had seized him the night before. Unable to move, he sat in a corner praying. Late in the afternoon, noticing the rays of the sun beginning to descend into the treetops, he came to the realization that his opportunity for a blessing from Shvartze Wolf would soon pass, that he would die without children.

"Maybe the answer is within me," he thought. "Maybe I should not give up hope. I will pray to the Almighty for children once more."

He moved to the wall where his prayers had welcomed the

Shabbos Queen the night before, and poured out his heart and soul to the Almighty.

Suddenly, he felt a soft hand on his shoulder. He turned from the wall and stood face to face with Shvartze Wolf who had been transformed into the most handsome man he had ever seen. He imagined that the face of Shvartze Wolf shone like the face of the High Priest when he emerged from the Holy of Holies on Yom Kippur.

Shvartze Wolf spoke. "I would like to invite you to join my family and me for *sholosh seudos*, the third meal of *Shabbos*." He felt Shvartze Wolf's hand tighten on his shoulder as he gently led him out of the stable toward the house.

Shvartze Wolf's wife and children had also been transformed into beautiful people. They were dressed in exquisite *Shabbos* clothes. The Rebbe imagined that Shvartze Wolf's house was as beautiful as the rebuilt Holy Temple. He hoped that the beauty he now saw meant that his character flaw had been corrected.

Shvartze Wolf was the first to speak. Gently, he said "I know why you came to spend *Shabbos* in the forest. I bless you that you will have a child in the coming year. I have only one request: please name your son after me!"

The Rebbe of Tzeznikov thought, "How can I name my son after him, when he is still alive?" Thanking Shvartze Wolf for his blessing, the rebbe departed after *havdalah*.

Excitedly, he ran through the forest to the outskirts of the *shtetl*. Panting, he burst into his house and yelled at the top of his lungs, "I received the blessing of Shvartze Wolf! I received the blessing of Shvartze Wolf!"

His joy was short-lived, for the next morning, when he arrived at the *shul* for the morning service, he was told that Shvartze Wolf had died during the night and no one wanted to go to his funeral! The Rebbe stood glued to the spot, aghast at the news. He murmured, "Shvartze Wolf, Shvartze Wolf, he was such a holy man. None of us ever extended any courtesy to him, we never spoke to him, we never wished him 'Good Shabbos,' we never gave him an *aliyah*, we never made him comfortable in our midst. But I want you to know that he was one of the *lamed vav tzaddikim*; in fact, he was the leader of the *lamed vav tzaddikim*."

Shvartze Wolf's blessing for a child for the rebbe and rebbetzen of Tzeznikov was fulfilled, but the story does not end there.

* * *

In 1944, the Belzer Rebbe, after escaping from Hitler's Europe, made *aliyah* to the Holy Land.[3]

On his first *Shabbos* in Tel Aviv, he invited the entire community for *kiddush* after the *Shabbos* morning service. It was his custom to bless everyone who came to partake of his *kiddush*. Men, one by one, walked up to the front of the room where he sat. They told him their names and the names of their parents, and he would bless them.

Everyone moved aside as an old *yiddele* made his way through the crowd. As he neared the front of the room, the Belzer Rebbe called out "*Mein ti-reh yiddele* (my precious Jew), what is your name?"

The *yiddele* called back, "Rebbe, my name is Shvartze Wolf ben Chanun."

The Belzer Rebbe then asked, "Are you the great grandson of the Shvartze Wolf who was named for the *lamed vav tzaddik?*"

Shvartze Wolf ben Chanun replied "Rebbe, do you really know the story?"

"Yes," sighed the Belzer Rebbe. "*I* know the story of Shvartze Wolf, but no one else does. I want *you* to tell the story, so everyone here will remember the original Shvartze Wolf." Some *chasidim* lifted the old *yiddele* onto a table, and he told the story.

[3]Rebbe Shalom Rokeach (1799–1855) was the founder of the Belz dynasty. Influenced by the Maggid of Koshnitz and the Seer of Lublin, he settled in Belz, a small *shtetl* north of Lemberg, where he guided followers from Galicia, Hungary, and Poland. In the magnificent *shul* he built there, his followers observed the meaning of devotion in prayer, intensity in learning, and no compromise with the alien influences that were beginning to penetrate Jewish life. The Belzer dynasty flourished for generations. During the Holocaust, the then Belzer rebbe, Aaron Rokeach (died 1957), was smuggled out of Hungary to Eretz Yisrael, and began the process of rebuilding the community that was decimated. Today, Belzer *chasidim* live all over the world, supporting institutions ranging from kindergartens to old-age homes, *yeshivos*, free dental and medical clinics, free loan societies, and food for the needy.

Rabbi Shlomo Carlebach heard the story from a man who was at the Belzer Rebbe's *Kiddush* that *Shabbos* in Tel Aviv in 1944. Recently, he retold it at a concert in *Binyanay Haumah* in Jerusalem. When he had finished, a young man waved his hand wildly to gain Shlomo's attention. When he was acknowledged, he recounted, "I want you to know that in my yeshiva class in B'nay B'rak, there is a young man named Shvartze Wolf. He is the grandson of the Shvartze Wolf who told the story to the Belzer Rebbe, who was the great-great-grandson of the Rebbe of Tzeznikov, who had named *his* son after the original *lamed vav tzaddik*."

Shlomo begged his audience, "In the future, when you walk down the streets of Jerusalem or B'nay B'rak, if you happen to meet someone named Shvartze Wolf . . . when you arrive home, tell the original story to your children for posterity."

Playing Rebbe

Today, in the ninth decade of the twentieth century, the imagination of children is fired by "Star Wars" and computer technology. The games they play imitate Luke Skywalker or Darth Vader. Because of the advancement in space exploration, visits to other planets are not unrealistic.

No such fantasies were possible in the *shtetlach* of the old country. The most exciting game children could play was imitating their elders.

So it was that the brothers Shalom Dov Ber, age 5, and Zorach Ahron, age 8, sitting on the steps of their front porch, decided to play rebbe and *chasid* one day.[1]

"Since I am the oldest," decided Zorach Ahron, "I will be the rebbe. You, Shalom Ber, can be my *chasid*. You come to me

Many Lubavitcher chasidim the authors consulted know this story; however, they were not able to pinpoint the source.

[1] Shalom Dov Ber and Zorach Ahron became leaders of the Lubavitch *chasidim* in the second-half of the nineteenth century. For the biography of the founder of Lubavitch and the history of the dynasty he founded, see footnote 3, pp. 210–211.

with a problem. We will start the game in ten mintues. I have to dress up.''

Quick as a flash, Zorach Ahron ran inside the house. He took his father's Shabbos *bekasheh*, *gartel*, and *shtreimel* from their place in the wardrobe and put them on. The coat trailed inches behind him as he sneaked into the study room, making sure no one saw him. He sat down on a chair, opened one of the holy books that his father had been studying, and began humming and shaking to the interior rhythm of the words that he as yet did not understand. After a few mintues, he called out, "Shalom Ber, you can come in now!" He closed his eyes, pretending to be deep in thought.

Shalom Ber hobbled into the study room. His facial expression was that of a deeply disturbed, heartbroken old man. Slowly, he moved toward the table where Zorach Ahron sat, emphasizing that the burden of his problem was weighing him down.

"Shalom Ber, it is always so good to see you, but today you look so troubled. How can I help you?"

Timidly, Shalom Ber answered, "Rebbe, something terrible happened."

He paused, waiting for the "rebbe's" reaction. Zorach Ahron picked up his cue. "Nu, nu, so tell me, what terrible thing happened?"

Shalom Ber put his hands on the edge of the table, shifted his weight from side to side, finally whispered in a strained voice, "You will never believe that this morning, after I finished my breakfast, I forgot to *bench* (recite the blessings after meals)!"

Zorach Ahron lifted his hand to his chin, pretending to stroke the beard that had not yet grown. He sat silently for a few moments, trying to evaluate the situation. Finally he said, "I'll tell you what you must do so it shouldn't happen again. The reason that you forget to *bench* is that you relied on your memory. To help you remember that you must *bench*, use a *siddur* at all times!"

Shalom Ber was not impressed with his brother's solution. He exploded. "Ha! You call yourself a rebbe? I came to you for help with a serious problem! And all you can tell me is to use a *siddur*? You're not a real rebbe!"

Zorach Ahron countered. "What are you talking about? What do you mean I'm not a real rebbe? Last week, a *chasid* came to our father with the same problem. Our father told him to *bench* with a *siddur*. What did I do wrong?"

Shalom Ber said triumphantly: "The difference between your answer and our father's answer is this. When the *chasid* told him what happened, our father *krechtzed* and cried out, "Oy Vey!" You could tell that he felt the pain of his *chasid*. You didn't even *krechtz*. My problem didn't even hurt you! You didn't play the part of the rebbe correctly!"

A Shining Jew

Rebbe Avraham of Slonim had occasion to spend a few days in an isolated inn located on the estate of a wealthy *poretz*.[1] The inn was leased to a Jew.

Each morning, when he emerged from his room to join the other guests for breakfast, he noticed that the innkeeper had a shining countenance and seemed exceptionally happy. He wondered why the innkeeper could possibly be so happy.

"Innkeeping is not a lucrative business," thought the rebbe. "It is apparent that this Jew barely ekes out a living. He has to serve peasants all day long. He has to keep the inn spotlessly clean. He is responsible to the *poretz* for the rent. I have to find the reason for his peaceful countenance."

After the other guests had gone, the rebbe approached the

Rebbe Avrahom Weinberg Saba Kadisha M'Slonim. *Baer Avrahom.* Jerusalem: Yeshivas Bays Avraham, 1975.

[1]Although he was the *rosh yeshiva* of Slonim, Rebbe Avraham Weinberg (died 1884) was very poor. A humble *tzaddik*, he insisted that his Torah thoughts not be published. Unlike most, when he prayed, his voice was inaudible, his body did not move. Yet his ecstatically glowing face reflected the intensity of his prayer.

innkeeper and introduced himself. "I am Rebbe Avraham, the Rebbe of Slonim," he said. "I have been traveling, and I decided to stay in your inn a few days to rest. From the day I arrived, something has intrigued me. Can you please tell me to what you attribute your cheerful face?"

At first the innkeeper was hesitant. Finally, he said softly, "I've lived in this isolated area, far from a Jewish community, all my life. I never had the benefit of a decent Jewish education. In fact, by most standards, you might call me an ordinary or illiterate Jew. I have very little contact with any of my people. I try to earn an honest living, but, believe me, it is very difficult to provide for my family."

The rebbe still did not know why the innkeeper had such a contented look. He persisted. "You live like many Jewish innkeepers, but none I have met have this special look that you have. Please, tell me your secret."

The innkeeper sighed, "You see, I don't even know how to pray from a *siddur*. However, I do know that a Jew is supposed to pray. So every evening, before I retire for the night, I recite this one prayer, 'O Master of the Universe, if You don't think that I will live up to Your expectations tomorrow, then don't awaken me. However, if You think that I will fulfill Your Will, then please bless me with another day.' "

Joyful tears streamed down the face of the rebbe, because he had never heard such a profound prayer. He now understood why the innkeeper was blessed with that look of peace and contentment.

An Unforgettable Melody

"Psst, Moshe Chasid, wake up, you overslept, you won't have time to but on *tallis* and *tefillin* before roll call. Hurry," urged Uri.

Moshe Chasid opened his eyes and stretched for a split second on the hard wooden plank that served as his bed. He jumped up, grabbed the threadbare shirt that also served as a blanket and put it on. He moved silently, not wanting to awaken the other men who slept on similar planks around him.

"I have been incarcerated here so long," he thought, "I wonder how much longer I will have to hide my religious observances; how much longer I will have to be the object of these people's scorn. It is almost impossible for Uri and me to live as Jews."

Moshe Chasid was one of the early Prisoners of Zion who were sent to the prison labor camp in Monchegorsk, near Murmansk, a port city just west of the Barents Sea.[1] It was a desolate place where the sun never rose in the winter, and only

Menachem Mendel. *Otzar Hachag, Shevuos,* op. cit. 1984, p. 198.
[1]The term "Prisoners of Zion" was already known in the 1920s.

shone for a few short months in the summer. He was one of the second generation of Zionist leaders, encouraging *aliyah* Palestine as an escape from the continuous pogroms in his motherland.[2] Therefore, he was accused of being an agent of British imperialism and sentenced to eight years in prison.[3]

It was here that he met Uri. Among all the prisoners, including many Jews who had been sent to labor camps as antigovernment agitators, they were the only religiously observant ones.

Somehow, the Jews gravitated toward Moshe Chasid and Uri, for in prison, cut off from their people, they yearned for familiar voices and faces. Sometimes, after a backbreaking day's work quarrying rock, which was freight-trained to Moscow for building purposes, fifty men gathered around Moshe Chasid's plank bed to listen to stories of how his father and his grandfather before him celebrated *Shabbos* and the holy days. The stories eased their pain and loneliness.

Now, as the month of Sivan approached, Moshe Chasid planned a clandestine celebration.[4]

"We have a problem," he told them three nights before the holiday. "We have to see if any of us can feign illness, so as not to be forced to work. The rest of us will have to celebrate the Day of Revelation, the day of the giving of Torah while at forced labor! Let's think of a plan to make this day different from any other work day."

"Maybe, we can all line up together," suggested Uri. "When the men begin to march toward the quarries, we can lag behind. As we march forward, slower than the rest, you can lead us in the holiday prayers. That way, at least, we will know that it is a special day."

"At lunchtime, let's all sit together," interrupted Yosef enthusiastically. "It will be as if we are eating a holiday meal. We can even recite the *kiddush* over our bread."

[2]During the 1930s, repression, persecution, and political purges characterized the Stalinist regime. The secret police concentrated on eliminating those elements of the population who might be disloyal in the event of war.

[3]The British government had promulgated the Balfour Declaration on November 2, 1917, pledging their support for the establishment of a Jewish national homeland in Palestine.

[4]The holiday of Shevuos is celebrated in Sivan.

"We might even be able to sing some holiday melodies, if we sit far enough away from the rest of the camp," added Beni.

"These are all great ideas," agreed Moshe Chasid. "Let's hope they work out."

Moshe Chasid could not sleep on Shevuos night. He remembered his childhood, how he used to go with his father to the rebbe, how the *shul* resounded with songs of joy in honor of the Revelation of the Torah. It was as if every Jew in that *shtetl* stood at Mt. Sinai. Tears rolled down his cheeks. Now he was lying on a hard wooden plank in a prison labor camp a million miles away from home with no Torah, no celebration, no joy.

"What can I do?" he thought helplessly. For a few minutes despair overtook him, but then a voice whispered, "Sad? Helpless? You, Moshe Chasid. They have imprisoned your body, but you know that they cannot imprison your mind!"

He sat up on the plank, startled. "I have no Torah scroll here to read, and no book to study, but I remember a lot by heart from my yeshiva days. I can celebrate Shevuos my own way here. I can review everything that I remember," he reasoned.

He threw his feet over the edge of the plank, lowered his head into his hands and began chanting softly:

"In the beginning God created heaven and earth and the earth was desolate and disordered and darkness was over the turmoil and the Breath of God hovered above the waters."[5]

He chanted what he remembered from the Torah throughout the night.

In the morning, the Jews stayed together during roll call. They looked quizzically at one another. No one understood what could have happened to make Moshe Chasid's face shine so in the desolate prison labor camp. He stepped into the center of the group and they paced around him slowly as he chanted the holy day prayers fervently.

As he chanted, Moshe Chasid noticed out of the corner of his eye that Yaakov Kovnoey, the recent arrival in the prison labor camp, stood apart from the worshipers, keeping his distance from them. He was not a part of them, but he was never far from them.

It was rumored that he was a native of Kovno, Lithuania,

[5]Genesis 1:1,2.

that he had agitated against the Communist party, that he had been arrested and imprisoned when the Soviets marched into his native country in 1940.

Moshe Chasid continued chanting fervently; his previous night's experience had added to his determination to strengthen his fellow prisoners. Fifty men joined him. Some repeated the almost-forgotten words barely audibly, others hummed softly along as they trudged to work. Yaakov Kovnoey drew closer and closer to the circle of marchers.

By the time Moshe Chasid reached the *Sh'ma Yisrael*, Yaakov Kovnoey was just behind him. When he reached the reader's repetition of the *amidah*, the silent devotion, and then sang out the words, "Our God and God of our forefathers . . . may the remembrance of your entire people Israel before You. . .on this day of the festival of Shevuos . . ." Yaakov Kovnoey was marching in step with him; his lips moved but there was no sound.

Finishing the last words of the *amidah*, Moshe Chasid turned to face Yaakov Kovnoey, who was shaking his shoulder, trying to get his attention. "Today is Shevuos. Aren't you going to recite *Akdamus*?" he demanded.[6]

Moshe Chasid was startled by the sudden intrusion. "*Akdamus*, yes, of course. Jews all over the world recite *Akdamus* on the first day of Shevuos. But unfortunately, the fact is that I don't remember more than the first line."

"Well, if *you* don't remember it," Yaakov Kovnoey lowered his voice still more, "would you mind if I sang it?"

Moshe Chasid looked at Yaakov Kovnoey incredulously. "How do you remember *Akdamus*?"

"That's a long story," he responded. "After we finish praying, if we are still able to stay together as a group, without the interference of the commander, I shall share my story with you. Right now. . ." He began

---

[6]The ninety verses of *Akdamus* were composed in Aramaic by Rabbi Mayer ben Yitzchak, who lived in the eleventh century in Worms, Germany. The prayer poem describes, through mysticism and allegory, God's creation of the world, the angels' praise of the Creator, the greatness of the Jewish people. It is therefore a fitting introduction to the theme of the Revelation at Sinai, the Torah reading on the first day of Shevuos.

Ak-da-mus mi-lin v'sha-ra-yus shu-sa
Av-la sha-kel-na har-man u're-shu-sa . . .

The marchers stopped in their tracks. They had never heard *Akdamus* chanted with such deep emotion. They could not believe their ears nor what they were seeing. The face of Yaakov Kovnoey, the anti-Communist, he who kept his distance from any form of religious observance, was flushed with joy and his voice sounded as if it had joined the ministering angels singing praises to God. His eyes peered into the distance, as if he were in a different world.

Never having heard *Akdamus* chanted with such feeling, Moshe Chasid concentrated on every word. Occasionally he blinked back the tears that had begun to well up in his eyes. Suddenly, he noticed the commander lurking at the edge of the circle. "I wonder if he overheard our chanting. Please, God, please, I hope I haven't endangered the safety of fifty Jews who tried to celebrate Your holy day."

His voice tapered off as the prayer ended. The marchers were forced to focus on the realities of their world, which had been transformed for a few short moments to the sphere of the Heavenly Court.

"What's going on here?" demanded the commander. "You, Yaakov Kovnoey, you haven't spoken a word since you arrived here. I thought that you didn't know how to speak! What were you singing there in the center of the circle? Answer me!"

Yaakov's lips were sealed again. It was as if he hadn't heard the commander demand an explanation. He knew that he didn't care about the consequences of his silence.

All at once, the harshness in the commander's voice eased. "I heard that somber melody you chanted as I walked beside the group at the edge of the circle. It was vaguely familiar. Somehow it brought back memories of my happy childhood. I just can't recall the exact circumstances." His voice trailed off for a moment before he shouted excitedly a few minutes later: "I remember now! I remember why I am familiar with that melody. I must have been about 9 or 10 years old. I grew up on a farm on the outskirts of a village almost entirely inhabited by Jews. My father used to take me into town as a treat. It seems that they all gathered in their synagogue two days each year at the beginning of the summer to celebrate something. When they left the synagogue, they would still be singing that melody as they walked home. Today must be that Jewish holiday, if you were singing that melody. Since you have brought back such happy childhood memories for me, I'll allow you to celebrate your holiday. The freight cars that you were scheduled to load today have not yet arrived. While we are waiting, you can all relax." He walked away.

The Jews looked at each other happily. Uri, turning to Moshe Chasid, urged, "Why don't you teach us Torah in honor of this holiday of Revelation?" And they studied together until their mid-day rations were distributed.

"Since we are still together as a group," suggested Yosef, "and since we are able to celebrate this holiday in some way, I think we should begin this meal with *Kiddush.*"

They recited the holiday *Kiddush* over their bread and then broke forth in joyous song. The sounds of *Akdamus* resounded through the quarry once more. Yaakov Kovnoey sat in the center of the group. When he finished eating, he began slowly, "Now I will tell you my story. My father was a rabbi and a judge in Kovno. He also chanted the Torah reading each *Shabbos* and holiday in the *shul.* I used to love to listen to him prepare the reading before he went to pray as I lay in my bed in the corner of the kitchen. I guess I grew up with the melody of Torah. The year before my *bar mitzvah,* my father taught me to read the Torah. He used to let me sit by his side as he prepared. And I sang the melody with him. He encouraged me to learn more and more and in this way he transmitted his love of Torah to me.

Before the Shevuos of my fifteenth birthday, he suggested, "Yaakov, if you learn *Akdamus* by heart, I will let you chant it before the reading of the Torah."

I desperately wanted to show my father that I was worthy and I did memorize the entire *Akdamus* in time for Shevuos. The people in the *shul* later said that my chanting must be similar to the chanting of the ministering angels. Still later, when I studied in the yeshiva in Kovno, I became the regular Torah reader.

Eventually I traded the world of the yeshiva for the secular world. I became involved with a group of agitators against the Communist government. We were all arrested and sentenced to long terms in prison labor camps. Last night, I had a terrifying dream. I saw the police break into my family's home in Kovno. I saw them shove my father out the door. As he crossed the threshold, he raised his hand to kiss the *mezzuzah*. One of the policemen slapped his hand with such force that he fell down. As he lay there, I heard him whisper "Yankele, Yankele, don't forget to recite *Akdamus* tomorrow."

I awoke startled. I tried to fall asleep again, but the dream repeated itself. This morning, I wondered why all of you marched off to work in a group. I decided to follow you. As you prayed, my father's words seemed to harmonize with the melody of your prayers. Then I knew I had to recite *Akdamus*. Yaakov Kovnoey's voice trailed off.

Uri pleaded, "Please, teach us what you know."

The remainder of that Shevuos day, the words and the melody of *Akdamus* echoed from hill to hill in the stone quarry of the prison labor camp near Monchegorsk.

Sh'ma Yisrael

Lieutenant Dan approached Rabbi Shlomo Carlebach after an outdoor concert he had given for thousands of Israeli soldiers soon after the Yom Kippur War.

"I want to tell you a story," he said, "so that you can tell it often at your concerts. It is a story that must be shared with Jews all over the world." He paused, waiting for Shlomo's reaction.

Shlomo put his arm around the soldier's shoulder and led him away from the crowd. They stopped near some boulders on the side of a road. Shlomo saw the soldier's body quiver and realized that he was crying.

"I want you to know," Lieutenant Dan sobbed, "that I had pretty much regained my composure in the past few days, but your songs reawakened some emotion that started me off once again."

Shlomo gripped his shoulders more vigorously, trying to calm him, as he waited for him to begin speaking.

* * *

During the war I fought in Sinai. The captain of my platoon was very religious,'' mumbled Dan. "His name was Avner. As we fought, side by side, he chanted, *Sh'ma Yisrael A-do-nay E-lo-hay-nu A-do-nay E-chad!*[1] (Hear O Israel, the Lord our God, the Lord is One.)

"I was very annoyed with his chanting, because I was the typical secular, nonobservant Jew. You see, I did not believe that there was a God. In fact, I had even raised my two children to believe that the concept of God is the biggest hoax and that the Jewish people are no more holy than any other people.

During the fighting, I was positioned behind Captain Avner. I heard his continuous, persistent chanting. As soon as he finished *E-chad*, he began all over again with *Sh'ma*. Raising his arm, motioning the soldiers to follow him into battle, he repeated over and over, "*Sh'ma Yisrael A-do-nay E-lo-hay-nu A-do-nay E-chad.*"

I think I was the only one in the platoon who was annoyed by his chanting. Can you imagine, day after day, hour after hour, minute after minute, the sound of *Sh'ma Yisrael*? I literally felt that the chanting would drive me out of my mind. I could not endure his foolish praying.

Finally, I could not contain myself any longer. At the top of my voice, I shrieked, "Why don't you stop chanting *Sh'ma Yisrael*? You are driving me crazy! You know that I don't believe the way you do. Why can't you just lead this platoon with neutral words of encouragement like *naylech* [let's go] or *halah*[forward]!"

Avner didn't pay too much attention to my shrieking at first, but at last he said patiently, "Know that the two of us have different ways of fighting. You remember, of course, King David's message to Goliath the Philistine, 'You come at me with a sword, but I come in the name of the Lord'?[2] Do me a favor. You fight your way, and I'll fight my way."

The fighting on the battlefield intensified. I never stopped pleading with Avner to stop chanting and he never changed his answer: You fight your way, and I'll fight my way.

The more the fighting intensified, the louder Avner

[1]Deuteronomy 6:4.
[2]1 Samuel 17:45.

chanted. It seemed that the rhythm of his chant kept pace with the exploding bombs in the distance.

On the fourth day of the battle, I thought that Avner had finally headed my pleas to stop chanting. He had advanced a short distance ahead of me when I realized why his chanting had stopped. He was lying on the sand of the Sinai desert, blood gushing from his mouth but still breathing. I ran forward and felt his chest. His breathing was painfully difficult. He opened his eyes, and I grasped his hand in mine.

Choking, I said, "Dearest friend, please forgive me for arguing with you, for insisting that your chanting was annoying me. I would do anything to retract those words."

As the tears streamed down my cheeks, I saw that he was trying to speak. I asked him if there was anything I could do for him. I laid my ear close to his mouth. He asked me to swear that I would chant *Sh'ma Yisrael* in his place!

I swore to him that I would fight chanting *Sh'ma Yisrael*. I don't know if he heard me, for he died a moment later. I lay beside him for a while, thinking about the holiness of the moment, realizing what *Sh'ma Yisrael* really meant. It was as if he had bequeathed me his message from Heaven, a message that suddenly turned on a light in my head. I knew then that there is only One God.

So with as much energy as I had denied God, I took it upon myself to proclaim Him. That night as I lay under the stars, trying to sleep, for the battle had turned in favor of Israel, I thought about my children. I had neglected to teach them what every Jewish father is supposed to teach his children. As soon as the rays of dawn appeared in the desert sky, I ran toward the regiment commander. Breathlessly, I shouted; "I must go home for twenty-four hours. It's a matter of life and death."

I was so agitated, that he did not even question me. He just nodded his head and waved his hand in the general direction of Israel.

All the way home, I chanted Captain Avner's melody "*Sh'ma Yisrael A-do-nay E-lo-hay-nu A-do-nay E-chad.*"

I burst into my house blurting out, I want you to know, children, *Sh'ma Yisrael, A-do-nay E-lo-hay-nu A-do-nay E-chad.* There is One God. The Jewish people are a holy people.

The next day, I returned to my unit. The war ended with

Israel's victory. Since then, I have more than fulfilled my vow. My family and I have become observant, and we try to inspire others to follow our example.

By repeating my story on the concert stage, you can teach the whole world to chant *Sh'ma Yisrael*.

Epilogue

We Wish You the Best

Zundel, a humble, hardworking *vasser trayger* who lived in a small *shtetl* a distance from Lublin, painstakingly saved spare kopeks all year in a glass jar so that he would have enough money to spend Rosh Hashanah with his Rebbe Yaakov Yitzchak Halayve Horowitz, the Chozeh of Lublin.

When his day's earnings were less than he needed for mere subsistence, he went to sleep hungry, never taking anything out of the jar to buy food. The clink of each additional coin resounded joyfully in his ears; his eyes sparkled with anticipation of the celebration of the holy days in the *bays midrash* in Lublin. His happiest time was spending Rosh Hashanah with his rebbe.

On the twenty-fifth day of Elul, one week before Rosh Hashanah, Zundel set out on foot for Lublin. He almost ran, so eager was he to arrive at his destination. By the time he reached the outskirts of Lublin, he was joined by hundreds of other *chasidim*. Rather than rest at the inn, he ran ahead. He wanted to be the first to greet the rebbe, visualizing the rebbe's warm greeting when he saw him.

The rebbe would say, "Zundel, it is so good of you to come

all the way from your *shtetl* to Lublin for the holy days. I am so happy to see you. I pray that you will be inscribed in the Book of Life."

However, when he got there, to Zundel's dismay, the rebbe shattered his vision. He said instead, "Zundel, go home! I don't want you to stay in Lublin for the holy days!"

Zundel was taken aback by the rebbe's words. Disappointed, he slunk out of the *bays midrash*, stoop-shouldered, red eyes staring blindly at the ground as he retraced his steps toward the inn.

Zundel's friends knew there was something wrong the minute he shuffled inside. They called out to him, "What are you doing back here?"

"I don't know what happened. I saved my kopeks all year so I could be here for Rosh Hashanah. I ran ahead of all of you. I wanted to be the first at the *bays midrash*. When the rebbe saw me, instead of greeting me joyfully as he usually does, he told me to go home."

"Wait, before you go, let's have a schnapps," called out one *chasid*.

"That's a great idea," agreed a second.

The innkeeper poured schnapps in little glasses for all the *chasidim*. One by one, they held up their glasses and shouted, "Zundel, we wish you the best, we wish you the best!"

Some of them started clapping, then the two men standing closest to Zundel lifted him up on their shoulders and started dancing with him. Everyone in the inn was singing, dancing, shouting, "Zundel, we wish you the best!"

Suddenly, the men dancing in a circle formed a procession, and they started marching toward the *bays midrash*, still carrying Zundel on their shoulders.

Zundel protested from above the shoulders of his friends, "Put me down, put me down. You are going toward the *bays midrash*, and the rebbe instructed me to go home. I can't go with you."

But they refused to listen. They quickened their gait, and in a few minutes Zundel was standing with them in the *bays midrash*.

This time the rebbe approached Zundel, and strangely, extended his hand. "Zundel," he said, "it is so good to see you. I pray that you will be inscribed in the Book of Life."

Zundel was clearly puzzled.

"Let me explain," said the rebbe quietly. "When you first arrived here, I perceived that evil was lurking behind you. If something were to happen, God forbid, I didn't want it to happen while you were separated from your family. Therefore, I told you to go home. When you stopped at the inn, and all your friends were so solicitous over your welfare, when they danced and sang with you, when they wished you the best, the evil that was lurking behind you retreated. Every time one of them wished you the best, it retreated one more step. Because the decree against you has been lifted, you are most welcome to stay here in Lublin for Rosh Hashanah. I want you to know that the greatest blessing one human being can bestow upon another is to sincerely wish him the best."

We too wish you the best! We too wish you the best!

Glossary

aliyah: going "up" from the lands of exile to Eretz Yisrael; also, to be called up to the *bimah* for a Torah reading.

Alt-neu schul: the oldest standing synagogue in Europe today. It is located in the medieval Jewish ghetto section in Prague. The exact date of the original building is unknown, but records, dating 1142–1171, describe its refurbishment; therefore it is called *Alt-neu schul,* the old new synagogue. Another interpretation of the name has its roots in the Hebrew *al tenai,* meaning "on condition." According to historical tradition, the Jews of Prague prayed in the *Alt-neu schul* on condition that when the Messiah arrived, they would all return to Eretz Yisrael.

ashkenazim: Those Jews who migrated from Eretz Yisrael to western Europe, following the trade routes and the conquerors northward to the Franco/Germanic lands, then eastward to the Polish/Russian lands.

auto-da-fe: burning at the stake

baal teshuvah: one who returns to Judaism
bahelfer: teacher's assistant
bar mitzvah: age of religious responsibility for a young man of thirteen
batim: outer black boxes of the *tefillin*
bays midrash: study hall

bekasheh, gartel, shtriemel: long black coat, belt, and broad brimmed
  fur hat
bimah: pulpit of the synagogue
bris milah: circumcision ritual

challah, challos: twisted loaves of freshly baked bread for *shabbos* and
  holy days
Chanukah: holiday commemorating the rededication of the Holy
  Temple and the Macabeean victory over the Greek/Syrians
chasidim: disciples of a rebbe
chazan: prayer leader
cheder: classroom for young children
chevra kadisha: the burial society
cholent: a mixture of meat, potatoes, beans, and barley that simmers
  from Sabbath eve until Saturday lunch meal
chuppah: the wedding canopy

daven: pray
diaspora: exile
din Torah: judgment

Eliyahu Hanavi: Elijah, the prophet of peace and redemption
Eretz Yisrael: ancestral homeland of the Jewish people
erev Shabbos: Friday afternoon, preceding the Sabbath

gut voch: a good week

hagadah: a set form of benedictions, prayers, and comments recited at
  the Passover *Seder*
havdalah: ritual separating the Sabbath from the weekdays, using
  wine, spices, by the light of a twisted, double-wicked candle

kaddish: a prayer exalting God, used to separate sections of the prayer
  service, and as a memorial for the deceased
kahal: an autonomous, central governing council
kiddush: sanctification of wine
kiddush hachayim: sanctification of life
kiddush hashem: martyrdom for the sanctification of God's Holy
  Name
kittel: white prayer robe
Kol Nidre: opening prayer of the Yom Kippur service, literally meaning
  "all the vows"
kugel: pudding made of potatoes, noodles, or rice
kvittel: a written request for a blessing

l'chayim: to life, usual toast when drinking wine

ma-ariv: evening prayer service

maggid: itinerant preacher and story teller; also a synonym for rebbe

ma-oz tzur: Chanukah song, "Rock of Ages"

matzah: unleavened bread

mazel: good fortune

megillah, megillas Esther: scroll of Esther, recited at Purim

melamed: a teacher of young children

melave malkah: farewell feast to the Sabbath Queen

menorah: candelabra that holds the Chanukah lights

Messiah: the redeemer

mezuzah: parchment scroll affixed to the doorposts of Jewish homes
   inscribed with the first two paragraphs of *Sh'ma* found in the *Torah*
   (Deuteronomy 6:4–8, 11:13–21)

midrash: legends and interpretations of verses in the Torah

mikveh: ritual bathing pool

minchah: afternoon prayer service

minyan: quorum of ten adult males gathered for a prayer service

mitzvah, mitzvas: commandment(s), good deed(s)

mohel: ritual circumciser

naches: pleasure or satisfaction one receives (usually from one's
   children)

niggun: melody

ofanim, chayos, serafim: names of angels

pale of settlement: In 1792, Catherine the Great decreed that the
   former Polish kingdom, which Russia had annexed, be called the
   Pale of Settlement. She prohibited Jews from leaving this territory.
   The word "pale" is derived from the Latin *palus*, meaning a stake or
   pole, for it was an area surrounded by poles that restricted or
   confined people who were under the jurisdiction of another country.
   The Pale of Settlement was located between the Baltic and Black Sea
   from north to south, and by the surrounding countries of Russia,
   Prussia, and Austria on the east and west sides. The Jews were
   confined to small villages in the western provinces of the empire, to
   prevent their spreading to other parts of Russia. They were treated
   as a hostile population, different from other Russian citizens, un-
   worthy of equal citizenship.

parnas: president of a medieval Jewish community

parsheyos: parchment upon which four sections of the Torah are
   inscribed for the black boxes of the *tefillin*

Pesach: Passover

poretz: landowner

Purim: holiday commemorating the downfall of Haman, arch enemy of
    the Jewish people, in the period between the destruction of the first
    Holy Temple and the building of the second

rebbe: rabbi of a chasidic sect

rebbetzen: the rabbi's wife

rosh chodesh: first day of the new month

Rosh Hashana: the beginning of the Jewish new year; also the name of
    a talmud tractate

rosh yeshiva: dean of a school of higher Jewish learning

Sephardim: referring to Jews who migrated eastward to the Asian
    countries, then followed the trade routes and the conquerors across
    North Africa to Spain

Shabbos: the Sabbath

shalom aleichem: greeting of "peace be with you"; in addition, it is the
    song sung before *Kiddush* to welcome the Shabbos angels who
    bring peace and blessings to the home

shamish: beadle

Shavuos: Pentecost

shlepper: someone without employment or visible means of support

Sh'ma: prayer affirming faith on One God

shofar: ram's horn

sholosh seudos: third meal of the Sabbath

shtetl, shtetlach: village(s) in eastern Europe, almost entirely inhab-
    ited by Jews

shtender: prayer desk

shtibel: a small house of prayer, usually associated with *chasidim*

shul: synagogue

siddur: a prayerbook

shiva: the seven-day mourning period, beginning after burial of the
    deceased

tallis: prayer shawl

tefillin: phylacteries

tefillos: prayers

tish: table where meals are eaten; a rebbe's *tish* is usually filled with
    guests, song, joy, and words of Torah

tzadik: righteous man

tzimmes: casserole of carrots and sweet potatoes

vasser trayger: water carrier

yahrzeit: anniversary of death

yeshiva, yeshivos: school(s) of higher Torah learning

yiddele: (diminutive) an aged Jew

yishuv: Jewish settlement in Eretz Yisrael, particularly in Jerusalem, around the turn of the century

Yom Kippur: the Day of Atonement

yom tov: holy day, literally a "good day"

zemiros: songs and melodies sung at the Sabbath and holy day table

zloty: Polish money

Zohar: a book that contains the mystical secrets of Torah